THE VULNERABLE CONSUMER

REVIEW OF MARKETING RESEARCH

Editor-in-Chief: Naresh K. Malhotra

EDITORIAL ADVISORY BOARD

REVIEW OF MARKETING RESEARCH   VOLUME 21

THE VULNERABLE CONSUMER: BEYOND THE POOR AND THE ELDERLY

EDITED BY

ANGELA Y. LEE
Northwestern University, USA

United Kingdom – North America – Japan
India – Malaysia – China

Emerald Publishing Limited
Emerald Publishing, Floor 5, Northspring, 21-23 Wellington Street, Leeds LS1 4DL

First edition 2024

Reprints and permissions service
Contact: www.copyright.com

British Library Cataloguing in Publication Data
A catalogue record for this book is available from the British Library

ISBN: 978-1-80262-956-9 (Print)
ISBN: 978-1-80262-955-2 (Online)
ISBN: 978-1-80262-957-6 (Epub)

ISSN: 1548-6435 (Series)

INVESTOR IN PEOPLE

CONTENTS

LIST OF FIGURES AND TABLES

ABOUT THE EDITOR-IN-CHIEF

Dr Naresh K. Malhotra was selected as a *Marketing Legend* in 2010, and his refereed journal articles were published in nine volumes by Sage with tributes by other leading scholars in the field. He is listed in Marquis *Who's Who in America*, and in *Who's Who in the World*. In 2017, he received the Albert Nelson Marquis *Lifetime Achievement Award* from Marquis Who's Who. In 2020, Dr Malhotra was listed in the published list of the *World's Top 2% Most-cited Researchers* across all disciplines (*22 major fields and 176 subfields*), according to research conducted by the Meta-Research Innovation Center at Stanford University. He is also listed in Research.com 2024 Ranking of Best Scientists in Business and Management, as well as Best Scholars. He has several *top* (number one) research rankings that have been published in the literature.

ABOUT THE EDITOR

Angela Y. Lee is the Mechthild Esser Nemmers Professor of Marketing at the Kellogg School of Management, Northwestern University. Dr Lee's expertise is in consumer learning, emotions, and motivation. Her research focuses on understanding what drives consumer attention, judgment, and choice. Dr Lee's publications appear in top marketing and psychology journals. She is the recipient of the 2006 Stanley Reiter Best Paper Award for her research on self-regulation and persuasion and the 2002 Otto Klineberg Award for best paper on international and intercultural relations. Dr Lee is a Fellow of the Society of Experimental Social Psychology, a Fellow of the American Psychological Society, and a Marketing Science Institute Academic Fellow. She is a Past President of the Association for Consumer Research and serves on the board of the Grant Park Music Festival and the Sheth Foundation.

ABOUT THE CONTRIBUTORS

Rohini Ahluwalia is the Curtis L. Carlson Trust Professor of Marketing at the Carlson School of Management at the University of Minnesota. She is an expert in the areas of persuasion, branding, and decision-making. Ahluwalia's research has been published in the top journals of the field, received the American Marketing Association's John A. Howard Dissertation Award, and reported in several media outlets including the National Public Radio and The New York Times. She has served on the Editorial Boards of top journals in the field, as well as the Associate Editor for the *Journal of Consumer Research*.

Tayler Bergstrom is a Behavioral Marketing PhD Student at UCLA Anderson School of Management. She studies how people think about their time and the implications this has on their behavior. Before UCLA, she studied Psychology and Business at the University of California, San Diego.

Ilana Brody is a PhD candidate at the UCLA Anderson School of Management. She studies the context and cues that shape judgment and decision-making, particularly as it relates to the process of giving and receiving aid. Prior to UCLA, Ilana worked as a social policy researcher and helped design, implement, and evaluate policies aimed at maximizing welfare in the United States.

Christopher Cannon is an Assistant Professor of Marketing at the Shidler College of Business, University of Hawai'i at Mānoa. He received his PhD in Marketing from the Kellogg School of Management at Northwestern University. He broadly studies consumer behavior from a psychological perspective. For his primary research, he explores consumers' perception of social hierarchies and how resource scarcity affects decision-making.

Casey Carder-Rockwell is an Assistant Professor and a Graduate Coordinator at the University of Arkansas at Little Rock. Her research centers on exploitation and capitalization in areas with limited regulation.

Lucy Joy Chase is a Graduate Student at the Gies College of Business at the University of Illinois, Urbana-Champaign. She received her BA in International Affairs from Elliott School for International Affairs at George Washington University, where she studied small business and personal development in low-income, international contexts. After over 15 years of experience practicing in the field of business management and administration, Lucy aspires to pursue further writing, teaching, and research opportunities, exploring the confluence of her interests in business, human development, and international development.

Nathan N. Cheek is an Assistant Professor of Psychological Sciences at Purdue University. He received his PhD in Psychology and Social Policy from Princeton University, where he also completed a postdoctoral fellowship. He studies prejudice, decision-making, and inequality with an eye to how behavioral science can inform and improve public policy.

David Crockett is a Professor of Marketing at the University of Illinois Chicago. His research explores sociological aspects of consumer behavior and marketing, particularly the consequences of social inequality along the lines of gender, race, and social class.

Lenita Davis is a Professor of Marketing and an Executive Director for Professional Sales and Sales Management Program at the University of Wisconsin Eau Claire. Her research examines the outcomes that occur when individuals intersect with established institutions across various contexts.

Aimee Drolet is a Professor of Marketing at UCLA Anderson School of Management. Her research looks at the mental processes underlying consumers' choices, specifically focusing on decision-making among older consumers (age 50 or older), consumer habits, and meta-preferences. She coauthored and coedited *The Aging Consumer: Perspectives from Psychology and Economics*, and was named one of Choice Magazine's Top 10 Outstanding Academic Titles in Business, Management and Labor in 2011. Dr Drolet's latest research focuses on the development of habits and on consumption moderation.

Kelly Goldsmith is a Behavioral Scientist whose research examines consumers' psychological and behavioral responses to goals and threats. She is the E. Bronson Ingram Professor of Marketing at Vanderbilt University, where she is an award-winning teacher and researcher. She is the Chairman of the Marketing Department and the Faculty Director of the Ingram Scholars Program and the Hoogland Undergraduate Business Program, in addition to serving as an Area Editor at several top marketing journals.

E. Tory Higgins is the Stanley Schachter Professor of Psychology, Professor of Business, and the Director of the Motivation Science Center at Columbia University. He is a *Fellow of the American Academy of Arts and Sciences*. He has received the *Ambady Award for Mentoring Excellence* (Society for Personality and Social Psychology) and the *Mentor Award for Lifetime Achievement* (Association for Psychological Science). He has received the *Donald T. Campbell Award for Outstanding Contributions to Social Psychology* (Society of Personality and Social Psychology), the *Distinguished Scientist Award* (the Society of Experimental Social Psychology), the *Anneliese Maier Research Award* (Alexander von Humboldt Foundation), the award for *Distinguished Contribution to Motivation Science* (Society for the Science of Motivation), the *William James Fellow Award for Distinguished Achievements in Psychological Science* (Association for Psychological Science), and the *American Psychological Association Award for Distinguished Scientific Contributions*.

Maria Jones is a Development Professional passionate about promoting women's economic empowerment. Her field research interests include gender equitable scaling of innovations, women's entrepreneurship, and improving rural women's livelihoods in South Asia and Sub-Saharan Africa. Maria holds an MBA and an MS in Environmental Engineering from the University of Illinois at Urbana Champaign.

Ronald Paul Hill, PhD, is the Dean's Professor of Marketing and Public Policy at the American University, Kogod School of Business. He has authored over 200 journal articles, books, chapters, and conference papers on topics that include impoverished consumer behavior, marketing ethics, corporate social responsibility, human development, and public policy using primarily qualitative methods. He served as the Vice President of Publications for the American Marketing Association, and he is Editor-in-Chief of the Responsible Research in Business and Management Honor Roll. He also was part of the founding of the Transformative Consumer Research Movement in ACR.

Emily Nakkawita is a PhD candidate at Columbia University interested in understanding the factors that lead to effective goal pursuit processes, with effectiveness defined in terms of both achievement and well-being. She studies the motivational underpinnings of different kinds of goal pursuit activities. In particular, she examines how the extent to which goal pursuit activities are accessible, enjoyable, and likely to be selected are affected by individual differences in the strength of fundamental motives for truth and control, combined with a focus on gains and nongains (promotion value) versus nonlosses and losses (prevention value). Prior to her graduate studies, Emily examined what motivates people through a career in brand marketing and advertising.

Ashley S. Otto is a Consumer Psychologist who specializes in the area of decision making and self-control. Her research has been published in various outlets within the domains of marketing and psychology, and her findings have been featured in media outlets from business magazines and news articles to edited academic volumes. She is currently an Associate Professor of Marketing at Baylor University.

Ryan Rahinel is an Associate Professor of Marketing, Judy and Hugh Oliphant Research Scholar at the Lundquist College of Business, University of Oregon. Rahinel's research on brands and the physical world has been published in the top outlets in marketing and psychology. Previously, Ryan spent nine years at the University of Cincinnati. He received his PhD in Marketing from the University of Minnesota in 2014.

Girish Ramani, PhD, is a Sr. Professorial Lecturer of Marketing at the Kogod School of Business, American University, Washington DC. He has authored journal articles, book chapters, and conference papers in the areas of marketing strategy, digital marketing analytics, and marketing research.

Marsha L. Richins is a Professor of Marketing at the University of Missouri, Columbia. Her research deals with materialism, consumption values, and the role those values play in consumer decisions and debt. Her measure of material values has become the standard by which scholars measure consumer materialism.

Caroline Roux is an Associate Professor of Marketing at Concordia University's John Molson School of Business. She also held the Concordia University Research Chair on the Psychology of Resource Scarcity (2018–2023). Her primary area of research explores how reminders of resource scarcity – or thinking about "not having enough" resources (e.g., money, time, food, etc.) – impact consumer decision-making and behavior.

Eldar Shafir is Class of 1987 Professor of Behavioral Science and Public Policy, and Professor of Psychology and Public Affairs at Princeton University. He is the Inaugural Director of Princeton's Kahneman-Treisman Center for Behavioral Science and Public Policy, cofounder of ideas42, a not-for-profit social science R&D lab, past president of the Society for Judgment and Decision Making, and an elected member of the American Academy of Arts and Sciences. He served as a member of President Barack Obama's Advisory Council on Financial Capability. He received a BA in Cognitive Science from Brown University and a PhD from MIT.

Ali Tezer is an Associate Professor of Marketing at HEC Montreal. His research broadly explores conditions under which the well-being of consumers, brands, and society at large intersect. His primary area of research examines sustainable consumption with a focus on consumer interactions with sustainable products and consumer responses to socially responsible brand behavior.

Madhu Viswanathan is a Professor of Marketing at Loyola Marymount University, Los Angeles, and Professor Emeritus, University of Illinois, Urbana-Champaign. His research programs are on measurement and subsistence marketplaces. His authored books include – *Measurement Error and Research Design, Subsistence Marketplaces,* and *Bottom-Up Enterprise.* He pioneered the area of subsistence marketplaces, adopting a unique bottom-up approach to research, education with content reaching educators worldwide, and social enterprise through marketplace literacy globally.

INTRODUCTION

OVERVIEW

Review of Marketing Research, now in its 21st volume, is a publication covering the important areas of marketing research with a more comprehensive state-of-the-art orientation. The chapters in this publication review the literature in a particular area, offer a critical commentary, develop an innovative framework, and discuss future developments, as well as present specific empirical studies. The first 20 volumes have featured some of the top researchers and scholars in our discipline who have reviewed an array of important topics. The response to the first 20 volumes has been truly gratifying, and we look forward to the impact of the 21st volume with great anticipation.

PUBLICATION MISSION

The purpose of this series is to provide current, comprehensive, state-of-the-art articles in review of marketing research. Wide-ranging paradigmatic or theoretical or substantive agendas are appropriate for this publication. This includes a wide range of theoretical perspectives, paradigms, data (qualitative, survey, experimental, ethnographic, secondary, etc.), and topics related to the study and explanation of marketing-related phenomenon. We reflect an eclectic mixture of theory, data, and research methods that is indicative of a publication driven by important theoretical and substantive problems. We seek studies that make important theoretical, substantive, empirical, methodological, measurement, and modeling contributions. Any topic that fits under the broad area of "marketing research" is relevant. In short, our mission is to publish the best reviews in the discipline.

Thus, this publication bridges the gap left by current marketing research publications. Current marketing research publications publish academic articles with a major constraint on the length. In contrast, *Review of Marketing Research* can publish much longer articles that are not only theoretically rigorous but also more expository, with a focus on implementing new marketing research concepts and procedures.

Articles in *Review of Marketing Research* should address the following issues.

- Critically review the existing literature.
- Summarize what we know about the subject – key findings.
- Present the main theories and frameworks.
- Review and give an exposition of key methodologies.

- Identify the gaps in literature.
- Present empirical studies (for empirical papers only).
- Discuss emerging trends and issues.
- Focus on international developments.
- Suggest directions for future theory development and testing.
- Recommend guidelines for implementing new procedures and concepts.

A FOCUS ON SPECIAL ISSUES

Since volume 8 published in 2011, *Review of Marketing Research* has a focus on special issues realizing that this is one of best ways to impact marketing scholarship in a specific area. The volume editors of all of the special issues have been top scholars. These special issues have focused on the following topics.

Volume, Year	Topic	Volume Editors
8, 2011	Marketing Legends	Naresh K. Malhotra
9, 2012	Toward a Better Understanding of the Role of Value in Markets and Marketing	Stephen L. Vargo and Robert F. Lusch
10, 2013	Regular Volume	Naresh K. Malhotra
11, 2014	Shopper Marketing and the Role of in-Store Marketing	Dhruv Grewal, Anne L. Roggeveen, and Jens NordfÄlt
12, 2015	Brand Meaning Management	Deborah J. Macinnis and C. Whan Park
13, 2016	Marketing in and for a Sustainable Society	Naresh K. Malhotra
14, 2017	Qualitative Consumer Research	Russell W. Belk
15, 2018	Innovation and Strategy	Rajan Varadarajan and Satish Jayachandran
16, 2019	Marketing in a Digital World	Aric Rindfleisch and Alan J. Malter
17, 2020	Continuing to Broaden the Marketing Concept: Making the World a Better Place	Dawn Iacobucci
18, 2021	Marketing Accountability for Marketing and Non-marketing Outcomes	V. Kumar and David W. Stewart
19, 2022	Measurement in Marketing	Hans Baumgartner and Bert Weijters
20, 2023	Artificial Intelligence and Marketing	K. Sudhir and Olivier Toubia

THIS VOLUME

This special issue focuses on the current state of the art of the literature on vulnerable consumers and thus provides a road map and agenda for future research in the field. Consumer vulnerabilities are defined very broadly to include not only scarcity of financial assets and materialistic resources but also a scarcity mindset, a lack of mental resources and self-knowledge, as well as the nonfulfillment of motivational needs. Together, the chapters in this volume lead to new insights, approaches, and directions for research on various aspects of the vulnerability of the consumer. It is hoped that collectively these chapters will substantially aid our efforts to theoretically conceptualize the constructs, collect data to empirically examine the measures, and formulate appropriate models to provide a broader arsenal of research methods as well as fertile areas for future research. I thank Angela Y. Lee for editing such an outstanding volume. The *Review of Marketing Research* continues its mission of systematically analyzing and presenting accumulated knowledge in the field of marketing as well as influencing future research by identifying areas that merit the attention of researchers.

Naresh K. Malhotra, Editor-in-Chief

THE VULNERABLE CONSUMER: BEYOND THE POOR AND THE ELDERLY

Angela Y. Lee

Northwestern University, USA

People experience obstacles and challenges on a daily basis. Some of these obstacles and challenges threaten our well-being and remind us of our vulnerability. The goal of this issue is to provide novel insights into the threats that consumers experience and how experiencing these threats shapes consumers' cognition, emotions, and behavior. Prior to the Great Recession, scant academic research in marketing directly examined the role(s) of threats in consumers' lives. The financial crises in the last two decades motivated some research that centered on threats emerging from micro-level socioeconomic factors, such as poverty, social class, and/or power. The nine articles in this issue on "The Vulnerable Consumer" adopt a wide lens to examine different types of consumer vulnerability that are the result of a range of factors such as poverty, low literacy, aging, underdeveloped cognitive or emotional systems, the lack of a clear sense of the self, and goal pursuit failures. Whereas some of the threats that consumers face are temporary, some are more persistent. Prominent scholars in the fields of marketing, management, and psychology have reviewed relevant literature, offered valuable insights into the risk factors and consequences of different types of consumer vulnerabilities, and provided directions for future research. I highlight some of their insights below.

Most people would agree that being poor puts people in a disadvantaged position. Several papers in this issue take a deeper dive to discuss how poverty disadvantages consumers. Starting with the paper titled "Vulnerability and Consumer Poverty," Hill and Ramani break down the various dimensions of consumption adequacy poor consumers are deprived of – potable water for drinking and sanitation, healthful foods for nourishment, proper shelter to shield and protect, appropriate clothing, preventative and remedial health care, education and training – and show how each dimension may compound the hardship

The Vulnerable Consumer
Review of Marketing Research, Volume 21, 1–5
Copyright © 2024 Angela Y. Lee
Published under exclusive licence by Emerald Publishing Limited
ISSN: 1548-6435/doi:10.1108/S1548-643520240000021001

of inadequacy in the other dimensions and further expose the poor consumers to deeper vulnerabilities. The authors call for more research in consumption adequacy measurement to enable governments, nongovernmental organizations (NGOs), and businesses big and small to more effectively allocate resources to enhance the well-being of all.

Cheek and Shafir adopt a more micro approach to examine sources of vulnerability. In particular, they examine how individuals with low socioeconomical status (SES) are disadvantaged. Their paper "From Stigma to Scarcity" highlights how the unfortunate phenomenon of "the rich gets richer and the poor gets poorer" is due largely to the negative stereotype many people have of low-SES individuals. In particular, many people have a "thick skin bias" – the belief that lower SES individuals are less harmed by negative life events, presumably because they experience so much more hardship that they are "toughened" by it. Hence, negative life events from domestic abuse to a flooded apartment to poor service at restaurants should be less upsetting to low-SES consumers. Not only do low-SES consumers receive less help when in need ("because they don't need it as much"), they also receive harsher punishment when they commit a transgression ("because it is necessary to achieve the same disciplinary effect"). In response, low-SES consumers often allocate their precious scarce resource to cope with the discrimination, such as paying a "safety tax" or making consumption choices such as cigarettes and alcohol that might work against their well-being just for the sake of building connections with others. Ironically, one potential upside is that low-SES consumers may be more vigilant and pay more attention to prices and hidden costs and hence are less prone to common financial decision biases.

But the constant worrying about one's finances does have profound impact on decision-making. In fact, just the thought of not having enough is known to exert systematic bias on judgments and behaviors. In their article "Yin and Yang of Hard Times," Goldsmith, Roux, Cannon, and Tezer identify the interesting dual effect of not-having-enough. In particular, they argue that while people who experience resource scarcity are often observed to conserve consumption, they at the same time are strategically considering how to invest in themselves to ensure future consumption adequacy. In fact, consumers who experience scarcity, even if only figuratively, are more willing to pay for products and services that offer self-improvement benefits. That is, people don't really have to experience actual consumption inadequacy – simply thinking or feeling that they do not have enough is sufficient to cause a shift in people's attention and behavior to become more self-focused. The authors report the results of an experiment whereby research participants who wrote about times when they "didn't have enough of something" or "when resources were scarce" (vs wrote about something they did during the past week) paid more for Post-it Notes featured as "Sticky Notes for Effective Knowledge Retention! The Secret Weapon of those Wishing to Improve," but not more for Post-it Notes simply featured as "Sticky Notes." Presumably, investments on the self is more justified in times of scare resources so one could be in a better position to handle scarcity in future.

And what does life look like for those who experience actual resource scarcity? Crockett, David, and Carder-Rockwell provide a different perspective on one aspect of consumption inadequacy – housing – by describing the lack of protection that renters who cannot afford to pay rent experience. In particular, the authors examine how eviction happens in the United States. In "A Consumer Vulnerability Perspective on Eviction," Crockett and his colleagues review how the rental market in Arkansas is regulated and find existing legislation to be more favorable to landlords, leaving renters more vulnerable to eviction threat. When assessed against national guidelines, the probusiness regulatory environment in Arkansas provides landlords with favorable provisions but little tenant protections. Interestingly, Arkansas reports one of the lowest displacement rates in the country despite high poverty rate and high rent burden, which leads to a rich set of research questions waiting to be explored – how do these low-income renters understand their rental obligations, and what strategies do they use to mitigate the unfavorable rental conditions?

Viswanathan, Chase, and Jones focus on a very different group of vulnerable consumers. In their paper "I Do Not Think of Myself as a Customer," the authors describe how a low-literate, low-income woman may experience vulnerability not just from poverty but from being at the bottom of the social hierarchy both inside as well as outside the home. Further, her low literacy makes her more vulnerable because it constrains her ability to think, exposes her to shame, and limits her ability to cope with life's challenges. The authors describe how a marketplace literacy education program could make a difference by helping to address these vulnerabilities that low-income, low-literacy consumers face. The program provides these individuals with not just the capacity to read but, more importantly, the social contexts that help them navigate the marketplace as customers and as entrepreneurs, and in turn instill in them the sense of self-confidence that completely transforms their lives.

These five papers make it very clear how the lack of financial and materialistic resources deprives consumers of many consumption adequacies and places them in vulnerable positions. However, vulnerability does not stop with not having enough material resources. Lacking the mental facilities to handle information or emotions also exposes consumers to vulnerabilities. The elderly (those age 65 and over) fall under this category. In their article "Aging and Vulnerabilities in Consumer Information Processing," Drolet, Bergstrom, and Brody review research on the effects of aging on how, and how much, aging consumers engage in sensory, cognitive, and emotional functioning. The authors find that for the elderly consumers, their working memory slows down, their sensory processing (i.e., vision, hearing, tasting, smelling, touching) is less sharp, and they attend more to emotions and emotional information. Thus, as many would suspect or even observe, elderly consumers more readily fall prey to misleading advertisements, illusionary truth effects, and even financial scams. But the authors also point out that the wisdom that elderly consumers possess through their lifelong experience offers them an edge. Wisdom development reflects a process of cognitive-affective integration that allows the elderly to optimize positive emotion and tolerate discomfort from the cognitive-affective complexity such as feeling happy and sad at the same time. More importantly, their accumulated experience may partially compensate for their age-related decline in cognitive functioning.

Impaired processing capabilities seem to happen to young people as well! In "Leaves in the Wind," Rahinel, Ahluwalia, and Otto identify a little-known segment of consumers with underdeveloped thinking systems. Many dual process models identify two systems that people draw on to process information – a system that relies on feelings and intuition (the experiential system) and another that relies on systematic, rational thinking (the rational system). These two systems are sometimes referred to as System 1 versus System 2, heuristic versus systematic processing, or central versus peripheral processing. The authors point out that the propensities of relying on one's experiential and rational systems are orthogonal. The implication is that there are people who chronically rely more on one system, or both systems equally, or neither system. The last group, referred to by the authors as low system thinkers, lack the motivation and/or the ability to access their experiential and their rational system for information processing and decision-making. Alarmingly, studies show that up to 35% of adolescents and 25% of young adults belong to this group of low system thinkers. As a result, these consumers often feel confused and overwhelmed, and they rely on whatever is most accessible or salient in the environment as the basis of their judgment and decisions. Their over-reliance on external cues regardless of their diagnostic values often leads to suboptimal consumption outcomes.

Yet another source of vulnerability may come from people feeling unsure of who they are, independent of their financial wealth or their age or their processing capabilities. In "Not Knowing Who I Am," Richins explains that people with high self-concept clarity (SCC) are certain in their beliefs about themselves; they perceive their traits to be generally consistent with each other, and that their self-perceptions are stable from day to day. A clear self-concept allows people to function and make decisions with confidence. In contrast, low SCC is a source of vulnerability that often leads to overspending, product dissatisfaction, and even self-harm. Richins reviews the literature to discuss how low SCC consumers rely on symbolic self-completion and social comparison to deal with their daily uncertainty about the self. This unfortunately leads to feelings of deficiency and reduced self-regulation and makes them more susceptible to external influences, which partially explains their materialistic behaviors. In the paper, Richins describes risk factors for low SCC and explains its association with materialism and proposes interventions and future research directions to help these consumers better cope with their vulnerabilities.

Does that mean that for the rest of the consumers – those not in the low SES segment, younger than 65, with a clear self-concept, and have access to either rational or experiential or both systems – are in the clear? Unfortunately, even for these consumers, there are situations when they may feel vulnerable. As argued by Goldsmith and her colleagues, whenever people find themselves in need of something, such as not having enough eggs to bake a cake, the printer runs out of paper, or forgot their credit cards at home...., they feel threatened and go into resource conservation and self-preservation mode. In their paper "Marketplace

Solutions to Motivational Threats," Nakkawita and Higgins propose a 2 (promotion vs prevention value) x 2 (control vs truth) framework to describe people's fundamental motivational drivers. Promotion value is about achieving growth and accomplishments, whereas prevention value is about attaining safety and security. When people pursue truth (i.e., effectively establishing what is real or right), they may engage in prevention-truth activities such as scrutinizing and verifying or promotion-truth activities such as wondering and discovering to understand the world. And when they seek control (i.e., having a good handle on life), they may engage in prevention-control activities such as defending and protecting or promotion-control activities such as launching and accelerating. They further propose that people become vulnerable when they fall short of attaining some desired outcomes, establishing truth, or losing control. These setbacks render consumers feeling confused, incompetent and insecure. The authors identify different marketplace offerings that can provide effective relief to these vulnerable consumers. For example, Wirecutter's analysis and recommendations for different products and services can offer comforting reassurances to consumers failing to meet their goals of prevention value and truth; while browsing on Pinterest to discover new fashions and home goods can satisfy those feeling vulnerable when they fail to attain promotion value and truth.

The goal of this issue is to enhance the awareness and understanding of consumer vulnerabilities so that consumers, marketers, policymakers, and society can exercise precautions and implement interventions to promote consumer and societal well-being. The nine papers collectively present a complex profile of the vulnerable consumer. Scarcity plays a dominant role as the key source of vulnerability. To be sure, scarcity is a lack of financial assets and materialistic resources (see Cheek & Shafir; Crockett et al.; Hill & Ramani; Viswanathan et al., in this volume), but scarcity threats also come from the mindset of not having enough (Goldsmith et al., in this volume), a lack of mental resources (see Drolet et al.; Rahinel et al., in this volume) and self-knowledge (Richins, in this volume), as well as the non-fulfillment of motivational needs (Nakkawita & Higgins, in this volume). That is, consumers do not have to be financially poor to be vulnerable. Also, there are many other sources of threats that are not covered in this issue – the climate crisis, the global food and water insecurity, pandemics, international conflicts, accelerating political polarization, crime, social and marketplace discrimination... the list goes on. My hope is that this issue will serve to inform and motivate researchers to consider other forms of vulnerabilities and explore ways to help improve the livelihoods of people around the world.

AGING AND VULNERABILITIES IN CONSUMER INFORMATION PROCESSING

Aimee Drolet, Tayler Bergstrom and Ilana Brody

UCLA Anderson School of Management, USA

ABSTRACT

This chapter reviews research on age-related differences in how consumers process information. Specifically, it discusses many of the effects of aging on the quality and quantity of consumers' sensory, cognitive, and emotional functioning. Some studies suggest that the manner in which elderly (age 65 and over) consumers process information may render them more vulnerable than young and middle-aged consumers to malign persuasion attempts. This chapter reveals that age has selective effects on information processing such that elderly consumers are sometimes more susceptible to marketing influence and sometimes they are less susceptible.

Keywords: Aging; information processing; vulnerability; elderly; sensory functioning; memory; emotional functioning

INTRODUCTION

Adults aged 65 and over now comprise the largest consumer segment of the US population. Indeed, nearly one out of six Americans are over the age of 65.[1] These consumers also represent the wealthiest segment of the US population. Their median net worth is more than double that of the average US adult ($266,400 vs $121,700; Federal Reserve Board, 2020). Accordingly, marketing researchers (and practitioners) have become increasingly interested in understanding the psychology and behavior of elderly consumers.

---

[1]"Fact Sheet: Aging in the United States," *Population Reference Bureau* (www.prb.org), 7/15/19.

The Vulnerable Consumer
Review of Marketing Research, Volume 21, 7–24
Copyright © 2024 Aimee Drolet, Tayler Bergstrom and Ilana Brody
Published under exclusive licence by Emerald Publishing Limited
ISSN: 1548-6435/doi:10.1108/S1548-643520240000021002

Recent studies have focused mainly on changes due to aging in how consumers process information. These studies reveal that the manner in which elderly consumers process marketing communications makes them more vulnerable than young adult consumers to malign persuasion attempts (for a recent review, see Bonifeld & Cole, 2021). For example, elderly consumers are more susceptible to misleading advertisements (Gaeth & Heath, 1987) and the truth-inflating effects of repetition (Skurnik et al., 2005). Not surprisingly, elderly consumers are frequent targets of financial scams.[2]

In this chapter, we review research on age-related differences in how consumers process information. Specifically, we review numerous effects of aging on the quality and quantity of consumers' sensory, cognitive, and emotional functioning. This review reveals that age has selective effects on mental processes which can make elderly consumers more vulnerable to marketing influence in some instances but not all. For example, age-related losses in fluid intelligence (e.g., working memory) occur alongside gains in crystallized intelligence (e.g., long-term memory) and the ability to regulate emotions. So, elderly consumers can be wiser.

OVERVIEW

In this chapter, we describe changes due to aging in consumers' sensory, cognitive, and emotional functioning. As we proceed, we describe how some, but not all, of these age-related changes make elderly consumers more vulnerable to certain kinds of marketing influence. Alternatively, some age-related changes may be protective.

Firstly, we discuss older consumers' increased vulnerability due to the harmful effects of aging on sensory functioning. Aging is associated with predictable declines in consumers' five senses (vision, hearing, smell, taste, and touch). These declines have widespread implications for consumers' mental processes and behavior. For example, degraded sensory inputs can affect consumers' understanding of and responsiveness to advertising, as well as their interactions with product design and service providers (e.g., Charness & Jastrzembski, 2009; Cole & Gaeth, 1990; Fisk et al., 2004).

Secondly, we review age-related changes in the cognitive system. In general, the impact of aging on cognition is detrimental but selective. Aging affects some aspects of memory and information processing (e.g., speed of processing), but not others (knowledge-based memory). Aging also affects some consumers (e.g., the uneducated) more than others.

Thirdly, we review age-related changes to the emotional system. Studies have shown that elderly (vs young) adults are more motivated to attend to emotions and emotional information (Carstensen et al., 1999) and as a result are better able to acknowledge and manage their emotions (Gross et al., 1997). We briefly review

---

[2]https://www.marketplace.org/2019/05/16/brains-losses-aging-fraud-financial-scams-seniors/

two accounts of why aging causes older adults to focus more on emotions, specifically wisdom development and time horizon perceptions.

Lastly, we consider how, together, changes in sensory, cognitive, and emotional functioning influence how older (vs young) consumers process information. Aging is associated with a decreased reliance on deliberative processing which can result in both increased and decreased vulnerability to varied marketing efforts.

AGING WORSENS SENSORY FUNCTIONING

The five senses (vision, hearing, smell, taste, and touch) receive information from the environment. This sensory information is converted into nerve signals that are carried to the brain where they are turned into meaningful sensations. Because aging raises the minimum level of sensation of 'threshold' needed for awareness, older consumers generally need more stimulation in order to recognize a change in the sensory environment. Put differently, (healthy) aging dulls consumers' sensory functioning.[3]

Vision

Vision worsens with age. Specifically, around the age of 40, the eye's lens becomes thicker, less elastic, and yellower, and near-vision declines (Kline & Scialfa, 1996). The pupil gets smaller, and less light reaches the retina (Emmett & Seshamani, 2015). The pupil also reacts more slowly in response to bright light or darkness. Together, the changes in the eye's lens and pupil structures cause slowed vision. The eye takes longer to focus on near objects or objects at different distances which makes it more difficult for consumers to identify objects. As a result, visual scanning becomes more difficult. So, for example, it becomes harder for elderly consumers to scan a shelf and find a specific brand.

Furthermore, changes in the eye's lens and pupil structures affect the refraction of light which can lead to blurred vision, distorted colors, and increased sensitivity to glare (Charness et al., 2010; Saxon & Etten, 2002). As a result, elderly consumers generally have more difficulty than younger and middle-age consumers recognizing brands in low-lighted areas and discerning between colors (e.g., black vs navy) (Margrain & Boulton, 2005).

However, importantly, these debilities in elderly consumers' vision can be offset by increasing illumination so consumers can more easily see brands clearly. For example, a retailer might physically position their brands in well-lit, low-glare areas. Or, a marketer might design brands labels with easy-to-read

---

[3]It is important to note that this review focuses exclusively on the effect of normal (i.e., healthy) aging on sensory functioning. Diseases such as Parkinson's, Alzheimer's, and diabetes have separable detrimental effects on consumers' abilities to see, hear, smell, taste, and touch.

visuals (i.e., bright colors, large high-quality font print, not all uppercase letters, matte finish paper, etc.).

Hearing

Our sense of hearing worsens with age. In particular, structures inside the ear start to change and their functions decline (Emmett & Seshamani, 2015). For example, the ability to pick up high-frequency sounds decreases. This condition, referred to as *presbycusis*, is the most common form of normal age-related hearing loss (Agrawal et al., 2008). Hearing occurs after sound vibrations cross the eardrum to the inner ear where the vibrations are changed into nerve signals in the inner ear and carried to the brain by the auditory nerve (National Institute of Health [NIH], 2022). *Presbycusis* is the result of degenerative changes in the cochlea or the auditory nerve fibers that lead from the cochlea to the brain (Nelson & Hinojosa, 2006). These changes result in a higher loss in hearing across high frequencies among elderly adults (Plack, 2014). The effects of presbycusis are generally noticeable around age 40 and then progress steadily over the life-span. This progression has clear implications for product design, given that auditory signals (beeps, bells, and whistles) are a common form of feedback in many products. Depending on the frequency of such signals, such feedback might or might not be lost on older consumers.

The intensity of such signals will also matter. For example, many older adults have difficulty discerning the difference between some sounds, for example, "s" and "th." When there is background noise, increasing the intensity of *some* sounds can improve hearing among older adults and thus their ability to have conversations with others (Schneider et al., 2005). However, increasing the intensity of *all* sounds may be unhelpful in the presence of other age-related hearing conditions, namely tinnitus (ringing in the ears).

Smell

The ability to smell declines with age. This decline renders elderly consumers more physically vulnerable since the sense of smell is important to overall health: A diminished sense of smell can decrease appetite and nutrition, and may pose other health-related problems. For example, people may accidentally consume soured or rancid foods because they are unable to detect odors that signal spoilage. People may also be less able to detect smoke and poisonous gases (Doty & Snow, 1988).

The decline in the sense of smell (*anosmia*) is linked to the loss of the nerve endings high in the lining of the nose and mucus production in the nose (National Institute of Health, 2022). In fact, studies have reliably found that roughly 30% of people age 70 and older can detect odors and correctly identify them (e.g., Doty et al., 1984). Interestingly, most people who have lost the ability to smell do not realize they have done so. However, if they expect something to smell citrusy, then they will "smell" citrus. Hence, elderly consumers may benefit from labeling products that (1) smell alike and (2) use visual cues to indicate what scent is present versus absent.

Taste

The ability to taste declines with age.[4] Dietary preferences change with age, and much of this change is related to changes in the ability to taste (Rolls, 1999). The majority of older adults can still identify sweet, sour, bitter, and salty foods, but it helps greatly when these flavors are concentrated because the number and size of taste buds decreases with age. In addition, the mouth produces less saliva which can cause dry mouth. With fewer taste buds and less saliva, elderly consumers gravitate to saltier foods and add larger amounts of salt to make foods more palatable, despite the increased health risks associated with a high sodium diet (Rolls, 1999).

Prescription drugs sometimes affect taste (e.g., leaves a bad after-taste). Since elderly consumers tend to take more prescription medicine than young adult consumers, they may be disproportionately negatively affected. A decreased sense of taste is one reason why some older adults exhibit poor appetite and distaste for foods prepared by someone with a stronger sense of taste (Rolls, 1999). Food designers make several recommendations with respect to pleasing elderly consumers' sense of taste, specifically avoiding bland foods, adding extra flavor, varying texture, and improving the food's appearance. They caution that "extra flavor" does not mean "extra spicy," as elderly consumers often have medical conditions that can be irritated by certain spices (Schiffman, 1997).

Touch

The brain interprets the type and amount of touch sensation. It also interprets the sensation as pleasant, unpleasant, or neutral (awareness of touching something). With aging, touch sensations may be reduced, mainly due to reductions in the amount of blood flow to nerve endings or to the spinal cord or brain (Katzman & Terry, 1983).

The sense of touch makes one aware of temperature, pain, vibration, and pressure. With decreased temperature sensitivity, it can be hard to tell the difference between cool and cold and between hot and warm (Verdu et al., 2000). Elderly adults have reduced sensitivity to pain. This can increase the risk of injury from frostbite and burns (Sherman & Robillard, 1964). Detection thresholds for vibration intensities are likewise higher among elderly adults (Verrillo et al., 2002). Accordingly, they may be less likely to notice and respond to haptic feedback, such as when using a cellular phone. Interestingly, however, older adults can become more sensitive to light touches because their skin is thinner. In

---

[4]Of course, the sense of smell and the sense of taste work together (Doty & Snow, 1988). Most tastes are linked with odors, and someone who cannot smell cannot taste food or enjoy it (Boyce & Shone, 2006).

contrast to temperature, pain, and vibration thresholds, tactile thresholds among elderly adults are significantly increased (Thornbury & Mistretta, 1981).

The spatial acuity of skin at the fingertips also deteriorates markedly with age. Impaired spatial acuity at the fingertips affects hand motor function in older adults. In brief, tactile sensory deficits can result in impaired manual control (e.g., grip) and greater difficulty with tasks requiring fine manipulations (Stevens & Patterson, 1995). This has many clear implications for elderly consumers' ability to use products and derive satisfaction from them, and in turn for how products should be designed for elderly consumers.

Summary

In summary, aging is associated with numerous declines in sensory functioning. These declines have implications for the integrity of consumer information processing, given its reliance on degraded sensory inputs. However, it is worth noting that many sensory declines can be corrected for situationally, for example, by improving lighting or simplifying communications.

AGING IMPAIRS SOME COGNITIVE PROCESSES

In general, age-related changes in the cognitive system can be characterized as selective, occurring in some but not all domains and to some but not all consumers. In particular, aging is associated with pronounced impairments in processing speed, that is, the speed with which one conducts mental operations (Salthouse, 1996). The decline in processing speed is thought to represent the decline in the speed of neural transmissions which is a key underlying cause of other age-related impairments in the cognitive system (Salthouse & Babcock, 1991).

Working Memory

Slower processing corresponds to lengthier and less efficient periods of information transfer between neural units, which is reflected in a weakened ability among older adults to hold information (digits and words) in working memory; that is, their ability to hold information in conscious memory declines. As processing speed slows, the efficiency and connectivity of neural units decreases, and as a result, the working memory of older adults often fails to meet the processing demands of complex computational tasks (Raz, 2000; Reuter-Lorenz et al., 1999). In addition, the ability to handle heavy information loads requires executive functioning capabilities that weaken with age (Babcock & Salthouse, 1990). As a result, and not unexpectedly, the performance of older adults on cognitively demanding tasks is generally worse relative to young adults (Mata et al., 2010).

Working memory and executive functioning tasks frequently require the inhibition or suppression of irrelevant information in order to protect attentional processes. This inhibitory ability is reduced in older adults (Hasher & Zacks, 1988). Aging is associated with changes in attentional capacity that compromise the ability to suppress irrelevant information (Conway & Engle, 1994; Engle, 2002; Hedden & Gabrieli, 2004). Consequently, older adults are poorer inhibitors of irrelevant information and are more susceptible to attentional distractions (Lustig et al., 2001). Whether these distractions arise from external sources (e.g., background noise) or internal sources (e.g., personal concerns), they interfere with the ability to comprehend information and make optimal choices. For example, the quality of older adults' choices worsens as the number of options in a choice set increases (Besedeš et al., 2012; Szrek & Bundorf, 2011).

Despite the detrimental effects that a degraded working memory ability can have on older adults' decision-making, an insufficiency in working memory can sometimes be advantageous in decision-making. For example, the ability to accurately detect correlations between variables, such as the correlation between price and quality, may be enhanced under conditions of insufficient working memory, which causes consumers to ignore specific numbers and focus instead on the holistic relationship between price and quality (DeCaro et al., 2008; Kareev et al., 1997).

Long-Term Memory

As with processing speed and working memory, long-term memory declines gradually over the lifespan (for a review, see Kausler, 1994). The declines in long-term memory occur primarily for episodic information (information about past personal events and experiences; Nilsson, 2003). There are also more noticeable deficits in explicit (vs implicit) recall (Light & Singh, 1987). People can better recognize words, objects, and faces learned earlier in life (Cortese & Khanna, 2007; Cuetos et al., 1999; Ellis et al., 2010; Ellis & Morrison, 1998; Juhasz, 2005; Moore & Valentine, 1999; Pérez, 2007). Indeed, older consumers can recognize extinct brands learned at a young age better than active brands learned later in life (Ellis et al., 2010).

Knowledge-based Memory. Older adults cope with declines in long-term episodic or source memory by using their stored knowledge or semantic memory, to fill information gaps (Umanath & Marsh, 2014). Accordingly, older adults tend to perform worse than young adults in free recall, cued recall, and recognition of recent exposures (i.e., episodic memory tasks) but not in category exemplar generation, word completion, and perceptual identification tasks, which rely on knowledge-based memory or implicit memory of a recent exposure (Light & Singh, 1987). Knowledge-based memory refers to general, world-based knowledge that is accumulated during the course of life (Tulving, 1972), while implicit memory represents memory trace of a recent exposure in the absence of one's conscious recollection of the event (Light & Singh, 1987). As people age, knowledge-based and implicit memory remain largely intact and can help elderly adults compensate for shortfalls in working memory. Specifically, expertise in a domain is protective against negative effects of aging on knowledge-based memory (Thornton & Dumke, 2005). Thus, an elderly consumer who has shopped regularly at a local supermarket for years may have acquired extensive knowledge of the price ranges of many products and the timing and amounts of price promotions. While cognitive decline makes it more difficult to recall the exact price they last paid for a product, more expert older consumers sense whether a given price is reasonable or unusual.

Source Memory. Long-term memory includes memory for when, where, or in what context information such as prices or other product features was learned – source memory. Older adults have worse source memory compared to young adults (Johnson et al., 1993; Spencer & Raz, 1995). They are also more likely to experience false recognition (i.e., mistakenly think they have previously encountered a novel item) (Pidgeon & Morcom, 2014; Schacter et al., 1999). Relatedly, older (vs young) adults are more likely to remember a warning message (e.g., "The claim X is false") as being true (Skurnik et al., 2005).

Further, a declining source memory has an unintended effect of repetition on older adults. For them, repetition increases familiarity with the warning claim itself but decreases recollection of the claim's original context. As a result, advertising that involves warning messages with a negation (e.g., "Don't do X" and "X is false") may be counterproductive for older adults because of their relatively poor source memory. Thus, if public policymakers want to convey a message to older adults, they may want to reduce negation words. For older consumers, a direct, positive message (e.g., "Do X)" without negation terms (e.g., "Don't") may be more effective in the long run.

Summary

In summary, the impact of aging on cognition is detrimental but selective. Aging affects some aspects of memory and information processing but not others. However, as just discussed, many studies specify simple ways in which marketing communications can be modified to improve comprehension. Overall, it is unclear how age-related declines in cognition may adversely affect elderly consumers. After all, the vast majority of consumer choice-making is habit-based, involving mental operations that have become automated and do not entail deliberative processing (Drolet et al., 2018).

CHANGES IN EMOTIONAL FUNCTIONING DUE TO AGING

Alongside changes in sensory and cognitive functioning, aging is associated with an increased focus on emotion. In brief, compared to young adults, elderly adults attend more to emotions and emotional information versus facts and nonemotional information (for a review, see Mather, 2004). As a result, they are better at acknowledging and regulating their emotions (Blanchard-Fields, 1986; Labouvie-Vief, 1998; Labouvie-Vief et al., 1989). For example, elderly adults are more predisposed to favor advertisements highlighting how a product or service can help them avoid a negative emotional experience (Williams & Drolet, 2005).

Indeed, both cross-sectional and longitudinal studies have found a so-called *positivity effect* whereby older adults report experiencing less negative emotion (e.g., anxiety) compared to young adults (Gross et al., 1997; Kennedy et al., 2004). And yet, older adults experience positive emotions as often as (Charles et al., 2001) or more often than do young adults (Mroczek & Kolarz, 1998; Ryff, 1989). The positivity effect appears partly due to older (vs young) adults' decreased memory for negative emotional information (Löckenhoff & Carstensen, 2007). For example, older adults recall fewer negative images versus positive or neutral images (Charles et al., 2003). Indeed, older (vs young) adults show less activation in the amygdala in response to negative versus positive images and have less encodings of negative emotional experiences (Mather & Carstensen, 2003). This finding suggests selective inactivity in responses to negative stimuli among older adults.

Past research reveals multiple motivation-based reasons for older adults' increased focus on emotions.

Wisdom Development

One reason is wisdom development. As people age and mature, they develop wisdom. Wisdom can be thought of as the ability to think and act using prior knowledge, past experiences, common sense, and insight (see Chapter 4, Castel, 2018). Wisdom development reflects a process of cognitive-affective integration that leads to a complex understanding of emotions and how facts are inextricably linked to emotions (Labouvie-Vief, 2003). Wisdom involves emotion as well as knowledge. In particular, it involves keeping emotions in check and deciding when to express them and to whom (Castel, 2018).

Labouvie-Vief's (2003) theory of cognitive-affective development states that individuals change along two dimensions during the life course. The first dimension is the ability to optimize positive emotion, an ability that increases with age. For example, older adults have more stable periods of highly positive affect and less stable periods of highly negative affect (Carstensen et al., 2000). The second dimension is the ability to tolerate the discomfort resulting from cognitive-affective complexity. For example, older adults are better able than young adults at enduring the discomfort of mixed emotional experiences (Aaker et al., 2008). As a result, older (vs young) adults show less emotional discomfort in response to mixed emotional advertisements (Williams & Aaker, 2002). The reason for these findings is that older adults have an increased tendency to accept contradiction, particularly in the domain of emotions. Wisdom development requires the integration of the two dimensions in order to optimize emotional well-being while maintaining an "objective" view of the world (Labouvie-Vief, 2003).

Perceptions of Time as Limited

A second reason for older adults' increased focus on emotion is their (chronic) perception of time as limited. According to socioemotional selectivity theory, the perception that time is limited leads people to shift their attention toward emotion and emotional information (Carstensen, 1992). People who view time as limited tend to focus more on the present and on what can be experienced and enjoyed now (Carstensen et al., 1999). In brief, they are more focused on achieving affective gain and experiencing positive emotion rather than avoiding affective loss or experiencing negative emotion. In contrast, people who view time as expansive tend to focus more on the future and on what can be experienced and enjoyed later.

Chronological age is a major determinant of the length of people's time horizon view. Older adults are more likely than young adults to describe their futures as limited (vs expansive; Carstensen et al., 1999). Older adults recognize that they are nearing the end of their lives and, as a result, are more intent on pursuing emotionally meaningful goals than knowledge-related goals (Lang & Carstensen, 2002).

Age is associated with increased attention to emotional aspects of relationships (Carstensen & Fredrickson, 1998; Carstensen & Turk-Charles, 1994). A limited time perception leads older adults to place greater significance on having emotionally meaningful relationships. Consequently, social networks shrink in size with age. The social networks of older adults have the same number of close relationship partners but fewer peripheral partners (English & Carstensen, 2014; Fung et al., 2001).

IMPLICATIONS OF AGING FOR THE QUALITY OF CONSUMER INFORMATION PROCESSING

Together, age-related changes in the sensory, cognitive, and emotional systems lead elderly consumers to process information differently than younger consumers do. In short, aging is associated with robust declines in the *deliberative* processing of information (Bjälkebring & Peters, 2021).

As mentioned above, aging is accompanied by declines in the speed and efficiency of controlled processing mechanisms associated with deliberation. Notably, many consumer choices involving numeric information usually require deliberative capacity to process. Consequently, numeracy (the ability to comprehend and use mathematical and probabilistic concepts) declines with age (e.g., Kirsch et al., 2002; Schaie & Zanjani, 2006). Lower numeracy is associated with lower comprehension which puts less numerate people at risk when making decisions that require numerical processing, such as financial and health-care decisions. And, lower comprehension due to numeracy has negative effects on the quality of older adults' decisions and in turn their well-being (e.g., Peters, 2010).

The decline in deliberative processing associated with aging also affects whether decision-makers will rely on a more top-down (beginning with the most important issue or question) versus bottom-up (focusing on tactical, specific details) processing style. Older (vs young) adults generally exhibit greater use of schema-based processing (Yoon, 1997). However, specific task conditions significantly impact processing strategy, with older adults demonstrating the ability to engage in detailed processing when exposed to high-incongruity cues during their optimal time of day (i.e., morning). Nevertheless, the presence of incongruity often leads to the use of schema-based processing during older adults' nonoptimal time of day (Yoon, 1997).

Likewise, research on the influence of aging on comprehension suggests that age-related declines in deliberative processes negatively impact decision-making (Chen, 2002, 2004; Chen & Blanchard-Fields, 2000). Elderly consumers demonstrate greater vulnerability to the influence of false information than younger consumers (Chen & Blanchard-Fields, 2000). Elderly consumers' performance worsens as the number of choice options under consideration increases. For example, elderly consumers make worse decisions in the Medicare prescription drug program when choosing among larger option sets (Tanius et al., 2009; Wood et al., 2011), although elderly adults perform similarly to young adults under full attention conditions (e.g., Castel & Craik, 2003). Taken together, these findings suggest that elderly adults may have more difficulty controlling attention and monitoring the accuracy of information in memory which in turn makes their judgments more prone to errors.

ARE ELDERLY CONSUMERS MORE VULNERABLE TO MARKETERS?

For numerous reasons, the general idea that older adults make worse decisions than young adults in many situations due to large declines in their deliberative capacity is overly simplistic. Blanket statements that elderly consumers are more vulnerable to marketing activities in comparison to young consumers are unhelpful insofar as they lack context. Older adults are able to selectively use their deliberative capacity. For example, compared to younger consumers, older adults show an increased preference for satisficing or making "good enough" choices (vs maximizing or choosing the very best options) (Bruine de Bruin et al., 2016). It is likely that older consumers maintain more positive well-being due to their choice to use satisficing strategies, since maximizing is associated with depression, perfectionism, social comparison, and regret (Schwartz et al., 2002).

Even when older adults lack sufficient deliberative capacity to solve a choice problem, their accumulated experience can compensate for this age-related decline. Thus, age-related changes in cognitive functioning can have both negative and positive impacts. Whereas "fluid abilities" (e.g., working memory ability) tend to decline with age from the 20s, "crystallized intelligence" (the accumulation of knowledge) increases from the 20s and remains relatively stable throughout most of adulthood (Horn, 1982). As such, older (vs young) consumers benefit from their ability to draw on larger stores of knowledge, experience, and expertise. For example, older adults are more financially literate than young adults, largely as the result of life experience (Li et al., 2013), and this literacy can compensate for a decline in numeracy (Eberhardt et al., 2019). Along similar lines, when older consumers are asked to remember realistic price information for groceries, they perform as well as young consumers (Castel, 2005). This pattern is in contrast to the age impairment for remembering unrealistic prices, as well as the typical poor performance of older adults when they must recall information in the absence of external cues (Craik & McDowd, 1987). Thus, the same pricing strategy may work differently for young and older consumers: older adults may remember realistic price information for groceries better than young adults.

Another reason why the notion that older adults make worse decisions is too simplistic is that older consumers appear to perform better than young adults at decision tasks that require affective and/or experiential inputs. Put differently, young adults may be better at decision tasks that require deliberative processes but worse at tasks that suffer from deliberation. For example, research by Damasio (1994) showed that older adults can outperform young adults in the Iowa Gambling Task, a decision task in which affective cues have been shown to be useful. In general, the extent to which cognitive versus affective/experiential cues may be useful in decision-making may differ at different age periods in life. Studies on financial decision-making have found an inverted U-shaped relationship between age and decision quality, with middle-aged adults outperforming both young and older adults (Agarwal et al., 2009; Read & Read, 2004). This is presumably because middle-aged adults achieve a balance between limited cognitive resources, increased emotional regulation, and accumulative experiences.

Finally, older consumers have also acquired extensive persuasion knowledge (i.e., knowledge that the consumer is a persuasion target; Friestad & Wright, 1994). Although older consumers may be less able to process advertisements in an elaborative way due to declines in the cognitive system, their many past experiences with marketing activities may help them avoid cons and scams and can render older adults less susceptible to misleading persuasive appeals (Yoon et al., 2009).

CONCLUSION

Aging causes changes in sensory functioning, emotion, and cognition which in turn change how elderly (vs younger) consumers make decisions. On the one hand, elderly consumers experience significant declines in cognitive ability that can negatively affect their comprehension of persuasive communications. On the other hand, elderly consumers are able to compensate for cognitive deficits by relying more on the affect and motivation system when forming judgments and making decisions. Further, elderly consumers are more experienced consumers, and their more extensive knowledge base has a protective effect on the quality of decision-making.

An important last note, our review provides a big picture perspective of the functional capabilities of the general population of older adults (age 60+) as a group, it is worth noting that older adults exhibit both greater interindividual variability and intraindividual variability in comparison to young adults (Hultsch et al., 2002). It is also worth noting that most of the age-related changes in consumer behavior may be moderated by numerous task and contextual characteristics. For example, age-related deficits in comprehension can be significantly reduced or even eliminated by changing how information is presented to consumers (Cole & Houston, 1987; Gaeth & Heath, 1987).

REFERENCES

Aaker, J., Drolet, A., & Griffin, D. (2008). Recalling mixed emotions. *Journal of Consumer Research*, *35*(2), 268–278. https://doi.org/10.1086/588570

Agarwal, S., Driscoll, J. C., Gabaix, X., & Laibson, D. (2009). The age of reason: Financial decisions over the life-cycle and implications for regulation. *Brookings Papers on Economic Activity*, *2009*(2), 51–117. https://doi.org/10.1353/eca.0.0067

Agrawal, Y., Platz, E. A., & Niparko, J. K. (2008). Prevalence of hearing loss and differences by demographic characteristics among US adults: Data from the National Health and Nutrition Examination Survey, 1999–2004. *Archives of Internal Medicine*, *168*(14), 1522–1530. https://doi.org/10.1001/archinte.168.14.1522

Babcock, R. L., & Salthouse, T. A. (1990). Effects of increased processing demands on age differences in working memory. *Psychology and Aging*, *5*(3), 421–428. https://doi.org/10.1037/0882-7974.5.3.421

Besedeš, T., Deck, C., Sarangi, S., & Shor, M. (2012). Age effects and heuristics in decision making. *The Review of Economics and Statistics*, *94*(2), 580–595. https://doi.org/10.1162/REST_a_00174

Bjälkebring, P., & Peters, E. (2021). Money matters (especially if you are good at math): Numeracy, verbal intelligence, education, and income in satisfaction judgments. *PLoS One*, *16*(11), e0259331. https://doi.org/10.1371/journal.pone.0259331

Blanchard-Fields, F. (1986). Reasoning on social dilemmas varying in emotional saliency: An adult developmental perspective. *Psychology and Aging*, *1*(4), 325–333. https://doi.org/10.1037/0882-7974.1.4.325

Bonifeld, C. M., & Cole, C. A. (2021). Comprehension of and vulnerability to persuasive marketing communications among older consumers. In A. Drolet & C. Yoon (Eds.), *The aging consumer: Perspectives from psychology and marketing* (pp. 182–199). Routledge/Taylor & Francis Group. https://doi.org/10.4324/9780429343780-12

Boyce, J. M., & Shone, G. R. (2006). Effects of ageing on smell and taste. *Postgraduate Medical Journal*, *82*(966), 239–241. https://doi.org/10.1136/pgmj.2005.039453

Bruine de Bruin, W., Parker, A. M., & Strough, J. (2016). Choosing to be happy? Age differences in "maximizing" decision strategies and experienced emotional well-being. *Psychology and Aging*, *31*(3), 295–300. https://doi.org/10.1037/pag0000073

Carstensen, L. L. (1992). Social and emotional patterns in adulthood: Support for socioemotional selectivity theory. *Psychology and Aging*, *7*(3), 331–338. https://doi.org/10.1037/0882-7974.7.3.331

Carstensen, L. L., & Fredrickson, B. L. (1998). Influence of HIV status and age on cognitive representations of others. *Health Psychology*, *17*(6), 494–503. https://doi.org/10.1037/0278-6133.17.6.494

Carstensen, L. L., Isaacowitz, D. M., & Charles, S. T. (1999). Taking time seriously. A theory of socioemotional selectivity. *American Psychologist*, *54*(3), 165–181. https://doi.org/10.1037/0003-066X.54.3.165

Carstensen, L. L., Pasupathi, M., Mayr, U., & Nesselroade, J. R. (2000). Emotional experience in everyday life across the adult life span. *Journal of Personality and Social Psychology*, *79*(4), 644–655. https://doi.org/10.1037/0022-3514.79.4.644

Carstensen, L. L., & Turk-Charles, S. (1994). The salience of emotion across the adult life span. *Psychology and Aging*, *9*(2), 259–264. https://doi.org/10.1037/0882-7974.9.2.259

Castel, A. D. (2005). Memory for grocery prices in younger and older adults: The role of schematic support. *Psychology and Aging*, *20*(4), 718–721. https://doi.org/10.1037/0882-7974.20.4.718

Castel, A. D. (2018). *Better with age: The psychology of successful aging*. Oxford University Press.

Castel, A. D., & Craik, F. I. (2003). The effects of aging and divided attention on memory for item and associative information. *Psychology and Aging*, *18*(4), 873. https://doi.org/10.1037/0882-7974.18.4.873

Charles, S. T., Mather, M., & Carstensen, L. L. (2003). Aging and emotional memory: The forgettable nature of negative images for older adults. *Journal of Experimental Psychology: General, 132*(2), 310–324. https://doi.org/10.1037/0096-3445.132.2.310

Charles, S. T., Reynolds, C. A., & Gatz, M. (2001). Age-related differences and change in positive and negative affect over 23 years. *Journal of Personality and Social Psychology, 80*(1), 136. https://doi.org/10.1037/0022-3514.80.1.136

Charness, N., Champion, M., & Yordon, R. (2010). Designing products for older consumers: A human factors perspective. In A. Drolet, N. Schwarz, & C. Yoon (Eds.), *The aging consumer: Perspectives from psychology and economics* (pp. 249–268). Routledge.

Charness, N., & Jastrzembski, T. S. (2009). Gerontechnology. In P. Saariluoma, & H. Isomäki (Eds.), *Future interaction design II* (pp. 1–30). Springer.

Chen, Y. (2002). Unwanted beliefs: Age differences in beliefs of false information. *Aging, Neuropsychology, and Cognition, 9*(3), 217–228. https://doi.org/10.1076/anec.9.3.217.9613

Chen, Y. (2004). Age differences in the correction of social judgments: Source monitoring and timing of accountability. *Aging, Neuropsychology, and Cognition, 11*(1), 58–67. https://doi.org/10.1076/anec.11.1.58.29359

Chen, Y., & Blanchard-Fields, F. (2000). Unwanted thought: Age differences in the correction of social judgments. *Psychology and Aging, 15*(3), 475–482. https://doi.org/10.1037/0882-7974.15.3.475

Cole, C. A., & Gaeth, G. J. (1990). Cognitive and age-related differences in the ability to use nutritional information in a complex environment. *Journal of Marketing Research, 27*(2), 175–184. https://doi.org/10.2307/3172844

Cole, C. A., & Houston, M. J. (1987). Encoding and media effects on consumer learning deficiencies in the elderly. *Journal of Marketing Research, 24*(1), 55–63. https://doi.org/10.2307/3151753

Conway, A. R., & Engle, R. W. (1994). Working memory and retrieval: A resource-dependent inhibition model. *Journal of Experimental Psychology: General, 123*(4), 354–373. https://doi.org/10.1037/0096-3445.123.4.354

Cortese, M. J., & Khanna, M. M. (2007). Age of acquisition predicts naming and lexical-decision performance above and beyond 22 other predictor variables: An analysis of 2,342 words. *Quarterly Journal of Experimental Psychology, 60*(8), 1072–1082. https://doi.org/10.1080/17470210701315467

Craik, F. I., & McDowd, J. M. (1987). Age differences in recall and recognition. *Journal of Experimental Psychology: Learning, Memory, and Cognition, 13*(3), 474–479. https://doi.org/10.1037/0278-7393.13.3.474

Cuetos, F., Ellis, A. W., & Alvarez, B. (1999). Naming times for the Snodgrass and Vanderwart pictures in Spanish. *Behavior Research Methods, Instruments, & Computers, 31*(4), 650–658. https://doi.org/10.3758/BF03200741

Damasio, A. R. (1994). *Descartes' error: Emotion, reason, and the human brain.* Putamen.

DeCaro, M. S., Thomas, R. D., & Beilock, S. L. (2008). Individual differences in category learning: Sometimes less working memory capacity is better than more. *Cognition, 107*(1), 284–294. https://doi.org/10.1016/j.cognition.2007.07.001

Doty, R. L., Shaman, P., Applebaum, S. L., Giberson, R., Siksorski, L., & Rosenberg, L. (1984). Smell identification ability: Changes with age. *Science, 226*(4681), 1441–1443. https://doi.org/10.1126/science.6505700

Doty, R. L., & Snow, J. B. (1988). Age-related alterations in olfactory structure and function. In F. L. Margolis & T. V. Getchell (Eds.), *Molecular neurobiology of the olfactory system* (pp. 355–374). Plenum Press.

Drolet, A., Bodapati, A. V., Suppes, P., Rossi, B., & Hochwarter, H. (2018). Habits and free associations: Free your mind and mind your habits. *Journal of the Association for Consumer Research, 2*(3), 293–305. https://doi.org/10.1086/695422

Eberhardt, W., de Bruin, W. B., & Strough, J. (2019). Age differences in financial decision making: The benefits of more experience and less negative emotions. *Journal of Behavioral Decision Making, 32*(1), 79–93. https://doi.org/10.1002/bdm.2097

Ellis, A. W., Holmes, S. J., & Wright, R. L. (2010). Age of acquisition and the recognition of brand names: On the importance of being early. *Journal of Consumer Psychology, 20*(1), 43–52. https://doi.org/10.1016/j.jcps.2009.08.001

Ellis, A. W., & Morrison, C. M. (1998). Real age-of-acquisition effects in lexical retrieval. *Journal of Experimental Psychology: Learning, Memory, and Cognition, 24*(2), 515–523. https://doi.org/10.1037/0278-7393.24.2.515

Emmett, S. D., & Seshamani, M. D. (2015). Otolaryngology in the elderly. In P. W. Flint, B. H. Haughey, V. J. Lund, J. K. Niparko, K. T. Robbins, J. R. Thomas, & M. M. Lesperance (Eds.) *Cummings otolaryngology: Head and neck surgery* (6th ed., pp. 270–296). Elsevier Saunders.

Engle, R. W. (2002). Working memory capacity as executive attention. *Current Directions in Psychological Science, 11*(1), 19–23. https://doi.org/10.1111/1467-8721.00160

English, T., & Carstensen, L. L. (2014). Selective narrowing of social networks across adulthood is associated with improved emotional experience in daily life. *International Journal of Behavioral Development, 38*(2), 195–202. https://doi.org/10.1177/0165025413515404

Federal Reserve Board. (2020). https://www.federalreserve.gov/publications/files/scf20.pdf

Fisk, A. D., Rogers, W. A., Charness, N., Czaja, S. J., & Sharit, J. (2004). *Designing for older adults: Principles and creative human factors approach.* CRC Press.

Friestad, M., & Wright, P. (1994). The persuasion knowledge model: How people cope with persuasion attempts. *Journal of Consumer Research, 21*(1), 1–31.

Fung, H. H., Carstensen, L. L., & Lang, F. R. (2001). Age-related patterns in social networks among European Americans and African Americans: Implications for socioemotional selectivity across the life span. *International Journal of Aging and Human Development, 52*(3), 185–206. https://doi.org/10.2190/1ABL-9BE5-M0X2-LR9V

Gaeth, G. J., & Heath, T. B. (1987). The cognitive processing of misleading advertising in young and old adults: Assessment and training. *Journal of Consumer Research, 14*(1), 43–54. https://doi.org/10.1086/209091

Gross, J. J., Carstensen, L. L., Pasupathi, M., Tsai, J., Götestam Skorpen, C., & Hsu, A. Y. (1997). Emotion and aging: Experience, expression, and control. *Psychology and Aging, 12*(4), 590–599. https://doi.org/10.1037/0882-7974.12.4.590

Hasher, L., & Zacks, R. T. (1988). Working memory, comprehension, and aging: A review and a new view. In G. H. Bower (Ed.). *The psychology of learning and motivation: Advances in research and theory* (Vol. 22, pp. 193–225). Academic Press. https://doi.org/10.1016/S0079-7421(08)60041-9

Hedden, T., & Gabrieli, J. D. (2004). Insights into the ageing mind: A view from cognitive neuroscience. *Nature Reviews Neuroscience, 5*(2), 87–96. https://doi.org/10.1038/nrn1323

Horn, J. L. (1982). The theory of fluid and crystallized intelligence in relation to concepts of cognitive psychology and aging in adulthood. In F. I. M. Craik & S. Trehub (Eds.), *Aging and cognitive processes* (pp. 237–278). Plenum Press. https://doi.org/10.1007/978-1-4684-4178-9_14

Hultsch, D. F., MacDonald, S. W. S., & Dixon, R. A. (2002). Variability in reaction time performance of younger and older adults. *Journals of Gerontology Series B: Psychological Sciences and Social Sciences, 57*(2), P101–P115. https://doi.org/10.1093/geronb/57.2.P101

Johnson, M. K., Hashtroudi, S., & Lindsay, D. S. (1993). Source monitoring. *Psychological Bulletin, 114*(1), 3.

Juhasz, B. J. (2005). Age-of-acquisition effects in word and picture identification. *Psychological Bulletin, 131*(5), 684–712. https://doi.org/10.1037/0033-2909.131.5.684

Kareev, Y., Lieberman, I., & Lev, M. (1997). Through a narrow window: Sample size and the perception of correlation. *Journal of Experimental Psychology: General, 126*(3), 278–287. https://doi.org/10.1037/0096-3445.126.3.278

Katzman, R., & Terry, R. D. (1983). *The neurology of aging.* F.A. Davis Company.

Kausler, D. H. (1994). *Learning and memory in normal aging.* Academic Press.

Kennedy, Q., Mather, M., & Carstensen, L. L. (2004). The role of motivation in the age-related positivity effect in autobiographical memory. *Psychological Science, 15*(3), 208–214. https://doi.org/10.1111/j.0956-7976.2004.01503011.x

Kirsch, I. S., Jungeblut, A., Jenkins, L., & Kolstad, A. (2002). *Adult literacy in America.* National Center for Education Statistics. https://nces.ed.gov/pubs93/93275.pdf

Kline, D. W., & Scialfa, C. T. (1996). Visual and auditory aging. In J. E. Birren & K. W. Schaie (Eds.), *Handbook of the psychology of aging* (4th ed., pp. 181–203). Academic Press.

Labouvie-Vief, G. (1998). Cognitive–emotional integration in adulthood. In K. W. Schaie & M. P. Lawton (Eds.), *Annual review of gerontology and geriatric cs: Vol. 17. Focus on emotion and adult development* (pp. 206–237). Springer.

Labouvie-Vief, G. (2003). Dynamic integration: Affect, cognition, and the self in adulthood. *Current Directions in Psychological Science*, *12*(6), 201–206. https://doi.org/10.1046/j.0963-7214.2003. 01262.x

Labouvie-Vief, G., DeVoe, M., & Bulka, D. (1989). Speaking about feelings: Conceptions of emotion across the life span. *Psychology and Aging*, *4*(4), 425–437. https://doi.org/10.1037/0882-7974.4. 4.425

Lang, F. R., & Carstensen, L. L. (2002). Time counts: Future time perspective, goals, and social relationships. *Psychology and Aging*, *17*(1), 125–139. https://doi.org/10.1037/0882-7974.17.1. 125

Li, Y., Baldassi, M., Johnson, E. J., & Weber, E. U. (2013). Complementary cognitive capabilities, economic decision making, and aging. *Psychology and Aging*, *28*(3), 595–613. https://doi.org/ 10.1037/a0034172

Light, L. L., & Singh, A. (1987). Implicit and explicit memory in young and older adults. *Journal of Experimental Psychology: Learning, Memory, and Cognition*, *13*(4), 531–541. https://doi.org/10. 1037/0278-7393.13.4.531

Löckenhoff, C. E., & Carstensen, L. L. (2007). Aging, emotion, and health-related decision strategies: Motivational manipulations can reduce age differences. *Psychology and Aging*, *22*(1), 134–146. https://doi.org/10.1037/0882-7974.22.1.134

Lustig, C., May, C. P., & Hasher, L. (2001). Working memory span and the role of proactive interference. *Journal of Experimental Psychology: General*, *130*(2), 199–207. https://doi.org/10.1037/ 0096-3445.130.2.199

Margrain, T. H., & Boulton, M. (2005). Sensory impairment. In M. L. Johnson (Ed.), *The Cambridge handbook of age and ageing* (pp. 121–130). Cambridge University Press.

Mata, R., von Helversen, B., & Rieskamp, J. (2010). Learning to choose: Cognitive aging and strategy selection learning in decision making. *Psychology and Aging*, *25*(2), 299–309. https://doi.org/10. 1037/a0018923

Mather, M. (2004). Aging and emotional memory. In D. Reisberg & P. Hertel (Eds.), *Memory and emotion* (pp. 272–307). Oxford University Press.

Mather, M., & Carstensen, L. L. (2003). Aging and attentional biases for emotional faces. *Psychological Science*, *14*(5), 409–415. https://doi.org/10.1111/1467-9280.01455

Moore, V., & Valentine, T. (1999). The effects of age of acquisition on processing famous faces and names: Exploring the locus and proposing a mechanism. In M. H. S. Stoness (Ed.), *Proceedings of the 21st Annual Meeting of the Cognitive Science Society* (pp. 749–754). Erlbaum.

Mroczek, D. K., & Kolarz, C. M. (1998). The effect of age on positive and negative affect: A developmental perspective on happiness. *Journal of Personality and Social Psychology*, *75*(5), 1333. https://doi.org/10.1037/0022-3514.75.5.1333

National Institute of Health: National Institute on Deafness and Other Communication Disorders. (2022, March 16). *How do we hear?* https://www.nidcd.nih.gov/health/how-do-we-hear

Nelson, E. G., & Hinojosa, R. (2006). Presbycusis: A human temporal bone study of individuals with downward sloping audiometric patterns of hearing loss and review of the literature. *The Laryngoscope*, *116*(S112), 1–12. https://doi.org/10.1097/01.mlg.0000236089.44566.62

Nilsson, L. G. (2003). Memory function in normal aging. *Acta Neurologica Scandinavica*, *107*(s179), 7–13. https://doi.org/10.1034/j.1600-0404.107.s179.5.x

Pérez, M. A. (2007). Age of acquisition persists as the main factor in picture naming when cumulative word frequency and frequency trajectory are controlled. *Quarterly Journal of Experimental Psychology*, *60*(1), 32–42. https://doi.org/10.1080/17470210600577423

Peters, E. (2010). Aging-related changes in decision making. In A. Drolet, N. Schwarz, & C. Yoon (Eds.), *The aging consumer: Perspectives from psychology and economics* (pp. 75–101). Psychology Press.

Pidgeon, L. M., & Morcom, A. M. (2014). Age-related increases in false recognition: The role of perceptual and conceptual similarity. *Frontiers in Aging Neuroscience*, *6*, 283. https://doi.org/10. 3389/fnagi.2014.00283

Plack, C. (2014). The temporal coding of pitch: Insights from human electrophysiology. *Journal of the Acoustical Society of America*, *135*(4), 2348. https://doi.org/10.1121/1.4877718

Raz, N. (2000). Aging of the brain and its impact on cognitive performance: Integration of structural and functional findings. In F. I. M. Craik & T. A. Salthouse (Eds.), *The handbook of aging and cognition* (pp. 1–90). Lawrence Erlbaum Associates.

Read, D., & Read, N. L. (2004). Time discounting over the lifespan. *Organizational Behavior and Human Decision Processes*, *94*(1), 22–32. https://doi.org/10.1016/j.obhdp.2004.01.002

Reuter-Lorenz, P. A., Stanczak, L., & Miller, A. C. (1999). Neural recruitment and cognitive aging: Two hemispheres are better than one, especially as you age. *Psychological Science*, *10*(6), 494–500. https://doi.org/10.1111/1467-9280.00195

Rolls, B. J. (1999). Do chemosensory changes influence food intake in the elderly? *Physiology & Behavior*, *66*(2), 193–197. https://doi.org/10.1016/S0031-9384(98)00264-9

Ryff, C. D. (1989). Happiness is everything, or is it? Explorations on the meaning of psychological well-being. *Journal of Personality and Social Psychology*, *57*(6), 1069–1081. https://doi.org/10.1037/0022-3514.57.6.1069

Salthouse, T. A. (1996). The processing-speed theory of adult age differences in cognition. *Psychological Review*, *103*(3), 403–428. https://doi.org/10.1037/a0023262

Salthouse, T. A., & Babcock, R. L. (1991). Decomposing adult age differences in working memory. *Developmental Psychology*, *27*(5), 763–776. https://doi.org/10.1037/0012-1649.27.5.763

Saxon, S. V., & Etten, M. J. (2002). *Physical change and aging: A guide for helping professions* (4th ed.). The Tiresias Press, Inc.

Schacter, D. L., Israel, L., & Racine, C. (1999). Suppressing false recognition in younger and older adults: The distinctiveness heuristic. *Journal of Memory and Language*, *40*(1), 1–24. https://doi.org/10.1006/jmla.1998.2611

Schaie, K. W., & Zanjani, F. A. K. (2006). Intellectual development across adulthood. In C. Hoare (Ed.), *Handbook of adult development and learning* (pp. 99–122). Oxford University Press.

Schiffman, S. S. (1997). Taste and smell losses in normal aging and disease. *JAMA*, *278*(16), 1357–1362. https://doi.org/10.1001/jama.1997.03550160077042

Schneider, B. A., Daneman, M., & Murphy, D. R. (2005). Speech comprehension difficulties in older adults: Cognitive slowing or age-related changes in hearing? *Psychology and Aging*, *20*(2), 261–271. https://doi.org/10.1037/0882-7974.20.2.261

Schwartz, B., Ward, A., Monterosso, J., Lyubomirsky, S., White, K., & Lehman, D. R. (2002). Maximizing versus satisficing: Happiness is a matter of choice. *Journal of Personality and Social Psychology*, *83*(5), 1178. https://doi.org/10.1037/0022-3514.83.5.1178

Sherman, E. D., & Robillard, E. (1964). Sensitivity to pain in relationship to age. *Journal of the American Geriatrics Society*, *12*(11), 1037–1044.

Skurnik, I., Yoon, C., Park, D. C., & Schwarz, N. (2005). How warnings about false claims become recommendations. *Journal of Consumer Research*, *31*(4), 713–724. https://doi.org/10.1086/426605

Spencer, W. D., & Raz, N. (1995). Differential effects of aging on memory for content and context: A meta-analysis. *Psychology and Aging*, *10*(4), 527. https://doi.org/10.1037/0882-7974.10.4.527

Stevens, J. C., & Patterson, M. Q. (1995). Dimensions of spatial acuity in the touch sense: Changes over a life span. *Somatosensory & Motor Research*, *12*(1), 29–47. https://doi.org/10.3109/08990229509063140

Szrek, H., & Bundorf, M. K. (2011). Age and the purchase of prescription drug insurance by older adults. *Psychology and Aging*, *26*(2), 308–320. https://doi.org/10.1037/a0023169

Tanius, B. E., Wood, S., & Hanoch, Y. (2009). Aging and choice: Applications to Medicare Part D. *Judgment and Decision Making*, *4*(1), 92–101.

Thornbury, J. M., & Mistretta, C. M. (1981). Tactile sensitivity as a function of age. *Journal of Gerontology*, *36*(1), 34–39. https://doi.org/10.1093/geronj/36.1.34

Thornton, W. J., & Dumke, H. A. (2005). Age differences in everyday problem-solving and decision-making effectiveness: A meta-analytic review. *Psychology and Aging*, *20*(1), 85. https://doi.org/10.1037/0882-7974.20.1.85

Tulving, E. (1972). Episodic and semantic memory. In E. Tulving & W. Donaldson (Eds.), *Organization of memory* (pp. 381–403). Academic Press.

Umanath, S., & Marsh, E. J. (2014). Understanding how prior knowledge influences memory in older adults. *Perspectives on Psychological Science*, 9(4), 408–426. https://doi.org/10.1177/1745691614535933

Verdu, E., Ceballos, D., Vilches, J. J., & Navarro, X. (2000). Influence of ageing on peripheral nerve function and regeneration. *Journal of the Peripheral Nervous System*, 5(4), 191–208. https://doi.org/10.1111/j.1529-8027.2000.00026.x

Verrillo, R. T., Bolanowski, S. J., & Gescheider, G. A. (2002). Effects of aging on the subjective magnitude of vibration. *Somatosensory & Motor Research*, 19(3), 238–244. https://doi.org/10.1080/0899022021000009161

Williams, P., & Aaker, J. L. (2002). Can mixed emotions peacefully coexist? *Journal of Consumer Research*, 28(4), 636–649. https://doi.org/10.1086/338206

Williams, P., & Drolet, A. (2005). Age-related differences in responses to emotional advertisements. *Journal of Consumer Research*, 32(3), 343–354. https://doi.org/10.1086/497545

Wood, S., Hanoch, Y., Barnes, A., Liu, P. J., Cummings, J., Bhattacharya, C., & Rice, T. (2011). Numeracy and Medicare Part D: The importance of choice and literacy for numbers in optimizing decision making for Medicare's prescription drug program. *Psychology and Aging*, 26(2), 295–307. https://doi.org/10.1037/a0022028

Yoon, C. (1997). Age differences in consumers' processing strategies: An investigation of moderating influences. *Journal of Consumer Research*, 24(3), 329–342. https://doi.org/10.1086/209514

Yoon, C., Cole, C. A., & Lee, M. P. (2009). Consumer decision making and aging: Current knowledge and future directions. *Journal of Consumer Psychology*, 19(1), 2–16. https://doi.org/10.1016/j.jcps.2008.12.002

VULNERABILITY AND CONSUMER POVERTY: AN EXPLICATION OF CONSUMPTION ADEQUACY

Ronald Paul Hill and Girish Ramani

American University, USA

ABSTRACT

There are multiple threats that cause consumers to be vulnerable in the marketplace, with poverty being a leading cause. Impoverishment often negatively impacts access to multiple categories of goods and services that consumers require to experience a reasonable quality of life. While there is research that explores the underlying factors that lead to resource deficits and marketplace restrictions, as well as their physical and emotional outcomes, an understanding of what is necessary to survive and thrive across societies is more elusive. To this end, our chapter carefully examines the concept of consumption adequacy (CA), which historically captures consumer needs for food and potable water, socially acceptable clothing adapted to weather conditions, safe housing that provides for privacy needs of occupants, preventative and remedial health care, and opportunities to grow and advance through education and training. After briefly summarizing the extant literature, each is described in turn, and ways of empirically investigating them across societies are advanced. This chapter closes with both marketer and public policy implications.

Keywords: Consumption adequacy; impoverished consumers; resource deficits and restrictions; consumer behavior; impoverished consumption; human development

INTRODUCTION

That many, if not most, people around the world struggle to meet their ordinary needs is well-known. One estimate is that only about 15% of the global

The Vulnerable Consumer
Review of Marketing Research, Volume 21, 25–48
Copyright © 2024 Ronald Paul Hill and Girish Ramani
Published under exclusive licence by Emerald Publishing Limited
ISSN: 1548-6435/doi:10.1108/S1548-643520240000021003

population lives as well as middle or higher socioeconomic classes in highly developed countries (Hill, 2022). The United Nations Development Program categorizes nations into four groupings, with the greatest disadvantages for women in Arab states, South Asia, and sub-Saharan Africa (UNDP, 2020). Concerns about impoverished consumers by marketing scholars began in the 1960s and 1970s, because of US racial discrimination and inner-city strife in places often designated as "ghettos" (see Andreasen, 1975; Sexton, 1971). This interest waxed and waned over the following years, regaining some prominence in the 1990s (e.g., Hill & Stamey, 1990). The renewed focus moved to different poverty communities (Bone et al., 2014, is an exception) to broaden marketer and public policymaker understanding of their lived experiences.

Some of these efforts focused on locations within the United States, including work by Saatcioğlu and Ozanne (2013) that involved examination of mobile-home dwellers and their search for social status both within and outside their neighborhoods. Viswanathan and a host of colleagues (e.g., Viswanathan & Venugopal, 2019; Viswanathan et al., 2010) moved beyond North America and have looked at how poor and often illiterate women in developing nations navigate markets typically dominated by the patriarchy. Prahalad (2005) attempted to show the viability of such marketplaces and their collective value, making the case that selling goods and services at the pyramid base is economically viable. While this perspective has its detractors (e.g., Hill, 2022; also see Karnani, 2011), it has had positive outcomes by redirecting attention away from only affluent communities to viable impoverished ones. Regardless, most research on poverty concentrates on restrictions faced by consumers and how they navigate them to acquire what they need or desire.

Much of this research is summarized by Hill and Sharma (2020) in their modeling of consumer vulnerability. Their article takes a resource-based perspective, noting how vulnerable consumers come up short on both sides of the exchange equation. By this, they mean consumers may lack the income or other means of purchasing or acquiring goods and services, and they can live in consumption environments that only contain meager options. Much effort is thus expended by vulnerable consumers to develop coping mechanisms under conditions of a lack of material fulfillment, which are termed defensive and non-defensive. The full set of differences is not germane to our arguments here, but it is important to recognize that the former suggests more proactive strategies, while the latter are more reactive. Proactive means they confront and seek to change the context, with reactive suggesting a more passive approach to this lacuna. What separates one from the other is the perceived mutability of the situation and the extent to which impoverished consumers can modify their circumstances (Cannon et al., 2019, provide a similar distinction in their work on scarcity). Martin and Hill (2012) looked at what happens at the base of the pyramid that drives them when the ability to meet basic needs are always denied (consumption [in]adequacy), and they find that psychological mechanisms of autonomy, competence, and relatedness do not operate to support life satisfaction when consumers are below the consumption adequacy (CA) threshold but are able to do so when consumers are above the threshold.

In the same article, Martin and Hill (2012) describe what constitutes CA, using five categories of goods and services to capture its essence. They are potable water for drinking and sanitation, as well as enough healthful foods prepared in culturally specified ways, shelter that yields adequate protection from possible outside interpersonal and climate threats and allows for needed levels of privacy, clothing consonant with weather conditions and local tastes, both preventative and remedial health-care options, and the ability to advance life prospects through education and training. While this step forward has benefits, the lack of measures makes it difficult to determine if adequacy exists along any of these dimensions or how they can best be understood objectively as well as subjectively from the perspectives of both observers and users. In this chapter, we emphasize the user perspective in the traditional sense of consumers. The next section provides more details on these products, using a multidisciplinary frame across literature. Once each is specified, we present a series of analyses that demonstrate how some have been measured and how they manifest individually and together for consumers. Of course, heterogeneity across cultural and religious contexts as well as development statuses suggest that there may be significant differences in national approaches to CA. Regardless, our goal is to find category definitions and measures that have universal appeal, allowing for some consensus that supersedes such differences.

DIMENSIONS OF CA

Water and Food

That humans require sustenance is a given, but what constitutes acceptable quantities has never been discussed in the consumer behavior or marketing literature. For the most part, nutritionists and other forms of health-care providers or public health experts seek to define formulae that will provide the exact number of calories an individual of a certain size and gender would need to ingest to maintain their current physicality. Other factors are important as well, including their lifestyle, physical health, age, and the types of foods and liquids that are normally accessible and allowable within the cultural and religious milieu. What is often missing is any differences in cultural tastes, preferences for certain foods because of individual history, and the value of prepared versus fresh-ingredient meals. The CA construct, then, can be expanded to mean enough potable water/water substitutes, along with access to healthful varieties of fruits, vegetables, lean meats, and other items prepared in ways that are both palatable and desirable. Further, water for the purposes of sanitation is also an additional and essential use.

The closest construct to the one proposed here is the low-cost but adequate (LCA) amount of food (with menus) that would provide a household of a particular size and makeup with a diet consistent with cultural/religious tastes and that satisfies guidelines for healthful consumption (Nelson et al., 2002). Yet these authors use the proxy of amount spent on food as the indicant of dietary sufficiency, especially for children (study completed in England). Other investigations followed suit, using indicators such as availability of foodstuffs in the region through supermarkets (Connell et al., 2007 – Mississippi Delta), a "simple" count of food items or groupings available in a particular home (Hatlùy et al., 1998 – Africa), subjective measures of food insecurity versus standardized poverty metrics (Bhattacharya et al., 2002 – US), and levels of dietary diversity and resulting micronutrients (Arimond et al., 2010 – five developing nations; Campbell et al., 2018 – Bangladesh). Taken together, they reveal little consistency in how CA in food is defined or measured, suggesting that uniform measures do not cover the necessary domain.

Acceptable Shelter

While some citizens around the world live in homes that dwarf the rest of the housing stock, most people, especially in developing nations or countries with vast differences between haves and have-nots, struggle with how to cope given insufficient utilities, the lack of enough privacy for household members, and structures that are not safe from intruders and changing weather patterns (Please see the many opinions and rulings on issues such as reasonable accommodations and fair market rents by the US Department of Housing and Urban Development fair housing – Housing and Urban Development Search Results [usa.gov]). Of course, there is a cultural element associated with what is acceptable or unacceptable to solve these difficulties. For example, in wealthy communities across the developed world, there are homes of 5,000 to 10,000 square feet (or more) that have two-to-four occupants, while the allocation of space in less-affluent nations and neighborhoods is miniscule by comparison. The former may have large yards and driveways to keep others at a distance and gates at the entrances to their homes or communities. For the latter, families may live in one crowded room for bedding, washing, and cooking, with the only other room for storage and sanitary purposes. Clearly, one moves beyond what is adequate by most standards, while the other is once again below acceptable. Thus, we reiterate that shelter should be safe from the elements and intruders, have the capacity to allow for functions like sleeping and eating without interference, and provide the necessary privacy for mental and physical health and security.

The literature on housing is global in nature but often has the same or similar concerns. There is a decided focus on what is "adequate" consistent with the CA construct (e.g., Mohamad et al., 2018 – Malaysia), emphasizing discrimination in the housing market (Mundra & Sharma, 2014 – US) and affordability for a reasonable shelter (Lerman & Reeder, 1987 – US). Other researchers have emphasized specific housing and locational conditions that include internal and external structures, access to various utilities and sanitation, and privacy considerations (Morton et al., 2004 – rural US). The most detailed description specifies hot and cold water in bathrooms for toilets and showers/baths, consistent heating in all rooms, constant availability of electricity, and freedom from water leaks, holes in floors, cracks on walls or ceilings, peeling paint, and rodents (Emrath & Taylor, 2012 – US). One vexing problem is how to determine a lack of shelter CA without extensive scrutiny of housing stock. One proposed indicant is the age of homes or complexes (Kutty, 1999 – multiple US cities). However, like concerns about measuring food CA, it is a gross indicator that may not capture the depth and breadth of problems worldwide.

Appropriate Clothing

Like other categories of goods and services, clothing has several roles for protection from weather and climate changes and for support of self-identity and religious mandates. For instance, consumers should have enough outer and inner wear such as shirts, pants, underwear, socks, shoes, and jackets, and other options depending upon taste, gender definition, social environment, and religious context. What makes this provision more complex is that certain identities, like high school student or restaurant worker, may also require purchasing uniforms that have little utility beyond the role function served. Still, it is unclear what condition each of these items must maintain to yield protection or signal acceptability in a particular society. To some extent, this function to determine CA may vary across nations and communities based on the necessary variety and its expression from individualistic to collectivistic countries and the need to standout versus blend into the social milieu. We close with another statement that captures the essence of CA: clothing should be provided in sufficient quantities in need categories that are consonant with identity formation in a cultural/religious context and the weather conditions faced.

Not surprisingly, most research on clothing examines more affluent consumers. For instance, Hwang et al. (2016 – US) modeled attitudes and purchase intentions, revealing factors like perceived usefulness and comfort, along with ease of use, aesthetic attributes, and environmental concerns as important. This last factor has also been demonstrated to involve considerations of sustainability (Harris et al., 2016 – UK) and avoidance of sweatshop labor products (Shaw et al., 2006 – UK). One exception looks at what they refer to as "the clothing disposal system," whereby individuals give each other clothing that is no longer useful to one but is for another (Cruz-Cárdenas et al., 2017 – Ecuador). The best available source for our research is a 1971 dissertation that studied clothing adequacy among impoverished children living in an urban setting (Patson, 1971 – US). Her work suggests that families make tradeoffs among CA categories of goods and service, prioritizing food then shelter before clothing. She also believes that clothing among these poor still must meet ecological and social needs (termed "health and decency") to be described as satisfactory. Further criteria for evaluating clothing adequacy include location and housing, jobs and other outdoor activities, and age or stage in the family lifecycle. Clothing may be the first indicant of social acceptability for most consumers.

Health Care

The levels of health protection, quality of life, and predicted longevity vary considerably around the world. More developed nations, for the most part, provide at least some health-care access for its citizenry. Others do not offer or offer considerably less if the consumer is without the financial wherewithal to cover fees or full payments. This often means that people suffering from illnesses typically do not get treated early on in their disease cycles unless they have far-ranging insurance. Physicians and public health experts note that these deficits cost a society more than if they had served the person earlier in disease progression. Thus, CA should be defined in this category as ready access to remedial health care at the onset of illness or disease to keep it from getting worse. As important is preventative care that could keep consumers from getting sick in the first place. Such options could save hospitals during times like the recent pandemic when they had to help people who failed to follow acceptable protocols, denying beds to other sick patients. Similar concerns exist in the United States for women following the recent overruling on Roe V. Wade.

There is considerable research on health care around the world, but most of it is consonant with studies in the United States. Firstly, it tends to concentrate attention on disparities between consumer groups, like differences in access within rural communities that lack a "network adequacy" of providers versus greater opportunities among urban patients (Casey et al., 2017). This situation has resulted in less access to services that are preventative in nature, suggesting failure in meeting standards for positive health outcomes (Casey et al., 2001). Other subpopulations of interest have included pregnant women of color and their use of prenatal care and levels of satisfaction (Tandon et al., 2013). Secondly, poverty is of great concern and homeless persons' views of mental health services and resulting stigma and prejudice have been studied (Bhui et al., 2006), as well as use of local or state safety nets for uninsured poor versus traditional avenues for insured patients and their relative abilities to successfully navigate the health-care system (Hall, 2011). Not surprisingly, the Affordable Care Act and its rollout on a state-by-state basis was scrutinized, revealing lack of uniformity or sophistication in its implementation (Haeder, 2014). Not surprisingly, continuous debate over access in the United States is a developed nation anomaly.

Education and Training

There are significant differences in access to education and training based on country development levels and cultural/religious expectations of women and children. In some developing countries, children are expected to work at very early ages, truncating their education options, even in countries that have prohibitions against child labor. In many rural areas, the need can be particularly great, and the patriarchal nature of the family may exacerbate this problem. Women suffer the most in this regard if they are from certain countries that hold a parochial and nondevelopmental perspective of the female gender. Training is different, and it includes opportunities to expand one's skill set to be more consistent with the dynamic nature of work and markets. Once again, some people may not be eligible depending upon their citizenship status, age, or gender. With our discussion in mind, this category should be described as widespread opportunities for schooling until at least they reach literacy and numeracy, and future options to go beyond these levels if the intelligence and desire are there.

Training and other resources should be provided to all adults who wish to change occupations or are victims of layoffs or declining markets.

Adequacy plays a role in these conversations as well. For example, concerns about access because of fees associated with school attendance and rights to a "basic education" have been discussed in the larger literature (Roithmayer, 2003 – South Africa). Such variations also include lower quality in terms of teachers, facilities, books, libraries, curriculum, and labs for poor versus more affluent children (Satz, 2007 – US), along with similar difficulties for children living in rural communities (Malhoit, 2005). Additional emphasis in more recent years concerns access to the technological advances that have changed the face of education, especially in the developed world, showing disparities across socioeconomic groupings and race (Roth, 2020 – US). Differences in resources necessary to support entrepreneurial ventures also have received much attention. For example, Bates (2002 – US) demonstrates that women-owned businesses face restrictions in their access to markets relative to men, and Brush et al. (2006 – US) find that women entrepreneurs have similar obstacles obtaining capital relative to men. As a result, women often are barred from growth-oriented enterprises and are more likely to be involved with smaller, local service-oriented, low-tech businesses (Roomi et al., 2009 – UK).

In summary, this brief review clearly indicates that adequacy across nations and categories of goods and services often does not exist because of disparities in affluence, racial prejudice, cultural and religious mandates, and gender discrimination. While much research has been done to understand various consumer needs and desires, a more expansive recognition of our CA construct has remained elusive. For example, even realizing when CA does not exist in various categories or countries is tangential to the lived experiences of people who must go without fulfillment. Objective measures used by observers are either burdensome to determine or are rough proxies that are designed to meet mostly public policy directives, and subjective measures of impacted consumers vary greatly and do not always align with global standards. Many applicable poverty measures offered by nongovernmental organizations like the UN are simple income-based dividing lines that translate poorly into consumption options. There also is little attention to differences in how a perceived lack in one category impacts consumer well-being or how multiple deficits operate simultaneously on this outcome. While this chapter does not resolve the objective–subjective argument, it does offer an approach to understanding uniform needs of people who lack prosperity with the end user in mind. Additionally, our research investigates the impact of multiple versus singular forms of deficit that have important implications for policy.

The next section presents results across nations with individual consumers to understand the impact of consumption *in*adequacy on their quality of life. The data come from highly reliable sources that have long histories of sensitive data collections. One difficulty is that our CA construct was not top-of-mind in their research decisions and protocols; hence, the measures we use do not perfectly fit our theoretical paradigm or all nuances of each category of goods and services. While our analyses are decidedly imperfect, even if we are accessing the best data available worldwide, the discussion that follows has much to offer about the global material environments of diverse people and subsequent impacts of them. An eventual goal is to proactively seek opportunities to influence future collection efforts to better align with the CA construct as it manifests globally.

DATA, METHODOLOGY, AND FINDINGS

The data for our analyses come from the World Values Survey wave 7 (WVS 7) (Haerpfer et al., 2022). The dataset consists of 87,882 observations collected from 59 countries. The WVS 7 dataset provides values for two quality of life variables: (1) life satisfaction and (2) happiness. The WVS 7 dataset also provides information on the extent of deprivation or vulnerability experienced by respondents across multiple categories of basic goods and services such as food, cash, shelter, medicine, and exposure to crime (impacts access and use of all categories of goods and services). We examine the influence of vulnerabilities experienced by respondents on both quality-of-life variables. The survey records, at the respondent level, show the extent to which they were subjected to multiple vulnerabilities in the past year that correspond to several dimensions of CA. The five vulnerability variables from the survey that serve as proxies for our analyses are food outage, cash outage, medicine outage, lack of shelter, and exposure to crime as the first attempt to look at multiple deficits or simultaneous access. See Appendix 1 for the questionnaire items corresponding to the full set of WVS 7 variables used in our analyses. Their study selected proxies for needed categories of goods and services, but they are unlikely to fully recognize the extent of need noted previously. We circle back to these concerns in the closing section.

Since we have a nested structure in our dataset, in that some variation across respondents on the dependent variables of life satisfaction and happiness is likely to be the result of their country affiliation, our analysis needed to account for this dependence. We adopted a multilevel modeling technique (see Bates et al., 2015; Oakley et al., 2006) to account for the hierarchy of individual (first level) and country (second level) effects. Additionally, life satisfaction and happiness have been identified as distinct components contributing to consumer well-being (Martin & Hill, 2012). While life satisfaction and happiness are interrelated, they have nuanced differences. The former is more of an enduring trait and moves/ changes more slowly, while the latter is about the day-to-day, impacted more by recent or current events. Hence, we separately explored the existence of multiplicative effects of the constituent dimensions of CA on each of these two quality of life variables. We seek to answer the following questions: Do consumers experiencing higher (lower) levels of vulnerabilities on multiple dimensions of CA report lower (higher) levels of life satisfaction and/or happiness? Does experiencing high levels of a single vulnerability dim or exacerbate the effects of being exposed to a higher level of a second vulnerability on quality of life?

To seek answers to the above questions, we test two models consisting of the CA variables in our dataset as predictors of quality of life and include two-way interaction terms for combinations of pairs of dimensions of CA. We do not include higher order interactions in our models. We expect that each of the vulnerabilities, food outage, cash outage, medicine outage, lack of shelter, and exposure to crime would individually have a significant effect in determining the level of life satisfaction and/or happiness of individuals across country borders. Hence, we expect our analysis to confirm the presence of these main effects. It is conceivable that the impact of one vulnerability, for example, food outage, would vary depending on the level of vulnerability experienced on a second vulnerability, such as lack of shelter. The interaction effect between food outage and lack of shelter may be such that when individuals experience higher levels of lack of shelter, the effect of food outage on quality of life is dimmed. On the other hand, it is also conceivable that when individuals experience higher levels of one vulnerability (such as cash outage), the negative impact of a second vulnerability (such as exposure to crime) on quality of life might be further heightened. It is also possible that some of the vulnerabilities identified do not interact, and the impact of one vulnerability on quality of life remains unaffected at different levels of the other vulnerability variables. Given these three distinct possibilities, we seek to empirically examine the nature of the interactions and report the findings of this analysis. Consequently, we identify if any single vulnerability plays a dominant role in impacting other vulnerabilities in terms of either dimming or exacerbating their effects on quality of life outcomes.

We estimate the main effects and the effects of the interaction terms for life satisfaction as the dependent variable in the first model and happiness as the outcome variable in the second. In our model specifications, we set the outcome intercept to randomly vary across the 59 countries. We include gender, age, social class, and income as level one control variables. Table 1 contains the correlations between the individual level variables.

Results From the Life Satisfaction Model

The results from the multilevel model for life satisfaction as the outcome variable are available in Table 2a. We report the results for the model containing the five main effects of the vulnerability variables from our dataset. These variables are food outage, exposure to crime, cash outage, medicine outage, and lack of shelter. We also include the 10 possible two-way interaction terms between each of the five variables in the model and report the estimated coefficients in Table 2a.

We find the coefficients for food outage (-0.288, $t(82,465) = -8.062, p < 0.001$), exposure to crime ($-0.158$, $t(82,497) = -6.262$, $p < 0.001$), cash outage (-0.289, $t(82,481) = -11.246, p < 0.001$), medicine outage ($-0.295$, $t(82,473) = -9.853 p < 0.001$), and lack of shelter ($-0.376$, $t(82,459) = -8.475, p < 0.001$) on the dependent variable life satisfaction are all negative and significant and, therefore, consistent with expectations. We also note that three interaction terms involving lack of shelter are significant. In particular, the interaction term for medicine outage and lack of shelter is significant (0.043, $t(82,453) = 3.538$, $p < 0.001$). Fig. 1 shows the plots of the interaction effects. Since all variables studied are continuous in nature, we plot values at $+/-$ standard deviation levels of the moderator variables (Martin & Hill, 2012).

The significant coefficients for lack of shelter, medicine outage, and the interaction term between the two variables (see Fig. 1a) suggest that both lack of

Table 1. Correlations.

	1	2	3	4	5	6	7	8	9	10	11
Happiness.	1										
Life_satisf	0.4358	1									
Food_outage.	−0.1219	−0.1949	1								
Crime_exp.	−0.0947	−0.1249	0.3691	1							
Med_outage.	−0.1359	−0.1944	0.5272	0.3942	1						
Cash_outage.	−0.1423	−0.2075	0.5398	0.3398	0.543	1					
Shelter_outage.	−0.0863	−0.1507	0.4467	0.3546	0.3991	0.3945	1				
Gender	0.0178	0.0087	0.0035	0.0012	−0.0037	0.0014	−0.0191	1			
Age	−0.0462	0.0236	−0.0934	−0.0326	−0.0624	−0.1058	−0.0849	−0.0218	1		
Social_Class.	0.1375	0.1559	−0.1855	−0.0994	−0.1838	−0.2276	−0.089	−0.0107	−0.0362	1	
Income	0.144	0.2004	−0.1914	−0.0968	−0.1828	−0.2399	−0.092	−0.0291	−0.0914	0.5045	1

Note: The following variables were reverse coded: Happiness, Food_outage, Crime_exp, Med_outage, Cash_outage, Shelter_outage, and Social_class.

Table 2a. Outcome Variable: Life Satisfaction (Observations = 82,528, Countries = 59).

Effect	Group	Term	Estimate	Std. Error	t Statistic	df[a]	p Value
Fixed	NA	(Intercept)	7.571	0.126	59.981	122	0.000
Fixed	NA	Food_outage.	-0.288	0.036	-8.062	82,465	0.000
Fixed	NA	Crime_exp.	-0.158	0.025	-6.262	82,497	0.000
Fixed	NA	Cash_outage.	-0.289	0.026	-11.246	82,481	0.000
Fixed	NA	Med_outage.	-0.295	0.030	-9.853	82,473	0.000
Fixed	NA	Shelter_exp.	-0.376	0.044	-8.475	82,459	0.000
Fixed	NA	Gender	0.058	0.014	4.115	82,456	0.000
Fixed	NA	Age	0.003	0.000	7.321	82,507	0.000
Fixed	NA	Social_Class.	0.124	0.009	14.289	82,484	0.000
Fixed	NA	Income	0.131	0.004	32.007	82,481	0.000
Fixed	NA	Cash_outage.:Med_outage.	0.014	0.010	1.483	82,461	0.138
Fixed	NA	Cash_outage.:Shelter_exp.	0.035	0.013	2.709	82,454	0.007
Fixed	NA	Med_outage.:Shelter_exp.	0.043	0.012	3.538	82,453	0.000
Fixed	NA	Food_outage.:Crime_exp.	0.002	0.011	0.164	82,458	0.869
Fixed	NA	Food_outage.:Cash_outage.	0.018	0.011	1.745	82,461	0.081
Fixed	NA	Food_outage.:Med_outage.	-0.001	0.011	-0.136	82,455	0.892
Fixed	NA	Food_outage.:Shelter_exp.	0.027	0.012	2.190	82,457	0.029
Fixed	NA	Crime_exp.:Cash_outage.	-0.002	0.010	-0.235	82,458	0.814
Fixed	NA	Crime_exp.:Med_outage.	0.017	0.010	1.745	82,457	0.081
Fixed	NA	Crime_exp.:Shelter_exp.	0.005	0.011	0.405	82,464	0.686
Ran_pars	Country_alpha	sd__(Intercept)	0.803	—	—	—	—
Ran_pars	Residual	sd__Observation	2.021	—	—	—	—

[a]Satterthwaite's degrees of freedom method.

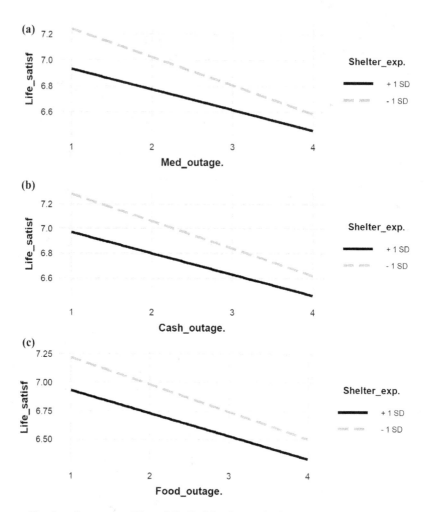

Fig. 1.   Interaction Plots: Life Satisfaction and Elements of Consumption Adequacy. Moderator: Shelter. (a) Medicine Outage × Shelter on Life Satisfaction. (b) Cash Outage × Shelter on Life Satisfaction. (c) Food Outage × Shelter on Life Satisfaction.

shelter and medicine outages significantly suppress life satisfaction, although the decline in life satisfaction brought on by medicine outage is much sharper at low levels of lack of shelter than at high levels of lack of shelter. That is, when people are not worrying about a lack of shelter, they are more distressed when they do not have access to medicine. However, as people become more concerned about lacking shelter, not having access to medicine does not distress them to the same extent, suggesting a primacy effect of lack of shelter.

We note that the interaction term for cash outage and lack of shelter is also significant (0.035, $t(82,454) = 2.709$, $p = 0.007$; see Fig. 1b). This suggests that the decline in life satisfaction brought on by cash outage is much sharper at low levels of lack of shelter than at high levels of lack of shelter. We also find that the interaction term for food outage and lack of shelter is significant (0.027, $t(82,457) = 2.190$, $p = 0.029$; see Fig. 1c). This suggests that the decline in life satisfaction brought on by food outage is much sharper at low levels of lack of shelter than at high levels of lack of shelter.

Given that the three two-way interaction terms for the three vulnerability variables medicine outage, cash outage, and food outage with lack of shelter as the moderator variable are significant, we conclude for this set of vulnerabilities that lower levels of one vulnerability magnify the impact of the second vulnerability variable on life satisfaction. Conversely, higher levels of one vulnerability variable dim the impact of the second variable on life satisfaction. This supports the notion that when people face challenges on multiple fronts, they may feel so numbed by life's hardships that their satisfaction with life does not drop as fast as it would when they experience severe hardship on a single front.

Results From the Happiness Model

The results from the model for happiness as the outcome variable are available in Table 2b. Like the life satisfaction models, we report the results for the effects from the same set of five CA variables and the corresponding two-way interaction effects. As Table 2b shows, the coefficients for food outage (-0.064, $t(82,336) = -5.534$, $p < 0.001$), cash outage (-0.052, $t(82,355) = -6.270$, $p < 0.001$), medicine outage (-0.063, $t(82,346) = -6.496$, $p < 0.001$), lack of shelter (-0.087, $t(82,328) = -6.011$, $p < 0.001$), and exposure to crime (-0.072, $t(82,371) = -8.703$, $p < 0.001$) on the dependent variable happiness are all negative and significant and, therefore, consistent with expectations.

Table 2b. Outcome Variable: Happiness (Observations = 82,394, Countries = 59).

Effect	Group	Term	Estimate	Std. Error	t Statistic	df[a]	p Value
Fixed	NA	(Intercept)	3.316	0.037	88.928	150	0.000
Fixed	NA	Food_outage.	−0.064	0.012	−5.534	82,336	0.000
Fixed	NA	Crime_exp.	−0.072	0.008	−8.703	82,371	0.000
Fixed	NA	Cash_outage.	−0.052	0.008	−6.270	82,355	0.000
Fixed	NA	Med_outage.	−0.063	0.010	−6.496	82,346	0.000
Fixed	NA	Shelter_exp.	−0.087	0.014	−6.011	82,328	0.000
Fixed	NA	Gender	0.026	0.005	5.707	82,324	0.000
Fixed	NA	Age	−0.001	0.000	−7.751	82,371	0.000
Fixed	NA	Social_Class.	0.054	0.003	19.218	82,359	0.000
Fixed	NA	Income	0.024	0.001	17.668	82,355	0.000
Fixed	NA	Cash_outage.: Med_outage.	0.003	0.003	0.872	82,331	0.383

(Continued)

Table 2b. *(Continued)*

Effect	Group	Term	Estimate	Std. Error	*t* Statistic	df[a]	p Value
Fixed	NA	Cash_outage.: Shelter_exp.	0.001	0.004	0.124	82,322	0.902
Fixed	NA	Med_outage.: Shelter_exp.	0.010	0.004	2.612	82,319	0.009
Fixed	NA	Food_outage.: Crime_exp.	0.009	0.004	2.427	82,327	0.015
Fixed	NA	Food_outage.: Cash_outage.	0.002	0.003	0.462	82,331	0.644
Fixed	NA	Food_outage.: Med_outage.	−0.005	0.003	−1.467	82,322	0.142
Fixed	NA	Food_outage.: Shelter_exp.	0.009	0.004	2.385	82,325	0.017
Fixed	NA	Crime_exp.: Cash_outage.	−0.008	0.003	−2.427	82,326	0.015
Fixed	NA	Crime_exp.: Med_outage.	0.007	0.003	2.028	82,325	0.043
Fixed	NA	Crime_exp.:Shelter_exp.	0.016	0.004	4.247	82,334	0.000
Ran_pars	Country_alpha	sd__(Intercept)	0.225	—	—	—	—
Ran_pars	Residual	sd__Observation	0.658	—	—	—	—

[a]Satterthwaite's degrees of freedom method.

We note that the interaction term for crime exposure and lack of shelter is significant (0.016, $t(82,334) = 4.247$, $p < 0.001$; see Fig. 2a). This suggests that the decline in happiness brought on by crime exposure is much sharper at low levels of lack of shelter than at high levels of lack of shelter. This may be taken to mean that when people do not have a roof over their head, the numbing effect of this hardship is such that the impact of crime exposure on their happiness levels tends to moderate. We note that the interaction term for medicine outage and lack of shelter is significant (0.010, $t(82,319) = 2.612$, $p = 0.009$). Fig. 2b is a plot of the interaction effect between medicine outage and lack of shelter. This suggests that the decline in happiness brought on by medicine outage is much sharper at low levels of lack of shelter than at high levels of lack of shelter. This result also suggests that, when a person does not have a roof over their head the numbing effect of this hardship is such that the impact of medicine outage on their happiness level tends to moderate. Fig. 2c which is a plot of the interaction effect between food outage and lack of shelter again highlights the numbing effect of lack of shelter.

We conclude there is a dimming of the effect of medicine outage, food outage, and crime exposure on happiness for higher levels of lack of shelter. The moderating effect of the variable lack of shelter on happiness is therefore clearly felt across three of the other vulnerability variables. We also note that two other interaction terms that do not involve the variable lack of shelter are also significant in the happiness model. The interaction between crime exposure and medicine outage is significant (0.007, $t(82,325) = 2.028$, $p = 0.043$). Interestingly, unlike all other significant interactions in both models, the interaction between

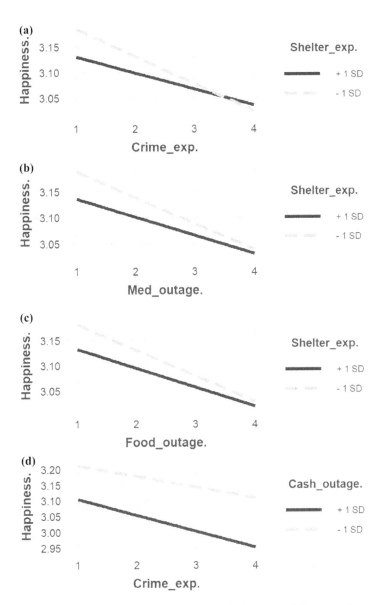

Fig. 2.   Interaction Plots: Happiness and Elements of Consumption
Adequacy. Moderators: Shelter, Cash Outage. (a) Crime Exposure × Shelter on
Happiness. (b) Medicine Outage × Shelter on Happiness. (c) Food Outage × Shelter
on Happiness. (d) Crime Exposure × Cash Outage on Happiness.

crime exposure and cash outage is negative and significant (-0.008, $t(82,326) =$ -2.427, $p = 0.015$). This suggests that cash outage exacerbates the effect of crime exposure on happiness (see Fig. 2d). The possibility exists that exposure to crime, such as being robbed, could itself be one of the reasons for cash outage. This finding further suggests that the relationship between these two variables may be deeper than our current analysis is able to uncover.

Floodlight Analysis

Since both the life satisfaction and happiness models involve moderator variables that were measured on a scale ranging from 1 to 4, we carried out floodlight analyses to examine the simple effects of independent variables across the entire range of the values of the moderator variables (Krishna, 2016; Spiller et al., 2013). We computed simple slopes and created Johnson Neyman (JN) plots (see Long, 2019) for the nine interactions that were reported as significant in the results of the two multilevel models. While later in this section we report the results from the simple slopes analysis for each of the nine significant interactions, for illustrative purposes we reproduce two of the JN plots obtained by visualizing changes in the effect (or slope) for the medicine outage variable on life satisfaction and happiness, as lack of shelter varies across the observed scale values ranging from 1 to 4. Fig. 3a represents the changing estimated effect of medicine outage on life satisfaction, as the value for the moderator variable lack of shelter is plotted to vary from one standard deviation below the range of the observed data to one standard deviation above the range of the observed data. As can be seen from the plot, the slope, while remaining significant for the entire range of the actual observed values of lack of shelter (for the range of 1–4), does diminish and approaches near zero for values of lack of shelter close to the upper bound of 4. The corresponding simple slopes analysis indicates that the slope estimates for medicine outage were all significant at $p < 0.05$ and took on the values -0.200, -0.157, -0.114, and -0.071, corresponding to the observed lack of shelter values of 1, 2, 3, and 4. Similarly, Fig. 3b is the plot representing the changing effect of medicine outage on happiness as the value for the moderator variable lack of shelter is allowed to change from one standard deviation below the range of the observed data to one standard deviation above the range of the observed data. The corresponding simple slopes analysis indicates that the slope estimates for medicine outage were significant at $p < 0.05$ and took on the values -0.045, -0.035, -0.025, corresponding to lack of shelter values of 1, 2, and 3. However, the effect of medicine outage changed to not significant at -0.014 ($p =$ 0.216), corresponding to the shelter exposure value of 4. The observed values in the significant region are high at 99.26%. However, the fact that the slope of medicine outage changes from being significant to not significant within the range of observed data lends strong support for the interaction effect between medicine outage and lack of shelter on happiness as the outcome.

Furthermore, in the case of the life satisfaction model, the simple slopes analyses of other variables involved in significant interaction terms indicated that the effect of the variables cash outage (-0.206, -0.171, -0.135, -0.100) and food outage (-0.227, -0.201, -0.174, -0.147), both remained significant ($p < 0.05$) but continually

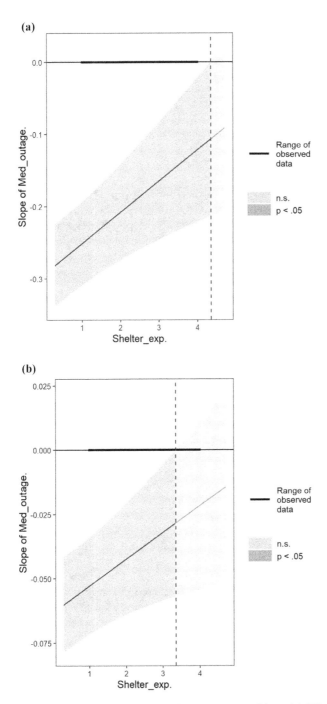

Fig. 3. Floodlight Analysis Using Johnson Neyman Plots. (a) JN plot:
Life_Sat ~ Med*Shelter. (b) JN plot: Life_Hap ~ Med*Shelter.

decreased as the value of the moderator variable lack of shelter took on the values 1, 2, 3, and 4.

In the case of the happiness model, a simple slopes analysis also indicated that the slope estimates for crime exposure were significant ($p < 0.05$) and took on the values -0.047, -0.031, -0.016, corresponding to lack of shelter values of 1, 2, and 3. However, the effect of crime exposure changed to not significant at -0.000 ($p = 0.983$) corresponding to the shelter exposure value of 4, further supporting the presence of a significant interaction effect. Also, the slope estimates for food outage took on these values (-0.047, -0.037, -0.028) and were significant ($p < 0.05$) corresponding to lack of shelter values of 1, 2, and 3. But, the effect of food outage changed to not significant (-0.019, $p = 0.102$) corresponding to the shelter exposure value of 4, further underscoring the role of lack of shelter's influence on the effects of other CA variables on life outcomes.

For completeness, we carried out simple slope analyses and examined Johnson Neyman plots for the happiness model with the moderator variables cash outage and medicine outage. The effect of crime exposure takes on these values (-0.047, -0.040, -0.034, -0.027), $p < 0.05$ for corresponding medicine outage values (1, 2, 3, and 4). The effect of crime exposure takes on increasing values (-0.036, -0.044, -0.052, and -0.060), all of which are significant at $p < 0.05$ for cash outage values (1, 2, 3, and 4), indicating once again that this is the only pair of interactions in our analysis where there is an exacerbating effect exerted by increasing levels of the moderating variable. This result might be due to the fact that a more complex relationship might exist between crime exposure and cash outage. For example, there might be a causal effect of crime exposure, such as burglary or theft, on cash outage.

Discussion of Key Findings

Our analysis shows that there are nine interactions that emerged as significant across both the life satisfaction and happiness models. The continuous nature of the CA variables in our data allows us to propose either variable in any given two-way interactions as the moderating variable. However, a simple count indicates that lack of shelter is the participating variable in six out of the nine significant interactions. In the life satisfaction model, lack of shelter is the variable in all the three interaction terms that are significant. Also, in the happiness model, lack of shelter is the variable in three out of six interactions that are significant. This underscores the role that lack of shelter plays in combination with the effects of the remaining four measures of CA of food outage, cash outage, medicine outage, and crime exposure on quality of life. Hence, our interaction plots and the analysis results consistently adopt lack of shelter as the reported moderating variable. Higher levels of lack of shelter consistently suppress the effect of the other vulnerability variables when it comes to both life satisfaction and happiness as measures of quality of life. Given our analysis examines data from individuals residing in 59 countries and allows for a multilevel hierarchy of a country effect and individual respondent level experiences, such a finding is of considerable significance for organizations, governments, and policymakers involved in uplifting the lives of the very poor, especially sections of countries' populations that may frequently lack basic access to shelter.

DISCUSSION

We began this research presentation by defining CA, describing its importance to understanding impoverished consumption, and offering more depth to the various goods and services that make up its portfolio. The next major section described a data set that informs how people across nations with different cultural contexts and levels of impoverishment endure their consumption lives as levels of access to different categories are assessed using the quality-of-life indicators of life satisfaction and happiness employed by Martin and Hill (2012). While not a test of CA as in that article, we show that increases/decreases in these items are associated with a lowering/advancement of quality of life. Our ability to articulate characteristics that make up each factor is important, but available secondary data at the national level often do not have a ready mix of subjective and objective indicators. One way to resolve this issue is for the consumer-behavior community of scholars to work with nongovernmental organizations such as the United Nations Development Program so that both parties gain from collaborations.

Regardless, our findings demonstrate some interesting outcomes that have value for future research and discovery. While previous research suggested that relatedness and autonomy can make up for certain levels of deficits in CA (Martin & Hill, 2012) on life satisfaction, no marketing or consumer scholar to date has attempted to see if the combination of different categories of goods and services has differential impacts on the focal quality-of-life variables. We do show here that for several combinations, the influence of one variable varies depending on the level of a second variable for both life satisfaction and happiness as outcome variables. This finding suggests the need for investigations across other combinations using different variables, while recognizing that any deficit does have a significant negative impact on quality of life.

This chapter makes clear the value of CA as a proxy for reasonable living in a material environment. It further suggests that progress has been made outside our marketing and consumer behavior fields, defining what is necessary to have or do to reach or exceed this marker. Of course, the capability of scholars to use these constructs in ways that result in similar measures for data collection and analyses will require cross-disciplinary cooperation that has eluded our field to date. The Transformative Consumer Research (TCR) movement has attempted to advance this cause by connecting TCR scholars with community organizers who have access to people living in diverse communities for the purposes of cocreating novel studies (see Blocker et al., 2013). We recommend seeking access to impoverished consumers who are struggling with one or more deficits below the adequacy threshold, especially combined with shelter concerns. Under these conditions, researchers can examine how tradeoffs occur among necessities and how they ultimately impact quality of life measures such as life satisfaction and happiness. Their ordering may also help policymakers in allocation decisions. Still, recognizing the impact of a single deficit remains essential, with adequate shelter at the top of this list.

The field is also seeing a melding of research on resource scarcity and lower income consumers (Hill, 2022). This work shows that people who have lower access, especially if that access is indeterminant in length, face much greater psychological and physical problems. One question is the extent to which these different negative consequences manifest and how they may come and go depending upon perceptions of restriction. This means that our concern with certain areas of deficit and their individual and cumulative impacts may need to be connected to these deleterious outcomes as an intermediate step that can moderate how poverty influences life satisfaction or happiness. Of course, this direction implies that poverty is more complex than many scholars realize, with tenacles into every facet of human functioning. It should be our goal to comprehend the fuller impacts and model our thinking accordingly.

CONCLUSION AND CLOSING REMARKS

The vulnerability of consumers living in poverty has and will continue to be at the forefront of societies' abilities to cope with restrictions associated with market-places. We freely admit that our analyses were not designed to rule on the objectivity–subjectivity debate, or that our measures co-align with the resource categories offered by Hill and Sharma (2020) or fully represent the CA construct. However, marketing and consumer scholars should continue to seek pathways to understanding impoverished consumers, as conditions within their consumption environments remain a global public policy concern. Our recommendation is that researchers begin their journey by looking at difficult situations and possible consequences for and reactions by impoverished consumers. These contexts are fertile terrain for discovery and can lead to successful investigations and eventual publication. However, it is essential that the next step involves making sure that these data are then available for distribution and discussion with people who play prominent roles in social enterprises or public policy, so that the loop is closed along the path from discovery to recovery that best serves all parties.

In our analysis, we limited ourselves to exploring interaction effects between the core CA variables of food outage, exposure to crime, cash outage, medicine outage, and lack of shelter. The model includes the self-reported control variable "Income" that captures individual respondent level data on wealth disparity within their respective countries. Future research could examine if the core CA variables also interact with country-level aggregate indicators of wealth and wealth disparity based on gross domestic product (GDP) or the Gini index. Analysis may also be further extended by examining country-level effects of cultural differences and other relevant variables.

REFERENCES

Andreasen, A. R. (1975). *The disadvantaged consumer*. The Free Press.

Arimond, M., Wiesmann, D., Becquey, E., Carriquiry, A., Daniels, M. C., Deitchler, M., Fanou-Fogny, N., Joseph, M. L., Kennedy, G., Martin-Prevel, Y., & Torheim, L. E. (2010). Simple food group diversity indicators predict micronutrient adequacy of women's diets in 5 diverse, resource-poor settings. *Journal of Nutrition, 140*, 2059S–2069S.

Bates, T. (2002). Restricted access to markets characterizes women-owned businesses. *Journal of Business Venturing, 17*, 313–324.

Bates, D., Mächler, M., Bolker, B., & Walker, S. (2015). Fitting linear mixed-effects models using lme4. *Journal of Statistical Software*, *67*(1), 1–48.

Bhattacharya, J., Currie, J., & Haider, S. (2002). *Food insecurity or poverty? Measuring need-related dietary adequacy*. Working Paper 9003. National Bureau of Economic Research. http://www.nber.org/papers/w9003

Bhui, K., Shanahan, L., & Harding, G. (2006). Homelessness and mental illness: A literature review and a qualitative study of perceptions of the adequacy of care. *International Journal of Social Psychiatry*, *52*, 152–165.

Blocker, C. P., Ruth, J. A., Sridharan, S., Beckwith, C., Ekici, A., Goudie-Hutton, M., & Rosa, J. A. (2013). Understanding poverty and promoting poverty alleviation through transformative consumer research. *Journal of Business Research*, *66*, 1195–1202.

Bone, S. A., Christensen, G. L., & Williams, J. D. (2014). Rejected, shackled, and alone: The impact of systemic restricted choice on minority consumers' construction of self. *Journal of Consumer Research*, *41*, 451–474.

Brush, C. G., Carter, N. M., Gatewood, E. J., Greene, P. G., & Hart, M. M. (2006). The use of bootstrapping by women entrepreneurs in positioning for growth. *Venture Capital*, *8*, 15–31.

Campbell, R. K., Hurley, K. M., Shamim, A. A., Shaikh, S., Chowdhury, Z. T., Mehra, S., Wu, L., & Christian, P. (2018). Complementary food supplements increase dietary nutrient adequacy and do not replace home food consumption in children 6–18 months old in a randomized controlled trial in rural Bangladesh. *Journal of Nutrition*, *148*(9), 1484–1492.

Cannon, C., Goldsmith, K., & Roux, C. (2019). A self-regulatory model of resource scarcity. *Journal of Consumer Psychology*, *29*, 104–127.

Casey, M. M., Call, K. T., & Klingner, J. M. (2001). Are rural residents less likely to obtain recommended preventive healthcare services? *American Journal of Preventative Medicine*, *21*, 182–188.

Casey, M., Henning-Smith, C., Abraham, J., & Moscovice, I. (2017). *Regulating network adequacy for rural populations: Perspectives of five states*. University of Minnesota Rural Research Center. Policy Brief, 1-4.

Connell, C. L., Yadrick, M. K., Simpson, P., Gossett, J., McGee, B. B., & Bogle, M. (2007). Food supply adequacy in the Lower Mississippi Delta. *Nutrition Education Behavior*, *39*, 77–83.

Cruz-Cárdenas, J., González, R., & Gascó, J. (2017). Clothing disposal system by gifting: Characteristics, processes, and interactions. *Clothing and Textiles Research Journal*, *35*, 49–63.

Emrath, P., & Taylor, H. (2012). Housing value, costs, and measures of physical adequacy. *Cityscape: A Journal of Policy Development and Research*, *14*, 99–125.

Haeder, S. F. (2014). Balancing adequacy and affordability?: Essential health benefits under the Affordable Care Act. *Health Affairs*, *118*, 285–291.

Haerpfer, C., Inglehart, R., Moreno, A., Welzel, C., Kizilova, K., Diez-Medrano, J., Lagos, M., Norris, P., Ponarin, E., & Puranen, B. (Eds.). (2022). *World values survey: Round seven – Country-pooled data file version 4.0*. JD Systems Institute & WVSA Secretariat. https://doi.org/10.14281/18241.18

Hall, M. A. (2011). Access to care provided by better safety net systems for the uninsured: Measuring and conceptualizing adequacy. *Medical Care Research and Review*, *68*, 441–461.

Harris, F., Roby, H., & Dibb, S. (2016). Sustainable clothing: Challenges, barriers and interventions for encouraging more sustainable consumer behaviour. *International Journal of Consumer Studies*, *40*, 309–318.

Hatlùy, A., Torheim, L. E., & Oshaug, A. (1998). Food variety—A good indicator of nutritional adequacy of the diet? A case study from an urban area in Mali, West Africa. *European Journal of Clinical Nutrition*, *52*, 891–898.

Hill, R. P. (2022). Poverty and consumer psychology. In L. R. Kahle, J. Huber, & T. M. Lowrey (Eds.), *APA handbook of consumer psychology* (pp. 243–265). American Psychological Association.

Hill, R. P., & Sharma, E. (2020). Consumer vulnerability. *Journal of Consumer Psychology*, *30*, 551–570.

Hill, R. P., & Stamey, M. (1990). The homeless in America: An examination of possessions and consumption behaviors. *Journal of Consumer Research*, *17*, 303–321.

Hwang, C., Chung, T., & Sanders, E. A. (2016). Attitudes and purchase intentions for smart clothing: Examining U.S. consumers' functional, expressive, and aesthetic needs for solar-powered clothing. *Clothing and Textiles Research Journal, 34*, 207–222.

Karnani, A. G. (2011). Doing well by doing good? The grand illusion. *California Management Review, 53*, 69–86.

Krishna, A. (2016). A clearer spotlight on spotlight: Understanding, conducting and reporting. *Journal of Consumer Psychology, 26*, 315–324.

Kutty, N. K. (1999). Determinants of structural adequacy of dwellings. *Journal of Housing Research, 10*, 27–43.

Lerman, D. L., & Reeder, W. J. (1987). The affordability of adequate housing. *AREUAE, 15*, 389–404.

Long, J. (2019). Interactions: Comprehensive, user-friendly toolkit for probing interactions, R package version 1.1.5. https://cran.r-project.org/package=interactions

Malhoit, G. C. (2005). *Providing rural students with a high quality education: The rural perspective on the concept of educational adequacy.* The Rural School and Community Trust, Rural Education Finance Center.

Martin, K. D., & Hill, R. P. (2012). Life satisfaction, self-determination, and consumption adequacy at the bottom of the pyramid. *Journal of Consumer Research, 38*, 1155–1168.

Mohamad, W., Wan, S. S., Syazwani, N. A., Rahman, B. A., & Ridzuan, M. R. B. (2018). Adequacy of low-cost housing: A study of the People's Housing Programme (PHP) at Kuala Lumpur. *The Journal of Social Sciences, 22*, 8–21.

Morton, L. W., Allen, B. L., & Li, T. (2004). Rural housing adequacy and civic structure. *Sociological Inquiry, 74*, 464–491.

Mundra, K., & Sharma, A. (2014). *Housing adequacy gap for minorities and immigrants in the U.S.: Evidence from the 2009 American Housing Survey.* IZA Discussion Papers, No. 8038. Institute for the Study of Labor (IZA).

Nelson, M., Dick, K., & Holmes, B. (2002). Food budget standards and dietary adequacy in low-income homes. *Proceedings of the Nutrition Society, 61*, 569–577.

Oakley, J., Iacobucci, D., & Duhachek, A. (2006). Multilevel, hierarchical linear models and marketing: This is not your advisor's OLS Model. In N. K. Malhotra (Ed.), *Review of marketing research* (Vol. 2). M.E. Sharpe. (Electronic Resource).

Patson, N. K. (1971). *Clothing adequacy of children six to eleven years old in low income families.* Dissertation in Home Economics. Ohio State University.

Prahalad, C. K. (2005). *The fortune at the bottom of the pyramid: Eradicating poverty through profits.* Wharton School Publishing.

Roithmayer, D. (2003). Access, adequacy and equality: The constitutionality of school fee financing in public education. *South African Journal on Human Rights, 19*, 382–429.

Roomi, M. A., Harrison, P., & Beaumont-Kerridge, J. (2009). Women-owned small and medium enterprises in England. *Journal of Small Business and Enterprise Development, 16*, 270–288.

Roth, K. (2020). *Technology in education: The ongoing debate of access, adequacy and equity.* https://educate.bankstreet.edu/independent-studies/248

Saatçioğlu, B., & Ozanne, J. L. (2013). Moral habitus and status negotiation in a marginalized working-class neighborhood. *Journal of Consumer Research, 40*, 692–710.

Satz, D. (2007). Equality, adequacy, and education for citizenship. *Ethics, 117*, 623–648.

Sexton, D. (1971). Comparing the cost of food to Blacks and Whites: A survey. *Journal of Marketing, 35*, 40–46.

Shaw, D., Hogg, G., Wilson, E., Shiu, E., & Hassan, L. (2006). Fashion victim: The impact of fair trade concerns on clothing choice. *Journal of Strategic Marketing, 14*, 427–440.

Spiller, S. A., Fitzsimons, G. J., Lynch, J. G., Jr., & McClelland, G. H. (2013). Spotlights, floodlights, and the magic number zero: Simple effects tests in Moderated Regression. *Journal of Marketing Research, 50*, 277–288.

Tandon, S. D., Cluxton-Keller, F., Colon, L., Vega, P., & Alonso, A. (2013). Improved adequacy of prenatal care and healthcare utilization among low-income Latinas receiving group prenatal care. *Journal of Women's Health, 22*, 1056–1061.

UNDP. (2020). *Tackling social norms: A game changer for gender inequalities.* UNDP.

Viswanathan, M., Rosa, J., & Ruth, J. A. (2010). Exchanges in marketing systems: The case of subsistence consumer-merchants in Chennai, India. *Journal of Marketing, 74*, 1–17.

Viswanathan, M., & Venugopal, S. (2019). Implementation of social innovations in subsistence marketplaces: A facilitated institutional change process model. *Journal of Product Innovation Management, 36*(6), 800–823.

APPENDIX 1
SUBSET OF WVS 7 QUESTIONNAIRE ITEMS USED IN THE ANALYSIS

Q46. Taking all things together, would you say you are (*read out and code one answer*):

(1) Very happy
(2) Rather happy
(3) Not very happy
(4) Not at all happy

Q49. All things considered, how satisfied are you with your life as a whole these days? Using this card on which 1 means you are "completely dissatisfied" and 10 means you are "completely satisfied" where would you put your satisfaction with your life as a whole? (*Code one number*):

Completely dissatisfied   Completely satisfied

| 1 | 2 | 3 | 4 | 5 | 6 | 7 | 8 | 9 | 10 |

In the last 12 months, how often have your or your family…?

		Often	Sometimes	Rarely	Never
Q51	Gone without enough food to eat	1	2	3	4
Q52	Felt unsafe from crime in your home	1	2	3	4
Q53	Gone without medicine or medical treatment that you needed	1	2	3	4
Q54	Gone without a cash income	1	2	3	4
Q55	Gone without a safe shelter over your head	1	2	3	4

Q260. Respondent's sex (*Code respondent's sex by observation, don't ask about it!*):

(1) Male
(2) Female

Q262. This means you are _____ **years old** (*write in age in two digits*).

Q287. People sometimes describe themselves as belonging to the working class, the middle class, or the upper or lower class. Would you describe yourself as belonging to the (*read out and code one answer*):

(1) Upper class
(2) Upper middle class
(3) Lower middle class
(4) Working class
(5) Lower class

Q288. On this card is an income scale on which 1 indicates the lowest income group and 10 the highest income group in your country. We would like to know in what group your household is. Please, specify the appropriate number, counting all wages, salaries, pensions and other incomes that come in. (*Code one number*):

Lowest group									Highest group
1	2	3	4	5	6	7	8	9	10

NOT KNOWING WHO I AM: IMPLICATIONS FOR MATERIALISM AND CONSUMPTION BEHAVIORS

Marsha L. Richins

University of Missouri, Colombia

ABSTRACT

This review identifies low self-concept clarity (SCC) as a source of consumer vulnerabilities and explains how the uncertainty associated with low SCC leads to processes that result in materialistic behaviors and overspending, product dissatisfaction, and potential self-harm. Processes include uncertainty reduction efforts through symbolic self-completion and social comparison, responses to everyday self-concept threats that result in feelings of deficiency and reduced consumption constraints, and susceptibility to interpersonal and marketer influences. In addition, the negative association between SCC and materialism is explained, risk factors for low SCC are described, and the need for research to help low SCC consumers deal with their vulnerabilities is explored.

Keywords: Self-concept clarity; uncertainty; materialism; compensatory consumption; vulnerable consumers

INTRODUCTION

All people have beliefs about themselves. Some of these beliefs are concrete, such as the knowledge that loud concerts give someone a headache or that they tend to sweat when they speak in public. Others are more abstract, such as the perception that one is conscientious, has high integrity, or tends to be pessimistic. The set of beliefs people have about themselves is the self-concept (Shavelson et al., 1976).

When people have confidence in their beliefs about themselves, they use this knowledge to guide their behavior and make choices (Setterlund & Niedenthal, 1993; Smith et al., 1996). A person who considers herself to be athletic would be

The Vulnerable Consumer
Review of Marketing Research, Volume 21, 49–68
Copyright © 2024 Marsha L. Richins
Published under exclusive licence by Emerald Publishing Limited
ISSN: 1548-6435/doi:10.1108/S1548-643520240000021004

more likely to accept an invitation for a canoe trip. Someone who knows he's an introvert would probably decide against applying for a job in fundraising. When a person has an unexpected setback, self-knowledge can help that individual decide a course of action to deal with it. And in the product choice arena, this confident self-knowledge allows people to make more satisfying choices (Mittal, 2015). However, for people who are uncertain about who they are, all these decisions are more difficult.

There is wide variation among people in how clear and confident they are in their self-perceptions. This difference is captured in the construct of self-concept clarity (SCC). People with high SCC are certain in their beliefs about themselves, they perceive their personal attributes to be generally consistent with each other (i.e., form a coherent whole), and their self-perceptions are stable from day to day (Campbell et al., 1996). Although self-construct clarity can fluctuate somewhat within the individual, longitudinal studies have shown it to be a relatively stable characteristic among both adolescents and adults (Campbell et al., 1996; Crocetti et al., 2016; Wu et al., 2010). Clarity in this context is subjective and is a characteristic of people's beliefs about their self-attributes; it is independent of the accuracy of those beliefs (Campbell et al., 1996).

It is important to note that SCC is different from self-esteem. SCC relates to beliefs about the self, while self-esteem is an evaluation of the self based on those beliefs. A person who clearly and confidently holds negative perceptions about herself would be high in SCC but probably low in self-esteem. Confidently held positive self-beliefs are associated with high self-esteem. Studies consistently show a negative correlation between self-esteem and SCC (e.g., Campbell et al., 1996; Cuperman et al., 2014).

This chapter makes the case that in the consumption arena, low SCC can make consumers vulnerable in a variety of ways, and these vulnerabilities can lead to materialistic behavior and overspending. Specifically, the discussions that follow will show that:

- Because uncertainty is aversive, low SCC people try to reduce uncertainty about themselves through self-relevant purchasing.
- Low SCC people also deal with uncertainty by comparing themselves with others or with societal standards. These comparisons tend to be biased in the upward direction and result in negative self-perceptions and unpleasant self-feelings that must be mitigated.
- Low SCC people are more affected than others by everyday self-concept threats. These threats reduce their confidence in their already-uncertain self-perceptions and result in negative self-perceptions that must be dealt with.
- To reduce uncertainty about themselves and to manage the damage to their self-concepts due to social comparison and other self-concept threats, low SCC consumers engage in materialistic behaviors. These materialistic behaviors include compensatory purchases that reduce uncertainty or bolster the damaged element of the self-concept and distraction activities such as shopping, purchasing self-gifts, and consumption of comforting or distracting products.

Self-concept threats also reduce consumption constraints for low SCC people, leading to more impulse purchasing and higher willingness to pay.
• Low SCC people are more vulnerable to persuasion attempts and other external influences. As a result, they may make purchases that are unneeded or suboptimal or spend more than necessary for an item.

MATERIALISTIC BEHAVIORS

Before going into detail about the processes described above, it is helpful to first define what constitutes materialistic behavior. Materialistic behavior involves making purchases for the purpose of transforming one's life (Richins, 2011), and especially to shape one's identity (Richins, 2017; Shrum et al., 2013). People commonly use products for self-definition and self-expression (Belk, 1988), but low SCC consumers do this more often than others; they *need* products more to support their identity because it's so wobbly. People with a firmer sense of self have less need to define themselves with products.

More than a dozen studies have shown that low SCC people are more materialistic (e.g., Martin et al., 2019; Noguti & Bokeyar, 2014), and there is also evidence that these consumers make more purchases and spend more on them than do those high in SCC (Sarial-Abi et al., 2016). However, scholars have not yet explained why this is so. This chapter provides a coherent set of explanations for the negative association between SCC and materialism observed in so many studies.

The sections below explain why people with low SCC rely excessively on purchases to define who they are and show how the vulnerabilities to materialistic behaviors and overspending created by low SCC are rooted in the uncertainty that accompanies this condition. These processes are summarized in Fig. 1. The uncertainty associated with low SCC is shown at the left of the figure, consumption responses to SCC are shown in the panel on the right, and the processes that lead to these responses are shown in the middle panel. Each of these processes is described in detail below. The final sections of this chapter identify consumers most at risk for low SCC and discuss implications of low SCC for consumers and consumer scholars.

UNCERTAINTY AND LOW SCC

A defining characteristic of low SCC is uncertainty. People low in SCC aren't sure of who they are or what personal qualities they possess and often don't know their own preferences or beliefs (Flury & Ickes, 2007). This uncertainty in preferences or beliefs increases their vulnerability in several ways. Firstly, the uncertainty they experience is in itself unpleasant; this unpleasantness motivates them to engage in behaviors that reduce the uncertain feeling they experience. Secondly, some uncertainty reduction activities, such as social comparison, can have an opposite effect from what's intended and produce further damage to the

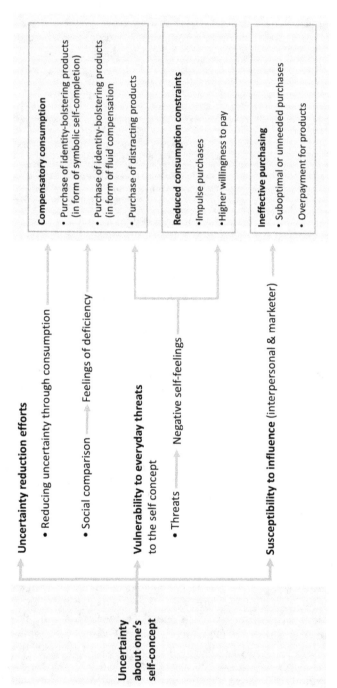

Fig. 1. Processes Initiated by the Uncertainty Associated With Low SCC and the Consumption Response to These Processes.

self-concept, resulting in negative feelings that require remedial action. Thirdly, uncertainty about the self increases vulnerability to threats experienced in everyday life because this uncertainty makes it difficult to dismiss self-relevant feedback or assess its accuracy. And finally, uncertainty causes low SCC consumers to be more susceptible to external influences. Each of these vulnerabilities and associated processes is reviewed in more detail below.

Uncertainty Reduction Tactics

It is widely accepted that uncertainty is an aversive state (e.g., Hogg, 2007; Sedikides et al., 2010). Because SCC is a trait-like condition, those low in SCC experience chronic unpleasant uncertainty and, as a result, experience more daily negative affect than those high in SCC. In one study in which community members completed daily diaries containing measures of affect, those with low SCC experienced more negative affect over a 7-day period, including guilt, nervousness, irritability, and fear, compared to those with higher SCC (Lee-Flynn et al., 2011). Other studies have found similar results (e.g., Ellison et al., 2020; Nezlek & Plesko, 2001).

Because uncertainty is unpleasant and is associated with reduced control over one's life, people have a strong motivation to reduce it (Hogg, 2007). Unfortunately, because SCC is a relatively stable trait (Crocetti et al., 2016), uncertainty reduction efforts are only temporarily successful. After a time, the uncertainty and associated unpleasant feelings return, and the quest to reduce that uncertainty begins again, leading to frequent oscillations between pleasant and unpleasant affective states. Accordingly, Nezlek and Plesko (2001) found that those with low SCC have greater within-day variability in self-esteem and both positive and negative affect. Affective instability increases the risk of depression (Thompson et al., 2011), and the long-term toll of this cycle is that people low in SCC experience more anxiety, depression, and stress on a day-to-day basis than others do (e.g., Butzer & Kuiper, 2006; Kusec et al., 2016; Smith et al., 1996).

There are many tactics that low SCC individuals use to reduce uncertainty about the self. In this chapter, we focus on two that are particularly relevant to consumer behavior: symbolic self-completion and social comparison (see Fig. 3.1).

Using products to reduce uncertainty about the self. One way that people low in SCC reduce their uncertainty about themselves is by purchasing or consuming products that bolster their uncertain personal attributes. The use of products to shore up an uncertain element of the self is described in symbolic self-completion theory. This theory posits that when people are incomplete (insecure or uncertain) in an important self-concept domain, they rely on symbols to complete that element of identity (Wicklund & Gollwitzer, 1981).

Numerous studies have shown how products with symbolic value are used for this purpose (e.g., Carr & Vignoles, 2011; Mead et al., 2011). For example, Wicklund and Gollwitzer (1982) found that MBA students who were less secure in their role as future business managers (e.g., were newer in their program, had lower grade point average (GPA), and had fewer job interviews) were more likely to display possessions that are symbolic of a successful businessperson, such as an expensive watch or business-appropriate footwear. In another study showing the use of possessions to bolster identity, Braun and Wicklund (1989) compared first-year students with fourth-year students at a university in terms of the number of articles they owned that displayed the university's logo or colors. First-year students, who presumably are less secure in their identity as university students, owned more these symbolic items.

One result of uncertainty about the self is a greater reliance, generally, on possessions to express one's identity. Consumers who are low in SCC are more likely to say they are "constantly seeking products in the marketplace to bolster my personality" (Mittal, 2015, p. 105). They are also more concerned about how they appear to others and purchase more appearance-management products (Wang & Yu, 2022). Similarly, people with low SCC are more likely to purchase and are willing to pay a higher price for a product that is strongly self-expressive or self-defining (Rozenkrants et al., 2017). Self-expressive products include those that have been customized (Kaiser et al., 2017), clothing and home décor items, and specific brands or products that consumers believe reflect one's inner self (Carroll & Ahuvia, 2006). Finally, people are more likely to describe their possessions as expressive of who they are after a self-concept uncertainty induction (Morrison & Johnson, 2011).

There is also evidence of uncertainty resulting in symbolic self-completion to shore up specific uncertain elements of the self. In experimental settings, when a self-view is made more uncertain, people choose products that bolster their original self-view over more neutral products. For example, Gao et al. (2009) found that when study participants' confidence in their intellectual ability was reduced, they were more likely to choose a gift of a fountain pen (a product shown in a pretest to be related to intelligence) than a gift of candy. Low SCC consumers are also more likely to purchase products that enhance their self-image by choosing items that accord more with their ideal self-image than their actual self-image (Noguti & Bokeyar, 2011).

All these findings are indicative of the use of products to reduce uncertainty about the self-concept. They also illustrate the materialistic tendency of low SCC people to rely on products to manage their identity. As we will see, this tactic of using products to address self-concept deficiencies and uncertainties is also used in other contexts by consumers low in SCC.

Engaging in social comparison to reduce uncertainty. The second tactic consumers low in SCC use to reduce uncertainty about themselves is social comparison, as shown in Fig. 1. When people are uncertain about themselves or their abilities, they tend to compare themselves with others on key elements of the self to reduce this uncertainty (Festinger, 1954; Schwartz & Smith, 1976). For example, a person who is unsure about their likeability will tend to compare themselves with other people they know in terms of number of friends they have or number of social invitations to see whether they measure up or fall short, thus reducing their uncertainty for a short time. Such comparisons can occur on many dimensions, including physical attractiveness, work competence, social skills, or any other personal characteristic. The chronic state of uncertainty experienced by those low in SCC leads them to engage in more frequent self-reassessment via social comparison (e.g., Cahill & Mussap, 2007; Servidio et al., 2021; Stapel & Tesser, 2001).

Unintended Consequences of Social Comparison

Although social comparison of personal qualities can reduce self-concept uncertainty at least temporarily, it also increases the chances of finding an undesirable discrepancy between the self and others (Tesser, 1991). In this section, we describe how low SCC consumers are especially likely to choose social comparison standards that result in feelings of deficiency and discuss how such consumers deal with the results of these comparisons.

Counterproductive comparison standards. Social comparison can result in feelings of deficiency when a person falls short in a comparison with another. This is most likely to happen when people engage in upward social comparison – comparisons with those who are better off (Wheeler & Miyake, 1992). Finding out that one is less intelligent, less attractive, or less well-liked than someone else can result in negative self-feelings, and the result of upward social comparisons is often reduced self-esteem and other unpleasant affect (Morse & Gergen, 1970; Salovey & Rodin, 1984; Wheeler & Miyake, 1992). Unfortunately, those low in SCC are especially likely to engage in upward social comparison – more so than those with high SCC (Butzer & Kuiper, 2006; Vartanian & Dey, 2013).

Compounding this tendency toward upward social comparisons, consumers who are low in SCC tend to have a stronger response to social comparison than their high SCC counterparts. For example, compared to high SCC women, low SCC women who viewed images of women with thin, toned bodies were more likely to compare their own bodies with those portrayed in the images and had a greater reduction in body satisfaction after this comparison (Carter & Vartanian, 2022). In another study, low SCC men who compared themselves with a highly competent person who was applying for the same job had a greater decrement in self-esteem after comparison than did men high in SCC (Morse & Gergen, 1970). Stronger responses to social comparison by low SCC individuals have also been observed in the context of academic performance (Zheng et al., 2018) and creativity (Ye et al., 2021).

While social comparison often involves comparison with others, people also compare themselves with abstract societal standards or role norms and expectations that have been internalized. There is some evidence that low SCC people are especially likely to internalize social norms. For example, they are more likely to internalize social norms for ideal body appearance, whether this be a thin body ideal for females (Carter & Vartanian, 2022; Posavac & Posavac, 2020) or a muscular body ideal for males (Cahill & Mussap, 2007).

It is not known if low SCC people are also more likely to compare themselves with other social norms and idealized role expectations, such as those relating to the roles of good parent, good partner, or "young professional." Given that those low in SCC tend to be high in conformity (Campbell et al., 1986; Cuperman et al., 2014), it is possible that they attempt to conform to social norm expectations in the same way that they conform to other people's expectations.

The expectations set by social and role norms are often difficult to meet. The requirements to be an ideal friend, parent, or spouse are impossible for most people to achieve on an everyday basis (e.g., Sperling, 2013). These standards are omnipresent and create opportunities for constant upward social comparisons. It is probable that low SCC individuals, with their uncertain sense of self, will engage in these social comparisons more frequently, experience a discrepancy between these ideals and how they see themselves more often, and will be more affected by these discrepancies.

This combination of more frequent social comparison by those low in SCC coupled with a stronger response to these comparisons means that these consumers frequently experience unpleasant feelings about themselves and perceptions of shortcomings in their self-concept that need to be remedied.

Remedies for social comparison shortcomings. There are many methods that consumers can use to deal with the perceived shortcomings or self-discrepancies that arise from social comparison and other sources (Mandel et al., 2017). This chapter focuses on three consumption tactics used by low SCC consumers to reduce feelings of deficiency resulting from social comparison (see column 3 in Fig. 1).

The first approach is to try to repair the damaged self-concept element by engaging in compensatory consumption that bolsters the deficient element of the self (e.g., Rucker & Galinsky, 2008). For example, after spending an evening out with a coworker who's more attractive and fashionable than she is, a young woman might go shopping for new clothes or cosmetics. This form of compensatory consumption is the same symbolic self-completion tactic, described above, that consumers low in SCC use to bolster uncertain elements of the self.

In the second compensatory consumption tactic, called fluid compensation by Mandel et al. (2017), consumers address a self-discrepancy in one element of the self by affirming some other unrelated element (see also Heine et al., 2006; Steele, 1988). For example, when students engaged in upward social comparison with advertising models who were more professional or more attractive, they experienced self-discrepancies concerning their own appearance, but subsequently bolstered other elements of their self-concept by expending effort to make more economically rational decisions (Sobol & Darke, 2014). The tendency to engage in fluid compensation seems to be especially strong among consumers low in SCC. For example, Zheng et al. (2018) found that after upward social comparison concerning academic achievement, students low in SCC preferred clothing items that had a conspicuous status brand logo, while high SCC students' logo preference was unaffected by social comparison.

A third tactic is to neutralize the bad feelings resulting from unfavorable social comparison with distracting product-related activities. Eating comfort foods and drinking alcohol are two activities that some consumers turn to when they feel bad (Evers et al., 2010; Rousseau et al., 2011). Shopping, for many, is an enjoyable distraction (Babin et al., 1994), and people in a bad mood are more likely to purchase an unplanned treat for themselves (Atalay & Meloy, 2011;

Rook & Gardner, 1993) or give themselves a purchased self-gift when shopping (McKeage et al., 1993). Evidence for the use of this tactic comes from Mittal (2015), who found that low SCC consumers are more likely than others to engage in shopping as a means of escape.

The upward social comparisons described in this section are a form of threat to the self-concept, but they are not the only such threat that consumers experience. Responses to other threats are discussed in the Uncertainty and Vulnerability to Daily Self-Concept Threats section.

Uncertainty and Vulnerability to Daily Self-Concept Threats

Threats to the self-concept are an everyday occurrence. Experiencing an awkward social interaction, not performing as well as hoped at work, and having someone question our judgment or opinions are all potential self-concept threats. People high in SCC are able to put such events in perspective and aren't much affected by them because they have a firm core set of beliefs about the self to rely on, but those low in SCC are more vulnerable to these threats because they are less able to dismiss self-relevant feedback that might challenge their already-uncertain sense of self (Guerrettaz & Arkin, 2016; Guerrettaz et al., 2014).

Those low in SCC have stronger responses to self-concept threats in four different contexts. The first context is threat from failure. Evidence for the effects of failure threat comes from a study by Stucke and Sporer (2002), who found that students low in SCC experienced more anger after receiving information that they had performed poorly on an intelligence test and displayed more verbal aggression than did high SCC students.

Disagreement from others can also constitute a potential threat. In a study of conflict resolution, people low in SCC (compared to those high in SCC) were more likely to engage in competitive communication and retaliatory responses to their negotiation partners when they anticipated or experienced opposition to their opinions or positions (De Dreu & Van Knippenberg, 2005). They also reported more negative perceptions of their partner.

Self-concept threat can also come from interpersonal relationships, for example, if an acquaintance intentionally or unintentionally snubs us or a friend stops replying to our text messages. Guerrettaz et al. (2014) found that when people received negative feedback about their likeability, those low in SCC subsequently wrote less positive essays about themselves than those high in SCC, indicating that low SCC people are more affected by perceived social affronts than those high in SCC.

A fourth source of self-concept threat comes from change. People low in SCC tend to avoid self-change because it increases the uncertainty they already feel about themselves (Emery et al., 2015). People rely on their romantic partners to provide stability in their lives. But when partners change, for example, by taking on a new hobby, changing careers, or choosing to improve their diet, it can be especially threatening to people low in SCC, and as a result, they are less supportive when their partners make these kinds of adjustments to their lives (Emery et al., 2018).

These kinds of self-concept threats occur on a frequent and regular basis and have an impact on low SCC individuals. These threats create negative self-feelings that are aversive and begging to be remedied, often by using the same remedies used to counter threats from social comparison (symbolic self-completion purchases, fluid compensation, and neutralizing negative affect through distracting consumption; see column 3 of Fig. 1). Gao et al. (2009) found that when people's confidence in an important element of their self-concept (intelligence, health consciousness) was shaken, they tended to engage in symbolic self-completion by choosing products that bolster those elements (fountain pen, apple) over products that do not (candy). Another study, involving fluid compensation, found that those whose self-concept was threatened (by negative performance feedback) later showed a higher willingness to pay for high status items than those whose self-concept was not threatened (Sivanathan & Pettit, 2010). Kim and Rucker (2012) demonstrated how threat to a self-concept element (perceptual intelligence, motivation level) resulted in higher consumption of distracting activities that reduce negative affect.

Because low SCC people are more affected by self-concept threats than those high in SCC, they are likely to more frequently engage in these compensatory consumption activities in response to all sorts of self-concept threats, and not just to the threat induced by upward social comparison described earlier.

Research has also demonstrated another response to self-concept threat, namely, reduced consumption constraints. Moran and Kwak (2015) found that people who experienced failure in a purported intelligence test subsequently had a higher online impulse buying tendency than those who didn't experience failure. Other studies have documented a higher willingness to pay for preferred brands (Chernev et al., 2011) or other items (Sivanathan & Pettit, 2010) after a self-concept threat has been experienced.

Uncertainty and Susceptibility to External Influences

In addition to being uncertain about who they are, low SCC individuals also tend to be uncertain about their product preferences (Flury & Ickes, 2007) and ambivalent in their opinions about social issues (Dummel, 2018). These uncertainties increase the vulnerability of low SCC consumers by making them susceptible to external influences, and this is especially true in their consumption behaviors. Low SCC individuals are more vulnerable than others to both interpersonal influence and marketer influence, and these vulnerabilities increase the likelihood of inefficient purchasing, as described below and shown in Fig. 1.

While everyone is influenced to some extent by friends and other people, low SCC consumers are especially likely to be influenced. They consistently score higher on the Consumer Susceptibility to Interpersonal Influence scale (Bearden et al., 1989), agreeing with statements like "It is important that others like the products and brands I buy" (Bharti et al., 2022; Isaksen & Roper, 2008; Mittal, 2015). They also score higher on measures of conformity (Campbell et al., 1986; Cuperman et al., 2014). Teens low in SCC are more likely to yield to peer pressure and purchase items they think will gain the approval of others (Gil et al.,

2017). This is perhaps a natural response to feelings of uncertainty: if a person doesn't have a firm set of self-beliefs to guide their opinions and behaviors, other people can be seen as useful guides when making decisions. The problem with this is that what is good for one person is not necessarily good for another, and leaning on others to make decisions can result in choices that might not necessarily be suitable for the purchaser. The outcome can be inefficient use of one's economic resources and lower satisfaction or increased doubt after a purchase is made (Mittal, 2015).

In terms of marketer influence, low SCC consumers are more likely than others to comply with product and service recommendations provided by marketers on their websites (Lee et al., 2010), and they rely more than others on the price-quality heuristic when making purchases (Chung & Saini, 2022), making it easier for them to overspend. The relationship between SCC and advertising response is unexplored territory, but given their vulnerability to interpersonal influence, it's plausible that low SCC consumers might be more vulnerable to advertising messages that use some sort of conformity or "fitting in" appeal than those high in SCC. In addition, because they are uncertain about who they are, they may be more susceptible to advertising for products that can bolster uncertain elements of their self-concept.

CONSEQUENCES OF LOW SCC

The processes described above show how low SCC people are vulnerable in a number of ways. Perhaps most importantly, low SCC people tend to have lower well-being and poorer mental health than people who are more confident and clearer about who they are, and there is an extensive literature documenting this relationship (e.g., Cicero, 2017; Lee-Flynn et al., 2011).

More pertinent to the field of consumer behavior, the discussion above has shown how low SCC creates vulnerabilities for people in the realm of consumption, and these vulnerabilities are for the most part a direct result of the uncertainties these consumers experience about who they are and what they believe about themselves. Summarizing these vulnerabilities (see also column 3 of Fig. 1), low SCC consumers:

- Are uncertain about who they are. This uncertainty is unpleasant and leads to efforts to reduce the uncertainty through the purchase of identity-bolstering products.
- More frequently engage in unfavorable social comparisons and are more affected by these unfavorable social comparisons than other consumers are. These social comparisons leave them with feelings of deficiency that they often attempt to mitigate through compensatory consumption and impulse purchasing, accompanied by a higher willingness to pay for these purchases.

- Are vulnerable to everyday self-concept threats that result in negative self-feelings that they often attempt to mitigate through purchasing.
- Are more susceptible to interpersonal and marketer influence, increasing the likelihood of making suboptimal or unneeded purchases or overpaying for products.

Problematic Outcomes for Low SCC Consumers

The responses of low SCC consumers to self-uncertainty and associated processes can lead to problematic outcomes for low SCC consumers, including debt, product dissatisfaction, and self-harm. These outcomes are described below.

The first problematic outcome is financial vulnerability. As discussed above, those low in SCC often deal with self-concept uncertainty by making purchases. Cumulatively, these expenditures can lead to overspending and eventually to debt. As described earlier, consumers low in SCC engage in more discretionary spending than others, and they do not benefit from self-regulatory practices such as elaboration on potential outcomes when making spending decisions (Sarial-Abi et al., 2016). Low SCC consumers also engage in more conspicuous consumption than others (Bharti et al., 2022), which can be expensive. Finally, these consumers tend to be more materialistic and are also more likely to be compulsive consumers (Claes et al., 2016; Noguti & Bokeyar, 2014); both of these conditions are associated with higher levels of debt (Richins, 2011; Spinella et al., 2014). Debt is harmful to consumers because it is expensive, reduces their freedom, and makes it difficult for them to deal with emergencies or other unexpected expenses.

The second problematic outcome is product dissatisfaction. Although the association between SCC and product satisfaction hasn't been studied much, we do know that those with low SCC are more likely to experience postpurchase doubt (Mittal, 2015). Because they are more susceptible to external influence, low SCC consumers may experience product dissatisfaction more frequently because their purchases are based on the needs and preferences of others instead of their own or because they are more influenced by marketer activities.

Recall, also, that low SCC people use purchases to bolster uncertain elements of their self-concept. However, because SCC is an enduring personal characteristic (Campbell et al., 1996; Crocetti et al., 2016), it is unlikely that any one purchase will increase certainty for very long. The utility of any one identity-bolstering purchase is likely to quickly decline and the need to make additional self-bolstering purchases will repeatedly arise, in a process similar to the hedonic treadmill (Brickman & Campbell, 1971). Indirect evidence for this decay of satisfaction over time comes from the fact that low SCC people tend to be materialistic, and product satisfaction decays more quickly for materialistic people than for those low in materialism (Richins, 2013).

The third undesirable outcome is potential self-harm resulting from unhealthy behaviors. As noted above, low SCC consumers are more likely to internalize idealized body norms of thinness (women) or athleticism (men and women), and in social comparisons, they are likely to fall short of these ideals. Besides being associated with eating disorders and unhealthy levels of exercise (Bell et al., 2016; Cahill & Mussap, 2007), internalization of idealized body types is associated with an increased willingness to undergo cosmetic surgery (Lunde, 2013) and the purchase and consumption of potentially harmful supplements or medications that promote weight loss or muscle development (Karazsia & Crowther, 2010; Strübel & Petrie, 2019).

MATERIALISM AND LOW SCC

In examining consumers' responses to low SCC, this chapter has shown how self-uncertainty leads to materialistic behaviors. Of the consumption responses shown in column 3 of Fig. 3.1, nearly all of them involve materialistic behaviors – the purchase of goods for the purpose of transforming one's life and shaping one's identity (Richins, 2011; Shrum et al., 2013). Further, as noted earlier, one of the most consistent findings about people with low SCC is that they are more materialistic than others. In this section, we come back to that observation and explain why this relationship occurs. To do so, we use an adaptation of the materialism reinforcement cycle described in Richins (2017), shown in Fig. 2. Evidence for the relationships described in this model was presented earlier in this chapter.

As shown at the left of the model, low SCC makes people vulnerable to threats in daily life, and an exposure to one of these threats leaves them in an unpleasant psychological state. Concomitantly, they believe in the value of products to bolster or shape the self. Richins (2011) refers to these beliefs as self-transformation expectations. Because of these beliefs, low SCC consumers purchase products to repair their sense of self and relieve the psychological discomfort they experience in response to uncertainty or threats. After the purchase, the psychological distress is temporarily relieved, reinforcing the belief that a purchase will transform the self or the way one feels about the self, which is a hallmark of materialism (Shrum et al., 2013).

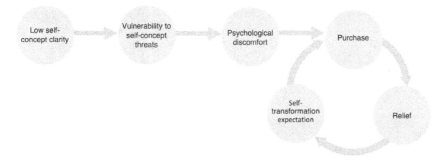

Fig. 2.   How Materialism is Reinforced in Consumers With Low
Self-Concept Clarity.

Materialism has several undesirable correlates, including lower marital satisfaction (Carroll et al., 2011), poorer interpersonal relationship quality more generally (Solberg et al., 2004), and greater loneliness (Pieters, 2013). Those high in materialism are less satisfied with their standard of living (Roberts & Clement, 2007), have more difficulty managing their money (Watson, 2003), and are less satisfied with their purchases (Fitzmaurice, 2008). These problems add to the vulnerabilities that low SCC people already experience due to their uncertain sense of self.

RISK FACTORS FOR LOW SCC

Above, we have described vulnerabilities created by low SCC. In this section, we identify the characteristics of people most likely to be low in SCC, and thus subject to these vulnerabilities.

As is the case for many other things in life, young people are more vulnerable than those who are older. Adolescents, especially those who lack good communication with their parents or experience family adversity, tend to be low in SCC (Van Dijk et al., 2014; Vartanian et al., 2016). Among adults, SCC has an inverted U-shaped relationship with age, with clarity increasing as young people take on more social roles as they move through adulthood and then peaking in midlife. A decline in SCC begins around age 60, especially among those who have lost important self-defining roles through job retirement or have lost loved ones, and among those whose health problems limit their social functioning (Lodi-Smith & Crocetti, 2017; Lodi-Smith & Roberts, 2010).

Slight gender differences have also been documented in the literature, with a few studies showing that males have slightly higher SCC than females, both in adolescence and adulthood (Cicero, 2019; Crocetti et al., 2016). However, these gender differences are overshadowed by the large variation in SCC within each gender group.

SCC is generally considered to be a relatively stable enduring characteristic, but SCC also fluctuates and is affected by external events of both long and short duration. Most noticeably, changes in social roles are associated with a reduction in SCC (Light & Visser, 2013). Making a career change, having a baby for the first time, or losing a romantic partner can cause people to question who they are and lower their confidence (Ruble & Seidman, 1996), hallmarks of low SCC. This reduction in SCC is especially likely to occur when the individual has negative feelings about the role transition (Slotter & Emery, 2017). Thus, people who normally are high in SCC but are experiencing an unwanted role change will be vulnerable in the same ways a person with chronic low SCC might be.

More transitory events can also temporarily change a person's SCC, as has been demonstrated in numerous studies that have manipulated SCC (Hertel, 2017). For example, negative feedback about an important self-belief can lower SCC, while supporting evidence about self-beliefs can increase it. Everyone from time-to-time encounters information that, at least for the moment, undermines the sense of self, thus temporarily influencing them to act more like people with low SCC and making them vulnerable to compensatory consumption urges.

IMPLICATIONS

Low SCC creates vulnerabilities that all people are susceptible to – either occasionally or chronically – but for those low in SCC, these vulnerabilities occur more often and the response to them is more severe. This, plus the fact that low SCC is associated with lower well-being, suggests that increasing SCC would be beneficial to individuals. SCC is a relatively stable personal characteristic, but there is some indication that it can be increased. Although research on the effect of counseling on self-concept is limited (a literature search identified only one article on this topic [Roepke et al., 2011]), some studies have shown that people can increase their SCC through the actions they take. Specifically, a willingness to positively commit to new roles and engage in other forms of self-expansion, such as living abroad, has been shown to increase SCC (Adam et al., 2018; Emery et al., 2022; Lodi-Smith & Crocetti, 2017). However, other research shows that low SCC people are especially resistant to self-expansion activities (Emery et al., 2015), suggesting that this route to increasing SCC may be undertaken by only a few of the people who might benefit from it the most.

Of particular importance to marketing scholars is the finding that low SCC consumers are vulnerable to marketer activities. Very little research has been done on this topic to date, but given the effects of low SCC observed in studies conducted in other contexts, it's likely that scholars have just scratched the surface of low SCC consumers' vulnerabilities in this regard.

One example of low SCC consumers' vulnerability to marketer activities concerns identity-related appeals made by companies. Marketers routinely promise that the purchase of some product will shore up or change a person's identity and then offer hard-to-resist invitations to purchase that product. High SCC consumers can put those offers in context and make a more-or-less reasoned judgment about whether they truly want to buy the product in question, but these offers can be harder for low SCC people to resist. Because marketers will continue to make claims that appeal to low SCC consumers, it is unfortunately up to these consumers to protect themselves from their own vulnerabilities and the marketers' potential exploitation of them.

CONCLUSION

Consumer researchers can help by investigating ways that low SCC consumers can protect themselves. For example, it is not known whether self-awareness of low SCC vulnerabilities acts as a prophylactic, allowing consumers to be on guard against unproductive consumption behaviors. Research could also identify activities, other than purchase, that would help consumers deal with the results of unfavorable social comparisons and other threats. And maybe, there could be an app for that. When low SCC consumers are experiencing negative affect due to uncertainty or the threats they experience, perhaps they could call up an app that helps them diagnose their feelings and suggests constructive ways to deal with their uncertainties and the negative affect that result. Artificial intelligence (AI) can allow such an app to provide increasingly effective suggestions as it learns which activities are most beneficial to each individual. Progress is being made in AI therapeutic applications (e.g., Pham et al., 2022), and in the future, these applications may be able to specifically address low SCC and its consequences. Much work remains to be done to help protect this vulnerable population of consumers.

REFERENCES

Adam, H., Obodaru, O., Lu, J. G., Maddux, W. W., & Galinsky, A. D. (2018). The shortest path to oneself leads around the world: Living abroad increases self-concept clarity. *Organizational Behavior and Human Decision Processes, 145*, 16–29.

Atalay, A. S., & Meloy, M. G. (2011). Retail therapy: A strategic effort to improve mood. *Psychology and Marketing, 28*(6), 638–659.

Babin, B. J., Darden, W. R., & Griffin, M. (1994). Work and/or fun: Measuring hedonic and utilitarian shopping value. *Journal of Consumer Research, 20*(4), 644–656.

Bearden, W. O., Netemeyer, R. G., & Teel, J. E. (1989). Measurement of consumer susceptibility to interpersonal influence. *Journal of Consumer Research, 15*(4), 473–481.

Belk, R. W. (1988). Possessions and the extended self. *Journal of Consumer Research, 15*(2), 139–168.

Bell, H. S., Donovan, C. L., & Ramme, R. (2016). Is athletic really ideal? An examination of the mediating role of body dissatisfaction in predicting disordered eating and compulsive exercise. *Eating Behaviors, 21*, 24–29.

Bharti, M., Suneja, V., & Bharti, M. (2022). Mindfulness as an antidote to conspicuous consumption: The mediating roles of self-esteem, self-concept clarity and normative influence. *Personality and Individual Differences, 184*, 111215.

Braun, O. L., & Wicklund, R. A. (1989). Psychological antecedents of conspicuous consumption. *Journal of Economic Psychology, 10*(2), 161–187.

Brickman, P., & Campbell, D. T. (1971). Hedonic relativism and planning the good society. In M. H. Appley (Ed.), *Adaptation level theory: A symposium* (pp. 287–302). Academic Press.

Butzer, B., & Kuiper, N. A. (2006). Relationships between the frequency of social comparisons and self-concept clarity, intolerance of uncertainty, anxiety, and depression. *Personality and Individual Differences, 41*(1), 167–176.

Cahill, S., & Mussap, A. J. (2007). Emotional reactions following exposure to idealized bodies predict unhealthy body change attitudes and behaviors in women and men. *Journal of Psychosomatic Research, 62*(6), 631–639.

Campbell, J. D., Tesser, A., & Fairey, P. J. (1986). Conformity and attention to the stimulus: Some temporal and contextual dynamics. *Journal of Personality and Social Psychology, 51*(2), 315.

Campbell, J. D., Trapnell, P. D., Heine, S. J., Katz, I. M., Lavallee, L. F., & Lehman, D. R. (1996). Self-concept clarity: Measurement, personality correlates, and cultural boundaries. *Journal of Personality and Social Psychology, 70*(1), 141.

Carr, H. L., & Vignoles, V. L. (2011). Keeping up with the Joneses: Status projection as symbolic self-completion. *European Journal of Social Psychology, 41*(4), 518–527.

Carroll, B. A., & Ahuvia, A. C. (2006). Some antecedents and outcomes of brand love. *Marketing Letters, 17*(2), 79–89.

Carroll, J. S., Dean, L. R., Call, L. L., & Busby, D. M. (2011). Materialism and marriage: Couple profiles of congruent and incongruent spouses. *Journal of Couple & Relationship Therapy, 10*(4), 287–308.

Carter, J. J., & Vartanian, L. R. (2022). Self-concept clarity and appearance-based social comparison to idealized bodies. *Body Image, 40*, 124–130.

Chernev, A., Hamilton, R., & Gal, D. (2011). Competing for consumer identity: Limits to self-expression and the perils of lifestyle branding. *Journal of Marketing, 75*(3), 66–82.

Chung, M., & Saini, R. (2022). Consumer self-uncertainty increases price dependency. *Journal of Business Research, 140*, 40–48.

Cicero, D. C. (2017). Self-concept clarity and psychopathology. In J. Lodi-Smith & K. G. deMarree (Eds.), *Self-concept clarity: Perspectives on assessment, research, and applications* (pp. 219–242). Springer.

Cicero, D. C. (2019). Measurement invariance of the Self-Concept Clarity Scale across race and sex. *Journal of Psychopathology and Behavioral Assessment, 42*(2), 296–305.

Claes, L., Müller, A., & Luyckx, K. (2016). Compulsive buying and hoarding as identity substitutes: The role of materialistic value endorsement and depression. *Comprehensive Psychiatry, 68*, 65–71.

Crocetti, E., Rubini, M., Branje, S., Koot, H. M., & Meeus, W. (2016). Self-concept clarity in adolescents and parents: A six-wave longitudinal and multi-informant study on development and intergenerational transmission. *Journal of Personality, 84*(5), 580–593.

Cuperman, R., Robinson, R. L., & Ickes, W. (2014). On the malleability of self-image in individuals with a weak sense of self. *Self and Identity, 13*(1), 1–23.

De Dreu, C. K., & Van Knippenberg, D. (2005). The possessive self as a barrier to conflict resolution: Effects of mere ownership, process accountability, and self-concept clarity on competitive cognitions and behavior. *Journal of Personality and Social Psychology, 89*(3), 345.

Dummel, S. (2018). Relating mindfulness to attitudinal ambivalence through self-concept clarity. *Mindfulness, 9*(5), 1486–1493.

Ellison, W. D., Gillespie, M. E., & Trahan, A. C. (2020). Individual differences and stability of dynamics among self-concept clarity, impatience, and negative affect. *Self and Identity, 19*(3), 324–345.

Emery, L. F., Gardner, W. L., Finkel, E. J., & Carswell, K. L. (2018). "You've changed": Low self-concept clarity predicts lack of support for partner change. *Personality and Social Psychology Bulletin, 44*(3), 318–331.

Emery, L. F., Hughes, E. K., & Gardner, W. L. (2022). Confusion or clarity? Examining a possible tradeoff between self- expansion and self-concept clarity. *Social Psychological and Personality Science*. https://doi.org/10.1177/19485506211067040

Emery, L. F., Walsh, C., & Slotter, E. B. (2015). Knowing who you are and adding to it: Reduced self-concept clarity predicts reduced self-expansion. *Social Psychological and Personality Science, 6*(3), 259–266.

Evers, C., Marijn Stok, F., & de Ridder, D. T. (2010). Feeding your feelings: Emotion regulation strategies and emotional eating. *Personality and Social Psychology Bulletin, 36*(6), 792–804.

Festinger, L. (1954). A theory of social comparison processes. *Human Relations, 7*(2), 117–140.

Fitzmaurice, J. (2008). Splurge purchases and materialism. *Journal of Consumer Marketing, 25*(6), 332–338.

Flury, J. M., & Ickes, W. (2007). Having a weak versus strong sense of self: The Sense of Self Scale (SOSS). *Self and Identity, 6*(4), 281–303.

Gao, L., Wheeler, S. C., & Shiv, B. (2009). The "shaken self": Product choices as a means of restoring self-view confidence. *Journal of Consumer Research, 36*(1), 29–38.

Gil, L. A., Dwivedi, A., & Johnson, L. W. (2017). Effect of popularity and peer pressure on attitudes toward luxury among teens. *Young Consumers, 18*(1), 84–93.

Guerrettaz, J., & Arkin, R. M. (2016). Distinguishing the subjective and the objective aspects of self-concept clarity. *Social and Personality Psychology Compass, 10*(4), 219–230.

Guerrettaz, J., Chang, L., von Hippel, W., Carroll, P. J., & Arkin, R. M. (2014). Self-concept clarity: Buffering the impact of self-evaluative information. *Individual Differences Research, 12*, 180–190.

Heine, S. J., Proulx, T., & Vohs, K. D. (2006). The meaning maintenance model: On the coherence of human motivations. *Personality and Social Psychology Review, 10*, 88–110.

Hertel, A. W. (2017). Sources of self-concept clarity. In J. Lodi-Smith & K. G. DeMarree (Eds.), *Self-concept clarity: Perspectives on assessment, research, and application* (pp. 43–66). Springer.

Hogg, M. A. (2007). Uncertainty–identity theory. *Advances in Experimental Social Psychology, 39,* 69–126.

Isaksen, K. J., & Roper, S. (2008). The impact of branding on low-income adolescents: A vicious cycle? *Psychology and Marketing, 25*(11), 1063–1087.

Kaiser, U., Schreier, M., & Janiszewski, C. (2017). The self-expressive customization of a product can improve performance. *Journal of Marketing Research, 54*(5), 816–831.

Karazsia, B. T., & Crowther, J. H. (2010). Sociocultural and psychological links to men's engagement in risky body change behaviors. *Sex Roles, 63*(9), 747–756.

Kim, S., & Rucker, D. D. (2012). Bracing for the psychological storm: Proactive versus reactive compensatory consumption. *Journal of Consumer Research, 39*(4), 815–830.

Kusec, A., Tallon, K., & Koerner, N. (2016). Intolerance of uncertainty, causal uncertainty, causal importance, self-concept clarity and their relations to generalized anxiety disorder. *Cognitive Behaviour Therapy, 45*(4), 307–323.

Lee, G., Lee, J., & Sanford, C. (2010). The roles of self-concept clarity and psychological reactance in compliance with product and service recommendations. *Computers in Human Behavior, 26*(6), 1481–1487.

Lee-Flynn, S. C., Pomaki, G., DeLongis, A., Biesanz, J. C., & Puterman, E. (2011). Daily cognitive appraisals, daily affect, and long-term depressive symptoms: The role of self-esteem and self-concept clarity in the stress process. *Personality and Social Psychology Bulletin, 37*(2), 255–268.

Light, A. E., & Visser, P. S. (2013). The ins and outs of the self: Contrasting role exits and role entries as predictors of self-concept clarity. *Self and Identity, 12*(3), 291–306.

Lodi-Smith, J., & Crocetti, E. (2017). Self-concept clarity development across the lifespan. In J. Lodi-Smith & K. G. DeMarree (Eds.), *Self-concept clarity: Perspectives on assessment, research, and application* (pp. 67–84). Springer.

Lodi-Smith, J., & Roberts, B. W. (2010). Getting to know me: Social role experiences and age differences in self-concept clarity during adulthood. *Journal of Personality, 78*(5), 1383–1410.

Lunde, C. (2013). Acceptance of cosmetic surgery, body appreciation, body ideal internalization, and fashion blog reading among late adolescents in Sweden. *Body Image, 10*(4), 632–635.

Mandel, N., Rucker, D. D., Levav, J., & Galinsky, A. D. (2017). The compensatory consumer behavior model: How self-discrepancies drive consumer behavior. *Journal of Consumer Psychology, 27*(1), 133–146.

Martin, C., Czellar, S., & Pandelaere, M. (2019). Age-related changes in materialism in adults – A self-uncertainty perspective. *Journal of Research in Personality, 78,* 16–24.

McKeage, K. R., Richins, M. L., & Debevec, K. (1993). Self-Gifts and the manifestation of material values. *Advances in Consumer Research, 20,* 359–364.

Mead, N. L., Baumeister, R. F., Stillman, T. F., Rawn, C. D., & Vohs, K. D. (2011). Social exclusion causes people to spend and consume strategically in the service of affiliation. *Journal of Consumer Research, 37*(5), 902–919.

Mittal, B. (2015). Self-concept clarity: Exploring its role in consumer behavior. *Journal of Economic Psychology, 46,* 98–110.

Moran, B., & Kwak, L. E. (2015). Effect of stress, materialism and external stimuli on online impulse buying. *Journal of Research for Consumers, 27,* 26–51.

Morrison, K. R., & Johnson, C. S. (2011). When what you have is who you are: Self-uncertainty leads individualists to see themselves in their possessions. *Personality and Social Psychology Bulletin, 37*(5), 639–651.

Morse, S., & Gergen, K. J. (1970). Social comparison, self-consistency, and the concept of self. *Journal of Personality and Social Psychology, 16*(1), 148.

Nezlek, J. B., & Plesko, R. M. (2001). Day-to-day relationships among self-concept clarity, self-esteem, daily events, and mood. *Personality and Social Psychology Bulletin, 27*(2), 201–211.

Noguti, V., & Bokeyar, A. (2011). Fantasy-shopping, self-concept clarity, and self-affirmation. *ACR Asia-Pacific Advances, 9,* 158–159.

Noguti, V., & Bokeyar, A. L. (2014). Who am I? The relationship between self-concept uncertainty and materialism. *International Journal of Psychology*, *49*(5), 323–333.

Pham, K. T., Nabizadeh, A., & Selek, S. (2022). Artificial intelligence and chatbots in psychiatry. *Psychiatric Quarterly*, *93*, 249–253.

Pieters, R. (2013). Bidirectional dynamics of materialism and loneliness: Not just a vicious cycle. *Journal of Consumer Research*, *40*(4), 615–631.

Posavac, S. S., & Posavac, H. D. (2020). Adult separation anxiety disorder symptomology as a risk factor for thin-ideal internalization: The role of self-concept clarity. *Psychological Reports*, *123*(3), 674–686.

Richins, M. L. (2011). Materialism, transformation expectations, and spending: Implications for credit use. *Journal of Public Policy and Marketing*, *30*(2), 141–156.

Richins, M. L. (2013). When wanting is better than having: Materialism, transformation expectations, and product-evoked emotions in the purchase process. *Journal of Consumer Research*, *40*(1), 1–18.

Richins, M. L. (2017). Materialism pathways: The processes that create and perpetuate materialism. *Journal of Consumer Psychology*, *27*(4), 480–499.

Roberts, J. A., & Clement, A. (2007). Materialism and satisfaction with over-all quality of life and eight life domains. *Social Indicators Research*, *82*(1), 79–92.

Roepke, S., Schröder-Abé, M., Schütz, A., Jacob, G., Dams, A., Vater, A., Rüter, A., Merkl, A., Heuser, I., & Lammers, C. H. (2011). Dialectic behavioural therapy has an impact on self-concept clarity and facets of self-esteem in women with borderline personality disorder. *Clinical Psychology & Psychotherapy*, *18*(2), 148–158.

Rook, D. W., & Gardner, M. P. (1993). In the mood: Impulse buyings' affective antecedents. In J. Arnold-Costa & R. W. Belk (Eds.), *Research in consumer behavior* (Vol. 6, pp. 1–28). JAI Press.

Rousseau, G. S., Irons, J. G., & Correia, C. J. (2011). The reinforcing value of alcohol in a drinking to cope paradigm. *Drug and Alcohol Dependence*, *118*(1), 1–4.

Rozenkrants, B., Wheeler, S. C., & Shiv, B. (2017). Self-expression cues in product rating distributions: When people prefer polarizing products. *Journal of Consumer Research*, *44*(4), 759–777.

Ruble, D. N., & Seidman, E. (1996). Social transitions: Windows into social psychological processes. In E. T. Higgins & A. W. Kruglanski (Eds.), *Social psychology: Handbook of basic principles* (pp. 830–856). Guilford Press.

Rucker, D. D., & Galinsky, A. D. (2008). Desire to acquire: Powerlessness and compensatory consumption. *Journal of Consumer Research*, *35*(2), 257–267.

Salovey, P., & Rodin, J. (1984). Some antecedents and consequences of social-comparison jealousy. *Journal of Personality and Social Psychology*, *47*(4), 780.

Sarial-Abi, G., Gürhan-Canli, Z., Kumkale, T., & Yoon, Y. (2016). The effect of self-concept clarity on discretionary spending tendency. *International Journal of Research in Marketing*, *33*(3), 612–623.

Schwartz, J. M., & Smith, W. P. (1976). Social comparison and the inference of ability difference. *Journal of Personality and Social Psychology*, *34*(6), 1268–1275.

Sedikides, C., De Cremer, D., Hart, C. M., & Brebels, L. (2010). Procedural fairness responses in the context of self- uncertainty. In R. M. Arkin, K. C. Oleson, & P. J. Carroll (Eds.), *The uncertain self: A handbook of perspectives from social and personality psychology* (pp. 142–159). Psychology Press.

Servidio, R., Sinatra, M., Griffiths, M. D., & Monacis, L. (2021). Social comparison orientation and fear of missing out as mediators between self-concept clarity and problematic smartphone use. *Addictive Behaviors*, *122*, 107014.

Setterlund, M. B., & Niedenthal, P. M. (1993). "Who am I? Why am I here?" Self-esteem, self-clarity, and prototype matching. *Journal of Personality and Social Psychology*, *65*(4), 769.

Shavelson, R. J., Hubner, J. J., & Stanton, G. C. (1976). Self-concept: Validation of construct interpretations. *Review of Educational Research*, *46*(3), 407–441.

Shrum, L. J., Wong, N., Arif, F., Chugani, S. K., Gunz, A., Lowrey, T. M., Nairn, A., Pandelaere, M., Ross, S. M., Ruvio, A., Scott, K., & Sundie, J. (2013). Reconceptualizing materialism as identity goal pursuits: Functions, processes, and consequences. *Journal of Business Research*, *66*(8), 1179–1185.

Sivanathan, N., & Pettit, N. C. (2010). Protecting the self through consumption: Status goods as affirmational commodities. *Journal of Experimental Social Psychology*, *46*(3), 564–570.

Slotter, E. B., & Emery, L. F. (2017). Self-concept clarity and social role transitions. In J. Lodi-Smith & K. G. DeMarree (Eds.), *Self-concept clarity: Perspectives on assessment, research, and application* (pp. 85–106). Springer.

Smith, M., Wethington, E., & Zhan, G. (1996). Self-concept clarity and preferred coping styles. *Journal of Personality*, *64*(2), 407–434.

Sobol, K., & Darke, P. R. (2014). "I'd like to be that attractive, but at least I'm smart": How exposure to ideal advertising models motivates improved decision-making. *Journal of Consumer Psychology*, *24*(4), 533–540.

Solberg, E. G., Diener, E., & Robinson, M. D. (2004). Why are materialists less satisfied? In T. Kasser & A. D. Kanner (Eds.), *Psychology and consumer culture* (pp. 29–48). American Psychological Association.

Sperling, J. H. (2013). Reframing the work-family conflict debate by rejecting the ideal parent norm. *Journal of Gender, Social Policy & the Law*, *22*, 47–90.

Spinella, M., Lester, D., & Yang, B. (2014). Compulsive buying tendencies and personal finances. *Psychological Reports*, *115*(3), 670–674.

Stapel, D. A., & Tesser, A. (2001). Self-activation increases social comparison. *Journal of Personality and Social Psychology*, *81*(4), 742.

Steele, C. M. (1988). The psychology of self-affirmation: Sustaining the integrity of the self. In L. Berkowitz (Ed.). *Advances in experimental social psychology* (Vol. 21, pp. 261–302). Academic Press.

Strübel, J., & Petrie, T. A. (2019). Appearance and performance enhancing drug usage and psychological well-being in gay and heterosexual men. *Psychology & Sexuality*, *10*(2), 132–148.

Stucke, T. S., & Sporer, S. L. (2002). When a grandiose self-image is threatened: Narcissism and self-concept clarity as predictors of negative emotions and aggression following ego-threat. *Journal of Personality*, *70*(4), 509–532.

Tesser, A. (1991). Emotion in social comparison and reflection processes. In J. Suls & T. A. Wills (Eds.), *Social comparison: Contemporary theory and research* (pp. 115–145). Lawrence Erlbaum.

Thompson, R. J., Berenbaum, H., & Bredemeier, K. (2011). Cross-sectional and longitudinal relations between affective instability and depression. *Journal of Affective Disorders*, *130*(1–2), 53–59.

Van Dijk, M., Branje, S., Keijsers, L., Hawk, S. T., Hale, W. W., & Meeus, W. (2014). Self-concept clarity across adolescence: Longitudinal associations with open communication with parents and internalizing symptoms. *Journal of Youth and Adolescence*, *43*(11), 1861–1876.

Vartanian, L. R., & Dey, S. (2013). Self-concept clarity, thin-ideal internalization, and appearance-related social comparison as predictors of body dissatisfaction. *Body Image*, *10*(4), 495–500.

Vartanian, L. R., Froreich, F. V., & Smyth, J. M. (2016). A serial mediation model testing early adversity, self-concept clarity, and thin-ideal internalization as predictors of body dissatisfaction. *Body Image*, *19*, 98–103.

Wang, J., & Yu, Y. (2022). Beautify the blurry self: Low self-concept clarity increases appearance management. *Journal of Consumer Psychology*, 1–17. https://doi.org/10.1002/jcpy.1298

Watson, J. J. (2003). The relationship of materialism to spending tendencies, saving, and debt. *Journal of Economic Psychology*, *24*(6), 723–739.

Wheeler, L., & Miyake, K. (1992). Social comparison in everyday life. *Journal of Personality and Social Psychology*, *62*(5), 760.

Wicklund, R. A., & Gollwitzer, P. M. (1981). Symbolic self-completion, attempted influence, and self-deprecation. *Basic and Applied Social Psychology*, *2*(2), 89–114.

Wicklund, R. A., & Gollwitzer, P. M. (1982). *Symbolic self-completion*. Lawrence Erlbaum.

Wu, J., Watkins, D., & Hattie, J. (2010). Self-concept clarity: A longitudinal study of Hong Kong adolescents. *Personality and Individual Differences*, *48*(3), 277–282.

Ye, J., Zhou, K., & Chen, R. (2021). Numerical or verbal Information: The effect of comparative information in social comparison on prosocial behavior. *Journal of Business Research*, *124*, 198–211.

Zheng, X., Baskin, E., & Peng, S. (2018). Feeling inferior, showing off: The effect of nonmaterial social comparisons on conspicuous consumption. *Journal of Business Research*, *90*, 196–205.

FROM STIGMA TO SCARCITY: ON INTERPERSONAL AND COGNITIVE SOURCES OF VULNERABILITY FOR CONSUMERS IN POVERTY

Nathan N. Cheek[a] and Eldar Shafir[b]

[a]*Purdue University, USA*
[b]*Princeton University, USA*

ABSTRACT

Poverty is a powerful context that affects billions of consumers around the world. An appreciation of this context and the ways it shapes thoughts, feelings, and behaviors is essential to understanding the vulnerabilities of low socioeconomic status (SES) consumers. We synthesize research on consumption in poverty by reviewing some of the social vulnerabilities and frequent neglect, discrimination, and stigmatization encountered by low-SES consumers, as well as the cognitive challenges emerging from the experience of financial scarcity. These social, cognitive, and societal vulnerabilities highlight the importance of behaviorally informed programs and policies to address consumer vulnerability in contexts of poverty.

Keywords: Stigma; poverty; consumer vulnerability; low socioeconomic status (or low SES); negative stereotypes; thick skin bias

INTRODUCTION

In research areas spanning consumer behavior, psychology, sociology, and other social and behavioral sciences, a growing recognition of inequalities both in the marketplace and throughout everyday life has brought increased attention to different sources of vulnerability among consumers. One powerful dimension of consumer vulnerability is *low socioeconomic status* (SES), a set of social and material conditions including financial difficulties that shapes the lives of many consumers.

The Vulnerable Consumer
Review of Marketing Research, Volume 21, 69–81
Copyright © 2024 Nathan N. Cheek and Eldar Shafir
Published under exclusive licence by Emerald Publishing Limited
ISSN: 1548-6435/doi:10.1108/S1548-643520240000021005

As an example of the frequency with which consumers experience vulnerabilities associated with low SES, in the United States, at least 37 million people meet the Census Bureau's definition of living in poverty (Shrider et al., 2021), though the official poverty measure is a substantial underestimate of those who are struggling with less than a living wage. Nearly 52 million US workers – or 32% of the country's workforce – earn less than $15 an hour, significantly below a living wage (Oxfam report, 2022). Recent reports estimate that an increase of more than 70% would be necessary to make a typical low-income American worker's earnings a living wage, while in some counties, a 229% increase would be needed (County Health Rankings National Findings Report, 2022).

In this chapter, we seek to add depth to the picture of consumers painted by these statistics of poverty. We review research from our lab and from others on social and cognitive sources of vulnerability among low-SES consumers. In doing so, we adhere to Antonoplis' (2023) definition of SES as referring to "individuals' possession of normatively valued social and economic resources" (p. 279), though our focus will be on "economic resources," including income and, in particular, poverty, as we investigate low-SES consumers. This focus is driven largely by existing research, which has often resorted to easier-to-gauge measures of income, financial scarcity, or related constructs to study SES and consumer vulnerability, though how to define and study SES, poverty, scarcity, and related constructs is the subject of ongoing discussion and innovative theoretical development (see, e.g., Blocker et al., 2023; Hill & Sharma, 2020; Tully & Sharma, 2022). We use terms such as "low-income" and "poverty" when referring to consumers who face persistent financial difficulties, while recognizing that SES encapsulates a broader set of conditions including characteristics such as social capital (Abbott & Reilly, 2019) and occupational prestige (Hughes et al., 2022) that have been less examined in the research we review.

We begin our discussion of low-SES consumers' experiences by exploring social vulnerabilities brought about by prejudice, stereotypes, and discrimination – often grouped together as *classism* (Lott, 2002). We outline some of the stereotypes that lead to discrimination and consider some of the effects that experiencing stigma and discrimination have on lower SES consumers' behavior and decision-making. We also review some recent research on biased beliefs that contribute to people's failure to appreciate the extent to which lower SES consumers need help and support. We then consider how financial scarcity, a common (perhaps defining) experience of low-SES consumers, often creates additional cognitive sources of vulnerability. Both the interpersonal and cognitive sources of vulnerability, we argue, can create insidious cycles that perpetuate and magnify the already-difficult circumstances low-SES consumers face.

PREJUDICE AND DISCRIMINATION AS SOURCES OF VULNERABILITY

Low-income consumers are burdened not only with the task of managing scarce resources but also with widespread stigma and discrimination routinely encountered by them in everyday life. Doctors and therapists undertreat lower

SES patients (Green et al., 2006; Kugelmass, 2016), teachers ignore lower SES students when they need help and punish them more when they misbehave (Calarco, 2018; Croizet et al., 2017; Mowen, 2017), and judges and juries assign harsher sentences to lower SES defendants (Clarke & Koch, 1976; Reiman & Leighton, 2017; Western, 2006). Businesses also pay lower SES employees lower wages even when they are well-credentialed (Laurison & Friedman, 2016), and basic financial services charge them higher fees (Barr, 2004).

In customer service contexts, lower SES consumers receive less attention, respect, and grace. In one study, for example, ostensible bus passengers who pretended not to be able to pay the fare were more likely to be given a free ride when their clothes suggested they were of higher SES, even though, presumably, a free ride would be more beneficial for lower SES individuals (Mujcic & Frijters, 2021). Illustrating how poverty intersects with other marginalized identities, this effect was especially strong when the lower SES passenger was Black.

Another provocative field demonstration found that a man received more contributions when asking for donations on the street while dressed in higher SES clothing than while dressed in lower SES clothing (Callaghan et al., 2022). More generally, consumers in low-SES contexts encounter extensive neglect, disdain, and mistreatment across different interpersonal interactions throughout their everyday lives (Lott, 2002).

Social–psychological perspectives on social class disparities emphasize the role of stereotypes and stigma in the discrimination experienced by low-SES consumers. Poverty is often attributed to the perceived incompetence, short-sightedness, or laziness of individuals (Bullock & Reppond, 2018; Cozzarelli et al., 2001; Feather, 1974; Fiske et al., 2002; Oh et al., 2020), who can be so harshly judged that they are denied basic humanity (Loughnan et al., 2014; Sainz et al., 2020). Interestingly, experiencing poverty does not guarantee better insight: those who grew up in poverty but then achieved higher SES can hold the least generous attitudes toward lower SES consumers because of an "if I did it, others can too" mentality (Hoo et al., 2023).

The harm of perceived incompetence is compounded by negative stereotypes about the motivations of consumers in poverty – that they could be working harder and pulling themselves up by their bootstraps but are instead choosing to free-ride on welfare programs and the taxes of "hard-working citizens" (Hunt & Bullock, 2016; Weiner et al., 2011). Because they are at least partially blamed for their limited resources, consumers who receive welfare benefits are judged harshly when they make purchases deemed to be anything but strictly necessary (Shepherd & Campbell, 2020). Those receiving government assistance are even viewed negatively when they help others if it means spending time that people think could be spent working (Olson et al., 2021).

Negative stereotypes about low-SES consumers help people preserve their beliefs in a just, meritocratic world and increase the blame they assign to low-income consumers for their own circumstances (Furnham & Gunter, 1984; Lerner, 1998). Even when they have some appreciation for the role of external factors as contributors to poverty, people tend to overweight dispositional explanations and underweight factors such as limited opportunity and mistreatment (Cozzarelli et al., 2001; Jones & Nisbett, 1972; Weiner et al., 2011). Not surprisingly, negative stereotypes about low-income consumers also under-mine support for policies intended to alleviate the hardships of poverty – when financial problems are attributed to individual failures and bad choices rather than to systemic factors, policy solutions intended to provide aid are viewed as less useful and unjustified (Bullock, 2013; Henry et al., 2004; McCall et al., 2017). Accordingly, acceptance of economic inequality is higher in countries such as the United States, where people widely attribute poverty to dispositional explana-tions, than, say, in Hungary, where people more commonly attribute poverty to situational factors (Piff et al., 2020).

CONSEQUENCES FOR LOW-SES CONSUMERS

Like other negative stereotypes, a pernicious consequence of stereotypes regarding low-SES consumers is that they may perpetuate the very circumstances they stigmatize. Stereotype threat processes, for instance, can cause lower SES students to perform worse academically when they are concerned with stereo-types about poverty and incompetence (Croziet & Claire, 1998). Research by Hall and colleagues (2014) suggests that poverty stigma undermines performance in low-SES adults as well, adding to the burden produced by a scarcity mindset reviewed later in this chapter. The shame of financial hardship can cause con-sumers to withdraw rather than trying to address their circumstances – in work by Gladstone et al. (2021), those who experienced greater hardship and shame were more likely to avoid looking at bills and refrained from asking for help from others. Shame and poverty stigma are also linked to more problematic financial decisions (e.g., incurring overdraft and late payment fees), can lead marginalized consumers to accept worse treatment in service contexts (Bone et al., 2023), and can ultimately undermine the efficacy of government assistance when low-income consumers become less likely to avail themselves of such programs (Allen et al., 2014; Gladstone et al., 2021; Hall et al., 2014).

Concerns about discrimination and stigma pervade the consumption experi-ences of low-SES individuals. Paralleling Shah et al.'s (2018) findings that many everyday situations can evoke thoughts about finances for lower SES individuals that do not occur to higher SES individuals, Jacob et al. (2022) showed that fears about and expectations of potential discrimination can be spontaneously triggered in everyday consumption experiences among lower SES but not higher SES consumers. Concerns about and attempts to avoid prejudice and discrimination can create a "lose-lose situation" for consumers in poverty, who may try to adopt strategies to reduce discriminatory treatment at the cost of their already limited financial resources. Such strategies might involve decisions about both *where* to buy and *what* to buy.

Regarding *where* to buy, Jacob et al. (2022), for instance, found that con-sumers in poverty often prefer to shop at more expensive stores if this allows them to avoid potentially negative cross-class interactions compared to cheaper stores where they are likely to encounter discrimination. Cues of exclusion and stigma can also deter low-SES consumers from formal banking and other institutions that would be beneficial in the long term if not for their threats to pride, identity, and belonging (Bertrand et al., 2006; Chaney et al., 2019; Jacob et al., 2022). In essence, low-SES consumers need to choose between paying a "safety tax" to shop at more inclusive stores or forgoing a safe environment to save money.

Understanding consumption as occasionally motivated by a desire to protect against mistreatment or to achieve higher status in social interactions can also help explain low-income consumers' choices that otherwise may appear confusing or maladaptive. A salient example are luxury purchases – consumers in poverty sometimes make seemingly extravagant purchases of designer clothing, accessories, or other items that challenge scarce financial resources. Such purchases often serve impression management goals – Cottom (2013), for instance, describes the better treatment low-SES people can receive when material purchases help meet others' expectations for respectable appearance. In illustrating the "logic of stupid poor people" who purchase status symbols over cheaper functional goods, Cottom (2013) writes,

> How do you put a price on the double-take of a clerk at the welfare office who decides you might not be like those other trifling women in the waiting room and provides an extra bit of information about completing a form that you would not have known to ask about? What is the retail value of a school principal who defers a bit more to your child because your mother's presentation of self signals she might unleash the bureaucratic savvy of middle-class parents to advocate for her child? (n.p.)

And research appears to back up this observation: people who wear higher status clothing are perceived as more competent, are treated better, and are helped more than those who wear lower status clothing (Callaghan et al., 2022; Nelissen & Meijers, 2011; Oh et al., 2020).

Other everyday purchases like cigarettes and alcohol, which might pose health risks or undermine longer term savings, can serve valuable social functions, such as helping someone fit in and build connections with others. Attending to others' choices and following social norms to fit in is particularly important in lower SES consumer contexts where building social resources can buffer against discrimination both psychologically and logistically (Carey & Markus, 2016; Snibbe & Markus, 2005). Hence, for low-SES consumers, "Many choices function to enhance social well-being even as they work against physical or financial well-being" (Carey & Markus, 2016, p. 580).

THE "THICK SKIN BIAS" AS A SOURCE OF VULNERABILITY

As low-SES consumers struggle and meet with challenges and discrimination, why aren't people more sensitized to their plight? In our recent work, we have looked not at beliefs about the causes of poverty but at potentially insidious beliefs about its *effects*. Specifically, we have documented what we termed the "thick skin bias" – the belief that lower SES individuals are less harmed or encumbered by negative life events than their higher SES counterparts (Cheek & Shafir, 2020). Previous research documented biases in perceived physical pain potentially attributable to the perception that Black individuals have experienced more hardship than white individuals and the assumption that hardship reduces vulnerability to physical pain (Hoffman & Trawalter, 2016). We extended this logic to propose that low-SES individuals are perceived as having been "toughened" by their hardship (see also Cheek & Murray, 2023), causing them to be less affected by new negative events. Across dozens of studies, we have found that laypeople, including a nationally representatively sample of US citizens, and professionals such as therapists and teachers believe that lower SES individuals are less impacted both by trivial and by more consequential negative events.

People believe that even five-year-olds would be less harmed by negative events if they have grown up in poverty (Cheek & Shafir, 2020), that sexual harassment and domestic abuse are less harmful for lower SES women (Cheek et al., 2023), and that, during the COVID-19 pandemic, restrictions such as being isolated at home and separated from loved ones were less upsetting for low-SES individuals (Cheek, 2023). The thick skin bias extends to situations where it would appear obvious that low-income consumers are more vulnerable, such as having a flooded apartment, or having the heating stop working in mid-winter, and it extends to judgments of physical pain as well (see also Bernardes et al., 2021; Summers et al., 2021). Directly relevant to consumer contexts, we found that employees in restaurants expected lower SES customers to be less upset with bad service or with low-quality food (Cheek & Shafir, 2020).

The thick skin bias offers further explanation, along with stigmatizing attributional stereotypes for much of the neglect low-SES consumers encounter. If low-income individuals are perceived as less harmed by negative events, from minor inconveniences to major harms, what happens to someone in poverty will appear less urgent or severe. The bias can explain why low-SES patients receive less treatment for mental or physical health problems, why teachers are less attentive to lower SES students in difficulty, and perhaps even why lower SES defendants receive harsher sentences – once perceived as less harmed by punishment, a harsher sentence may be perceived as necessary to achieve the same "level" of discipline.

Along with being seen as less harmed when things go wrong, low-SES individuals in our studies were also perceived as more positively impacted when things go right (Cheek et al., 2023; Cheek & Shafir, 2020). This would suggest a perception that consumers in poverty may be happier with less, potentially exacerbating neglect. It is also consistent with findings that many purchases, not only luxuries but even some necessities, are perceived as less "necessary" for lower SES consumers (Hagerty & Barasz, 2020). The belief that low-SES consumers are happier with less suggests that even minor pleasures will provide an outsized benefit, compared with greater pleasures needed to provide higher SES consumers with a similar experience.

In summary, stigma, stereotypes, and discrimination represent a serious social challenge and threat to low-SES consumers. They constitute not only a direct menace of mistreatment by others but also social and cognitive challenges around stereotype threat, chronic concerns about mistreatment, and the need to make costly financial tradeoffs to protect oneself and avoid further prejudice and discrimination. Consumers in poverty are judged harshly for their financial circumstances, yet these harsh judgments only perpetuate and exacerbate the tough circumstances low-SES consumers find themselves in.

COGNITIVE SOURCES OF VULNERABILITY

In addition to causing exposure to stigma and discrimination, living with financial scarcity, as many (but not all, e.g., Blocker et al., 2023) low-SES consumers do, requires near-constant juggling of problems and priorities, including the persistent need to balance burning present needs versus important future costs, navigating ubiquitous tradeoffs and carefully tracking expenses near the edge – not to mention the occasional yet highly predictable "financial shock." Managing all this imposes a cognitive load on low-income consumers' attention and can undermine executive function and lead to the neglect of important concerns outside the immediate focus of attention. Sometimes, people in poverty fall into patterns of maladaptive behaviors – for example, neglecting important things that fall outside their immediate and urgent concerns. Lower income individuals are more likely to miss important appointments (e.g., court appearances), stray from healthy diets, forget to take their medications, and fail to avail themselves of opportunities to increase their savings or earnings (Fernandez-Lazaro et al., 2019; Fishbane et al., 2020).

These patterns, often interpreted by laypeople as well as policymakers through the lens of negative stereotypes about incompetence and laziness, can be more accurately understood from a behavioral perspective that helps identify the source of many suboptimal behaviors as scarcity itself. Indeed, research on scarcity, including both the financial scarcity common among low-SES consumers as well as other forms of scarcity such as insufficient time, calories, or other resources people feel they need, has found that the same person may perform better, pay greater attention, or show higher cognitive functioning when experiencing abundant resources than when confronting scarcity (Mullainathan & Shafir, 2013).

In one study, for example, the same farmers exhibited higher cognitive functioning in contexts of plenty (after having been paid for their harvest) compared to contexts of scarcity (before they'd been paid and after they'd run out of money; Mani et al., 2013). Clearly, it is not the farmers' disposition but the context of scarcity that undermined performance on cognitive tasks. Studies ranging from lab experiments with undergraduates to field experiments involving high-stakes outcomes such as debt relief have illuminated the extent to which salient concerns about scarce resources and intrusive thoughts about money and debt can capture attention and undermine reasoning (e.g., Ong et al., 2019; Shah et al., 2012).

To be sure, we are not arguing that low-SES consumers do not often develop strategies to effectively navigate their financial circumstances. On the contrary, people in contexts of poverty have been found, not surprisingly, to be highly attentive to the everyday use of their limited funds. Low-income consumers have been shown to pay more attention to pricing and to hidden costs compared to higher income consumers, to remember costs more accurately, and to attend to tradeoffs more consistently (Binkley & Bejnarowicz, 2003; Goldin & Homonoff, 2013; María Rosa-Díaz, 2004; Mullainathan & Shafir, 2013). In fact, because they are more likely to think about tradeoffs and opportunity costs (Spiller, 2011), lower income consumers can be more consistent in their valuation of money and of discounts and less prone to some well-documented behavioral finance biases (Shah et al., 2015). But recognizing the strengths of low-SES consumers does not conflict with recognizing that the cognitive experience of scarcity can exacerbate the existing challenges of managing constrained budgets. Rather, it appears that what is often attributed to individual failings or to problematic "cultures" of poverty can be more accurately located in contextual factors that perpetuate economic hardship despite the persistent efforts and potential strengths of low-SES consumers (see Frankenhuis & Nettle, 2020).

Research on the impact of financial scarcity on low-SES consumer behavior continues to explore the various conditions that lead to substantial versus little effects of immediate financial difficulties on cognition (Carvalho et al., 2016; Mani et al., 2013, 2021; Ong et al., 2019; Shah et al., 2019). Some new research explores the differences between shorter and longer time horizons when theorizing about the relative adaptiveness of behaviors under scarcity (Sharma et al., 2023), while other work highlights some new consequences of scarcity, such as a study by Kaur and colleagues (2021) showing that financial concerns undermine employee productivity and cause more frequent workplace mistakes and accidents. Our own recent work (Wu et al., 2024) suggests that a scarcity mindset may even influence imagination, mindfulness, and the ability to think for pleasure.

In sum, when low-SES consumers face persistent money concerns, juggling finances can diminish cognitive performance and undermine decision-making, leisure, and well-being. Remarkably, as summarized earlier, instead of respect for their ongoing struggles, consumers in low-SES contexts and contexts of poverty often encounter disrespect and discrimination rather than the greater care and support they need (and which so many higher income and higher SES citizens typically receive).

CONCLUSION: FUTURE DIRECTIONS TO ADDRESS CONSUMER VULNERABILITY IN CONTEXTS OF POVERTY

Vulnerable consumers often inhabit challenging environments, including noisy neighborhoods, higher crime rates, substandard housing, inferior schools, unreliable transportation, fear, distrust, disrespect, and uncertainty. We have focused on some of the cognitive and social sources of vulnerability inherent to the consumption experience of low-SES individuals, especially those in poverty.

Consumers in poverty experience a wide range of vulnerabilities, yet they are often met with uncaring institutions, hostile environments, and policies driven by punishment and shame rather than care and understanding. Burdensome paperwork, unforgiving deadlines, judgmental bureaucrats, and indifferent professionals introduce new obstacles instead of paving a smoother path to economic subsistence. In recent years, marketing, psychology, economics, and other behavioral sciences have helped explain how the context of poverty functions to perpetuate and even magnify financial hardship. In light of that work, it is clear that society's approach to poverty is overly focused on the individual instead of the context and overly punitive when it should be supportive.

Behavioral public policy offers a way forward that takes into account the contextual vulnerabilities faced by low-SES consumers. Indeed, there are several directions for future research that could address some of the vulnerabilities we have explored in this chapter. For instance, we see potential for the development of behaviorally informed interventions. Some might aim to intervene on common biases toward those of lower SES, with the goal of reducing discrimination and increasing helping behaviors; others might work to affirm lower SES consumers' capabilities and identities with the goal of buffering them from the harmful effects of experiencing stigma and discrimination. Relevant to the first goal, some recent research suggests that making inequality more salient to people or giving them clear evidence of contextual (i.e., external rather than dispositional) causes of poverty can improve attitudes toward low-SES individuals and increase support of poverty-alleviation policies (McCall et al., 2017; Piff et al., 2020). With regard to the second goal, there is some evidence that affirming lower SES consumers' sense of pride and capability may counteract the harm of stigma and improve their financial well-being (e.g., by increasing their willingness to avail themselves of government assistance programs; Hall et al., 2014). There is much work to be done on these kinds of behaviorally motivated interventions, on the potentially harmful self-views of lower SES consumers, on the prejudices of all consumers, and on the extent to which different contextual features (e.g., identity safety cues vs identity threatening cues; Chaney et al., 2019) can help or hinder low-SES consumers.

Future research may also further elucidate the varieties of scarcity experiences, financial and otherwise by, for example, comparing the effects of temporary versus chronic scarcity (including scarcity induced in the lab vs scarcity experienced "in the field") and the fluctuations in the perception of scarcity, within and across individuals, over time (e.g., Wu et al., 2024). We can think of many relatively minor interventions that could ease the many burdens imposed on low-SES consumers in their challenging circumstances. Complicated forms can be simplified, reminders can be automated, loans can be more effectively regulated, and even debt collection could be made more cooperative (Carmichael, 2013), freeing up mental bandwidth to deal with other aspects of life. Of course, minor interventions of this kind, however useful, should not replace real attempts to lessen the occurrence of poverty and scarcity. Earnings below a living wage will not be alleviated by minor policy tweaks, and the evidence is clear that living in contexts of scarcity tends to be debilitating and harmful. As we gain further insights behavioral scientists should communicate and explain the vulnerabilities that threaten low-SES consumers, with the ultimate aim of achieving a better informed and equitable social, political, and policy environment for all consumers.

REFERENCES

Abbott, M., & Reilly, A. (2019). The role of social capital in supporting economic mobility. *Office of the Assistant Secretary for Planning and Evaluation, US Department of Health and Human Services, Office of Human Services Policy, 42*(2), 33.

Allen, H., Wright, B. J., Harding, K., & Broffman, L. (2014). The role of stigma in access to health care for the poor. *The Milbank Quarterly, 92*(2), 289–318. https://doi.org/10.1111/1468-0009.12059

Antonoplis, S. (2023). Studying socioeconomic status: Conceptual problems and an alternative path forward. *Perspectives on Psychological Science, 18*, 275–292. https://doi.org/10.1177/17456916221093615

Barr, M. S. (2004). Banking the poor. *Yale Journal on Regulation, 21*, 121.

Bernardes, S. F., Tomé-Pires, C., Brandão, T., Campos, L., Teixeira, F., & Goubert, L. (2021). Classism in pain assessment and management: The mediating role of female patient dehumanization and perceived life hardship. *Pain, 162*, 2854–2864. https://doi.org/10.1097/j.pain.0000000000002278

Bertrand, M., Mullainathan, S., & Shafir, E. (2006). Behavioral economics and marketing in aid of decision making among the poor. *Journal of Public Policy and Marketing, 25*, 8–23. https://doi.org/10.1509/jppm.25.1.8

Binkley, J. K., & Bejnarowicz, J. (2003). Consumer price awareness in food shopping: The case of quantity surcharges. *Journal of Retailing, 79*, 27–35. https://doi.org/10.1016/S0022-4359(03)00005-8

Blocker, C., Zhang, J. Z., Hill, R. P., Roux, C., Corus, C., Hutton, M., Dorsey, J., & Minton, E. (2023). Rethinking scarcity and poverty: Building bridges for shared insight and impact. *Journal of Consumer Psychology, 33*, 489–509. https://doi.org/10.1002/jcpy.1323

Bone, S. A., Christensen, G. L., Williams, J. D., Cross, S. N. N., & Dellande, S. (2023). Moving beyond perceptions: Examining service disparities among consumers. *Journal of the Association for Consumer Research, 8*, 107–119. https://doi.org/10.1086/722689

Bullock, H. E. (2013). *Women and poverty: Psychology, public policy, and social justice*. John Wiley and Sons.

Bullock, H. E., & Reppond, H. A. (2018). Of "takers" and "makers": A social psychological analysis of class and classism. In P. L. Hammack Jr. (Ed.), *The Oxford handbook of social psychology and social Justice* (pp. 223–244). Oxford University Press.

Calarco, J. M. (2018). *Negotiating opportunities: How the middle class secures advantages in school*. Oxford University Press.

Callaghan, B., Delgadillo, Q. M., & Kraus, M. W. (2022). The influence of signs of social class on compassionate responses to people in need. *Frontiers in Psychology, 13*, 936170. https://doi.org/10.3389/fpsyg.2022.936170

Carey, R. M., & Markus, H. R. (2016). Understanding consumer psychology in working-class contexts. *Journal of Consumer Psychology, 26*, 568–582. https://doi.org/10.1016/j.jcps.2016.08.004

Carmichael, S. G. (2013, August 16). The debt-collection company that helps you get a job. *Harvard Business Review*. https://hbr.org/2013/08/the-debt-collection-company-th#:~:text=Bill%20Bartmann%2C%20CEO%20of%20debt,resume%20help%20and%20interview%20prep

Carvalho, L. S., Meier, S., & Wang, S. W. (2016). Poverty and economic decision-making: Evidence from changes in financial resources at payday. *The American Economic Review, 106*, 260–284. https://doi.org/10.1016/j.joep.2018.12.001

Chaney, K. E., Sanchez, D. T., & Maimon, M. R. (2019). Stigmatized-identity cues in consumer spaces. *Journal of Consumer Psychology, 29*, 130–144. https://doi.org/10.1002/jcpy.1075

Cheek, N. N. (2023). People think the everyday effects of the COVID-19 pandemic are not as bad for people in poverty. *Journal of Experimental Psychology: Applied, 29*, 425–439. https://doi.org/10.1037/xap0000442

Cheek, N. N., Bandt-Law, B., & Sinclair, S. (2023). People believe sexual harassment and domestic violence are less harmful for women in poverty. *Journal of Experimental Social Psychology, 107*, 104472. https://doi.org/10.1016/j.jesp.2023.104472

Cheek, N. N., & Murray, J. (2023). Why do people think individuals in poverty are less vulnerable to harm? Testing the role of intuitions about adaptation. *Personality and Social Psychology Bulletin.* https://doi.org/10.1177/01461672231202756

Cheek, N. N., & Shafir, E. (2020). The thick skin bias in judgments about people in poverty. *Behavioural Public Policy.* https://doi.org/10.1017/bpp.2020.33

Clarke, S. H., & Koch, G. G. (1976). The influence of income and other factors on whether criminal defendants go to prison. *Law and Society Review, 11*, 57–92. https://doi.org/10.2307/3053204

Cottom, T. M. (2013). The logic of stupid poor people. Some of us are brave: The archive. https://tressiemc.com/uncategorized/the-logic-of-stupid-poor-people/. Accessed on November 23, 2022.

County Health Rankings. (2022). *National findings report.* https://www.countyhealthrankings.org/sites/default/files/media/document/2022%20County%20Health%20Rankings%20National%20Findings%20Report.pdf

Cozzarelli, C., Wilkinson, A. V., & Tagler, M. J. (2001). Attitudes toward the poor and attributions for poverty. *Journal of Social Issues, 57*, 207–227. https://doi.org/10.1111/0022-4537.00209

Croizet, J.-C., Goudeau, S., Marot, M., & Millet, M. (2017). How do educational contexts contribute to the social class achievement gap: Documenting symbolic violence from a social psychological point of view. *Current Opinion in Psychology, 18*, 105–110. https://doi.org/10.1016/j.copsyc.2017.08.025

Croziet, J.-C., & Claire, T. (1998). Extending the concept of stereotype threat to social class: The intellectual underperformance of students from low socioeconomic backgrounds. *Personality and Social Psychology Bulletin, 24*, 588–594. https://psycnet.apa.org/doi/10.1177/0146167298246003

Feather, N. T. (1974). Explanations of poverty in Australian and American samples: The person, society, or fate?. *Australian Journal of Psychology, 26*, 199–216. https://doi.org/10.1080/00049537408255231

Fernandez-Lazaro, C. I., Adams, D. P., Fernandez-Lazaro, D., Garcia-González, J. M., Caballero-Garcia, A., & Miron-Canelo, J. A. (2019). Medication adherence and barriers among low-income, uninsured patients with multiple chronic conditions. *Research in Social and Administrative Pharmacy, 15*, 744–753. https://doi.org/10.1016/j.sapharm.2018.09.006

Fishbane, A., Ouss, A., & Shah, A. K. (2020). Behavioral nudges reduce failure to appear for court. *Science, 370*, eabb6591. https://doi.org/10.1126/science.abb6591

Fiske, S. T., Cuddy, A. J. C., Glick, P., & Xu, J. (2002). A model of (often mixed) stereotype content: Competence and warmth respectively follow from perceived status and competition. *Journal of Personality and Social Psychology, 82*, 878–902. https://psycnet.apa.org/doi/10.1037/0022-3514.82.6.878

Frankenhuis, W. E., & Nettle, D. (2020). The strengths of people in poverty. *Current Directions in Psychological Science, 29*, 16–21. https://doi.org/10.1177/0963721419881154

Furnham, A., & Gunter, B. (1984). Just world beliefs and attitudes towards the poor. *British Journal of Social Psychology, 23*, 265–269. https://psycnet.apa.org/doi/10.1111/j.2044-8309.1984.tb00637.x

Gladstone, J. J., Jachimowicz, J. M., Greenberg, A. E., & Galinsky, A. D. (2021). Financial shame spirals: How shame intensifies financial hardship. *Organizational Behavior and Human Decision Processes, 167*, 42–56. https://doi.org/10.1016/j.obhdp.2021.06.002

Goldin, J., & Homonoff, T. (2013). Smoke gets in your eyes: Cigarette tax salience and regressivity. *American Economic Journal: Economic Policy, 5*, 302–336. https://doi.org/10.1257/pol.5.1.302

Green, C., Todd, K. H., Lebovits, A., & Francis, M. (2006). Disparities in pain: Ethical issues. *Pain Medicine, 7*, 530–533. https://doi.org/10.1111/j.1526-4637.2006.00244.x

Hagerty, S. F., & Barasz, K. (2020). Inequality in socially permissible consumption. *Proceedings of the National Academy of Sciences, 117*, 14084–14093. https://doi.org/10.1073/pnas.2005475117

Hall, C. C., Zhao, J., & Shafir, E. (2014). Self-affirmation among the poor: Cognitive and behavioral implications. *Psychological Science*, *25*, 619–625. https://doi.org/10.1177/0956797613510949

Henry, P. J., Reyna, C., & Weiner, B. (2004). Hate welfare but help the poor: How the attributional content of stereotypes explains the paradox of reactions to the destitute in America. *Journal of Applied Social Psychology*, *34*, 34–58. https://doi.org/10.1111/j.1559-1816.2004.tb02536.x

Hill, R. P., & Sharma, E. (2020). Consumer vulnerability. *Journal of Consumer Psychology*, *30*, 551–570. https://doi.org/10.1002/jcpy.1161

Hoffman, K. M., & Trawalter, S. (2016). Assumptions about life hardship and pain perception. *Group Processes and Intergroup Relations*, *19*, 493–508. https://doi.org/10.1177/1368430215625781

Hoo, H. J., Piff, P. K., & Shariff, A. F. (2023). If I could do it, so can they: Among the rich, those with humbler origins are less sensitive to the difficulties of the poor. *Social Psychological and Personality Science*, *14*, 333–341. https://doi.org/10.1177/19485506221098921

Hughes, B. T., Srivastava, S., Leszko, M., & Condon, D. M. (2022). Occupational prestige: The status component of socioeconomic status. PsyArXiv. https://psyarxiv.com/6qgxv/

Hunt, M. O., & Bullock, H. E. (2016). Ideologies and beliefs about poverty. In D. Brady & L. M. Burton (Eds.), *The Oxford handbook of the social science of poverty* (pp. 93–116). Oxford University Press.

Jacob, J., Vietes, Y., Goldszmidt, R., & Andrade, E. B. (2022). Expected socioeconomic-status-based discrimination reduces price sensitivity among the poor. *Journal of Marketing Research*, *59*, 1083–1100. https://doi.org/10.1177/00222437221097100

Jones, E. E., & Nisbett, R. E. (1972). The actor and the observer: Divergent perceptions of the causes of behavior. In E. E. Jones, D. E. Kanouse, H. H. Kelley, R. E. Nisbett, S. Valins, & B. Weiner (Eds.), *Attribution: Perceiving the causes of behavior* (pp. 79–94). General Learning Press.

Kaur, S., Mullainathan, S., Oh, S., & Schilbach, F. (2021). *Do financial concerns make workers less productive?* NBER. http://www.nber.org/papers/w28338

Kugelmass, H. (2016). "Sorry, I'm not accepting new patients": An audit study of access to mental health care. *Journal of Health and Social Behavior*, *57*, 168–183. https://doi.org/10.1177/0022146516647098

Laurison, D., & Friedman, S. (2016). The class pay gap in higher professional and managerial occupations. *American Sociological Review*, *81*, 668–695. https://doi.org/10.1177/0003122416653602

Lerner, M. J. (1998). The two forms of belief in a just world: Some thoughts on why and how people care about justice. In L. Montada & M. J. Lerner (Eds.), *Responses to victimizations and belief in a just world* (pp. 247–269). Plenum Press.

Lott, B. (2002). Cognitive and behavioral distancing from the poor. *American Psychologist*, *57*, 100–110. https://doi.org/10.1037//0003-066X.57.2.100

Loughnan, S., Haslam, N., Sutton, R. M., & Spencer, B. (2014). Dehumanization and social class: Animality in the stereotypes of "white trash," "chavs," and "bogans.". *Social Psychology*, *45*, 54–61. https://psycnet.apa.org/doi/10.1027/1864-9335/a000159

Mani, A., Mullainathan, S., Shafir, E., & Zhao, J. (2021). Scarcity and cognitive function around payday: A conceptual and empirical analysis. *Journal of the Association for Consumer Research*, *5*, 365–376. https://doi.org/10.1086/709885

Mani, A., Mullainathan, S., Shafir, E., & Zhao, J. (2013). Poverty impedes cognitive function. *Science*, *341*, 976–980. https://doi.org/10.1126/science.1238041

María Rosa-Díaz, I. (2004). Price knowledge: Effects of consumers' attitudes towards prices, demographics, and socio-cultural characteristics. *The Journal of Product and Brand Management*, *13*, 406–428. https://doi.org/10.1108/10610420410560307

McCall, L., Burk, D., Laperrière, M., & Richeson, J. A. (2017). Exposure to rising inequality shapes Americans' opportunity beliefs and policy support. *Proceedings of the National Academy of Sciences*, *114*, 9593–9598. https://doi.org/10.1073/pnas.1706253114

Mowen, T. J. (2017). The collateral consequences of "criminalized" school punishment on disadvantaged parents and families. *The Urban Review*, *49*, 832–851. https://doi.org/10.1007/s11256-017-0423-z

Mujcic, R., & Frijters, P. (2021). The colour of a free ride. *The Economic Journal*, *131*, 970–999. https://doi.org/10.1093/ej/ueaa090

Mullainathan, S., & Shafir, E. (2013). *Scarcity: Why having too little means so much*. Macmillan.

Nelissen, R. M. A., & Meijers, M. H. C. (2011). Social benefits of luxury brands as costly signals of wealth and status. *Evolution and Human Behavior, 32*, 343–355. https://doi.org/10.1016/j. evolhumbehav.2010.12.002

Oh, D., Shafir, E., & Todorov, A. (2020). Economic status cues from clothes affect perceived competence from faces. *Nature Human Behaviour, 4*, 287–293. https://doi.org/10.1038/s41562-019-0782-4

Olson, J. G., McFerran, B., Morales, A. C., & Dahl, D. W. (2021). How income shapes moral judgments of prosocial behavior. *International Journal of Research in Marketing, 38*, 120–135. https://doi.org/10.1016/j.ijresmar.2020.07.001

Ong, Q., Theseira, W., & Ng, I. Y. H. (2019). Reducing debt improves psychological functioning and changes decision-making in the poor. *PNAS, 116*, 7244–7249. https://doi.org/10.1073/pnas. 1810901116

Oxfam Report. (2022). *The crisis of low wages in the US.* https://www.oxfamamerica.org/explore/ research-publications/the-crisis-of-low-wages-in-the-us/

Piff, P. K., Wiwad, D., Robinson, A. R., Aknin, L. B., Mercier, B., & Shariff, A. (2020). Shifting attributions for poverty motivates opposition to inequality and enhances egalitarianism. *Nature Human Behaviour, 4*, 496–505. https://doi.org/10.1038/s41562-020-0835-8

Reiman, J., & Leighton, P. (2017). *The rich get richer and the poor get prison.* Pearson.

Sainz, M., Martínez, R., Sutton, R. M., Rodríguez-Bailón, R., & Moya, M. (2020). Less human, more to blame: Animalizing poor people increases blame and decreases support for wealth redistribution. *Group Processes & Intergroup Relations, 23*, 546–559. https://doi.org/10.1177/ 1368430219841135

Shah, A. K., Mullainathan, S., & Shafir, E. (2012). Some consequences of having too little. *Science, 338*, 682–685. https://doi.org/10.1126/science.1222426

Shah, A. K., Mullainathan, S., & Shafir, E. (2019). An exercise in self-replication: Replicating Shah, Mullainathan, and Shafir (2012). *Journal of Economic Psychology, 75*, 102127. https://doi.org/ 10.1016/j.joep.2018.12.001

Shah, A. K., Shafir, E., & Mullainathan, S. (2015). Scarcity frames value. *Psychological Science, 26*, 402–412. https://doi.org/10.1177%2F0956797614563958

Shah, A. K., Zhao, J., Mullainathan, S., & Shafir, E. (2018). Money in the mental lives of the poor. *Social Cognition, 36*, 4–19. https://doi.org/10.1521/soco.2018.36.1.4

Sharma, E., Tully, S. M., & Wang, X. (2023). Scarcity and intertemporal choice. *Journal of Personality and Social Psychology, 125*, 1036–1054. https://doi.org/10.1037/pspa0000353

Shepherd, S., & Campbell, T. (2020). The effect of egocentric taste judgments on stereotyping of welfare recipients and attitudes toward welfare policy. *Journal of Public Policy and Marketing, 39*, 1–14. https://doi.org/10.1177/0743915618820925

Shrider, E. A., Kollar, M., Chen, F., & Semega, J. (2021). *Income and poverty in the United States: 2020.* U.S. Census Bureau, U.S. Department of Commerce. https://www.census.gov/content/ dam/Census/library/publications/2021/demo/p60-273.pdf

Snibbe, A. C., & Markus, H. R. (2005). You can't always get what you want: Educational attainment, agency, and choice. *Journal of Personality and Social Psychology, 88*, 703–720. https://psycnet. apa.org/doi/10.1037/0022-3514.88.4.703

Spiller, S. A. (2011). Opportunity cost consideration. *Journal of Consumer Research, 38*, 595–610. https://doi.org/10.1086/660045

Summers, K. M., Deska, J., Almaraz, S. M., Hugenberg, K., & Lloyd, E. P. (2021). Poverty and pain: Low-SES people are believed to be insensitive to pain. *Journal of Experimental Social Psychology, 95*, 1041116. https://doi.org/10.1016/j.jesp.2021.104116

Tully, S. M., & Sharma, E. (2022). Consumer wealth. *Consumer Psychology Review, 5*, 125–143. https://doi.org/10.1002/arcp.1073

Weiner, B., Osborne, D., & Rudolph, U. (2011). An attributional analysis of reactions of poverty: The political ideology of the giver and the perceived morality of the receiver. *Personality and Social Psychology Review, 15*, 199–213. https://doi.org/10.1177/1088868310387615

Western, B. (2006). *Punishment and inequality in America.* Russel Sage Foundation.

Wu, S. J., Cheek, N. N., & Shafir, E. (2024). *Scarcity undermines pleasurable thinking.* Manuscript in preparation.

THE YIN AND YANG OF HARD TIMES: WHEN CAN STATES OF VULNERABILITY MOTIVATE SELF-IMPROVEMENT?

Kelly Goldsmith[a], Caroline Roux[b], Christopher Cannon[c] and Ali Tezer[d]

[a]Vanderbilt University, USA
[b]Concordia University, Canada
[c]University of Hawai'i at Mānoa, USA
[d]HEC Montréal, Canada

ABSTRACT

This chapter advances our understanding of vulnerable consumers by exploring new relationships between resource scarcity and consumer decision-making. Although resource scarcity often prompts individuals to pull back on spending, recent research has shown that it can also increase consumers' motivation to engage in behaviors that fulfill their need for personal control. We extend this stream of research by offering the novel proposition that because resource scarcity motivates the desire for control, activating thoughts about scarcity will increase consumers' interest in products offering self-improvement benefits. We offer initial empirical evidence for when resource scarcity causes consumers to forgo their desire to save by increasing their willingness to pay for products that offer self-improvement benefits. In doing so, this chapter (i) highlights resource scarcity, a state of vulnerability, as an antecedent to the desire for self-improvement, (ii) provides a more nuanced perspective on the motivational underpinnings of resource scarcity and its effects on consumption, and (iii) sheds light on when resource scarcity can increase rather than decrease consumer spending.

Keywords: Scarcity; vulnerability; self-improvement; psychological threat; compensatory consumption

The Vulnerable Consumer
Review of Marketing Research, Volume 21, 83–96
Copyright © 2024 Kelly Goldsmith, Caroline Roux, Christopher Cannon and Ali Tezer
Published under exclusive licence by Emerald Publishing Limited
ISSN: 1548-6435/doi:10.1108/S1548-643520240000021006

INTRODUCTION

The self-improvement industry is a large and thriving enterprise. Many retailers stock a diverse array of products that offer the promise of bettering relevant aspects of the self (e.g., beverages that promise to enhance one's physical and/or psychological health; Ross, 2015). Interestingly, consumers' desire for products and services offering self-improvement benefits did not flag during recent periods of resource scarcity. For example, consumers' likelihood of investing their money and time into retreats that offered the promise of self-improvement (e.g., Tony Robbins' six-day, $3,500 "Date with Destiny" program) did not wane during the 2008 economic recession (O'Keefe, 2014). Similarly, consumers' spending on expensive workout equipment (e.g., Peloton's $2,245 exercise bike) soared during the COVID-19 pandemic (Griffith, 2020). In addition, markets related to self-improvement, such as fitness tracking (e.g., smartwatches, wearables, trackers) and personal development (e.g., books, videos, seminars) – each valued at approximately $45 billion globally in 2022 (Grand View Research, 2023a, 2023b) – rose during the COVID-19 pandemic and are forecasted to keep growing in its aftermath. A preponderance of market data thus attests to the fact that the abundant supply of goods and services offering self-improvement benefits in the marketplace is warranted given commensurate levels of demand from consumers, even during times of resource scarcity.

The desire for self-improvement is defined as "the motivation to pursue outcomes that will facilitate bettering some self-relevant aspect of the self, including personal attributes or performance in domains important to the self, such as the intellectual, moral, social, or physical self" (Allard & White, 2015, p. 403). This definition bears relevance to why consumers may be drawn to products offering self-improvement benefits; improvements to one's personal attributes and/or performance in domains that are important to the self are generally positive for the enhancement of individual consumer welfare. This implies that if self-improvement was costless, a rational consumer would generally pursue this outcome because the net result would only be positive for the self.

However, both the academic definition of self-improvement and the marketplace examples noted above highlight the fact that although self-improvement benefits may generally be appealing, they are also often costly in terms of the resources that must be invested to attain such benefits (Grewal et al., 2022). These resources can come in the form of the effort one must exert (e.g., exercise to gain benefits to one's physical health), the money that must be spent (e.g., money spent toward self-help programs), and/or the opportunity costs that must be sacrificed (e.g., spending time studying vs socializing). Taken together, this implies that although self-improvement benefits are likely to be attractive to most – if not all – consumers, the likelihood that such benefits will be pursued will vary as a function of their willingness to tradeoff their resources in favor of this objective.

Consequently, we could expect consumers experiencing resource scarcity to be less willing to use their limited resources for the pursuit of self-improvement benefits (and thus to curb their related spending) in order to conserve them for more pressing scarcity-related needs (Mullainathan & Shafir, 2013). However, this intuition does not fit with the marketplace examples showing consumer spending related to self-improvement rose during times of scarcity. In this chapter, we build on prior research on the effects of resource scarcity on consumption (Cannon et al., 2019) to help explain when and why vulnerable consumers experiencing resource scarcity may invest in self-improvement during hard times.

RESOURCE SCARCITY AND SELF-IMPROVEMENT

Reminders of resource scarcity are pervasive throughout consumers' lives, and it is very common for people to feel as if they "do not have enough" resources (Shah et al., 2012). Building on prior work, we define resource scarcity as "sensing or observing a discrepancy between one's current level of resources and a higher, more desirable reference point" (Cannon et al., 2019, p. 105). In this chapter, we focus on *incidental* forms of scarcity. Incidental scarcity is experienced through everyday deficits in one's perceived levels of resources. These are commonly experienced by consumers irrespective of their objective resource levels (e.g., socioeconomic status) and engender a sense of vulnerability (Blocker et al., 2023). For instance, a consumer comparing their financial situation to someone better off (Sharma & Alter, 2012), reading a news article about an impending economic recession (Griskevicius et al., 2013), or facing stockouts of their preferred brands at the grocery store (Khan & DePaoli, forthcoming) would experience incidental scarcity due to an unfavorable comparison to a more desirable reference point (i.e., their friends' affluence, macroeconomic stability, and product availability, respectively).

Integrating extant research on how resource scarcity shapes consumption with the fact that pursuing self-improvement benefits is often costly, one might predict that considerations of resource scarcity should generally decrease consumers' interest in products and services offering such benefits. For example, prior research on how resource scarcity affects attentional allocation has revealed that it generally shifts consumers' attention toward the scarcity-related threat and away from other concerns (Mullainathan & Shafir, 2013; Sharma et al., 2023). This suggests that resource scarcity may direct attention away from other goals (i.e., self-improvement) when those goals are not directly implicated in the scarcity-related problem. Given that consumers' likelihood of pursuing any goal increases to the extent that goal is cognitively accessible (Kruglanski et al., 2002), this prior research suggests that resource scarcity might decrease consumers' interest in goods that offer self-improvement benefits.

This attentional shift, however, occurs when consumers believe they can directly resolve their experienced resource scarcity by investing a reasonable amount of effort (i.e., high mutability) toward acquiring or protecting the scarce resource (i.e., scarcity reduction; Cannon et al., 2019). For instance, a consumer feeling financially deprived would attempt to directly resolve their experienced scarcity by trying to find other means to acquire money and/or expenses to cut from their budget. By contrast, when consumers believe that no reasonable amount of effort will help them directly address their scarcity-related situation (i.e., low mutability) or when the experienced resource scarcity is not due to one specific resource constraint, consumers instead attempt to resolve their resource scarcity threat indirectly (i.e., control restoration; Cannon et al., 2019). For example, a consumer feeling financially deprived who has no additional means of acquiring money and/or already has a very tight budget, or a consumer who experiences a general sense of scarcity when watching the news during a world-wide pandemic, would have to find ways to indirectly cope with their experienced scarcity.

Importantly, prior research has argued that incidental resource scarcity, which is the focus of this chapter, is linked to low mutability (Cannon et al., 2019). When consumers perceive their incidental scarcity as being low in mutability, they are motivated to address the psychological threat to personal control that resource scarcity presents by pursuing strategies aimed at restoring their personal control (Cannon et al., 2019). Such strategies can take the form of compensatory consumption or competitive motives, which could both help explain consumers' sustained desire for self-improvement during times of scarcity (see Table 1).

Firstly, consumers experiencing resource scarcity can restore their personal control by engaging in compensatory consumption in related (i.e., symbolic self-completion) or unrelated (i.e., fluid compensation) domains (Cannon et al., 2019; Mandel et al., 2017). For instance, financial deprivation has been shown to increase consumers' preference for long-lasting material possessions over expe-riences (Tully et al., 2015) and the desire for unique products that other con-sumers do not possess (Sharma & Alter, 2012). In addition, prior research has shown that upward (vs downward) comparisons can increase consumers' desire for self-improvement, by making them feel less satisfied with their current standing (Schlosser & Levy, 2016). Given that experiences of resource scarcity are prompted by comparing one's level of resources to a superior benchmark (Cannon et al., 2019), such experiences could thus prompt a desire for self-improvement. Consuming products and services offering such benefits can therefore offer consumers a means to compensate for their perceived self-deficits and restore their personal control.

Table 1. The Effects of Resource Scarcity on Consumption (Cannon et al., 2019).

Perceived Mutability of the Resource Scarcity	Focus	Psychological Mechanism	Examples of Impacts on Consumption
High mutability	Resource discrepancy	Scarcity reduction	• Planning and prioritization of scarce resource(s) • Increase valuation and consump-tion of scarce resource(s)
Low mutability	Psychological threat	Control restoration	• Compensatory consumption • Enacting competitive motives to accrue compensatory resources

Secondly, resource scarcity has been shown to activate self-focused competitive motivations, which can prompt consumers to acquire compensatory resources as a means of providing security and adopt aggressive tendencies that can help them feel more in control (Cannon et al., 2019). For instance, prior research has shown that considerations of resource scarcity tend to prompt self-focused allocation decisions (e.g., keeping more money for the self when playing the dictator game; Roux et al., 2015), and that exposure to limited-quantity promotions can promote incidental aggressive behavior (e.g., shooting more bullets or throwing more punches at opponents in a video game; Kristofferson et al., 2017). Interestingly, prior research has argued that competitive motivations can either be directed toward improving one's condition through maximizing one's absolute gains (i.e., "constructive" competition) or be directed toward pulling down and/or derogating rivals to improve one's standing through the maximization of relative gains (i.e., "destructive" competition; Fülöp, 2004).

Importantly, Roux et al. (2015) found that considerations of resource scarcity increase concerns related to both one's relative *and* absolute (vs joint) gains, such that considerations of resource scarcity prompt consumers to consider both their relative *and* absolute standing. However, maximizing one's absolute (vs relative) gains has been argued to be a more adaptive and socially accepted response to competitive motives (Sedikides & Skowronski, 2000). In addition, consumers' ability to maximize their relative gains through the derogation of rivals is impoverished in the context of everyday consumer decision-making (i.e., few goods are directly positioned around offering ways to harm one's competitors), whereas opportunities to maximize their absolute gains through improvements to the self are comparatively abundant in the marketplace (as discussed previously). Self-improvement thus offers consumers experiencing resource scarcity a means to enhance their absolute standing (Sedikides & Skowronski, 2000) by allowing them to gain superior skills and/or acquire compensatory resources (Brock & Brannon, 1992). Further, such resources can be particularly useful to restore one's personal control in contexts of heightened interpersonal competition (e.g., economic recession; Griskevicius et al., 2013).

Consequently, we contend that considerations of resource scarcity will increase consumers' desire for self-improvement and, accordingly, will increase their interest in products and services offering self-improvement benefits. Our theorizing is consistent with both a general compensatory mechanism as well as competitive motivations. In this chapter, we will remain agnostic about whether the proposed effect of resource scarcity on self-improvement is due to a general compensatory process or more specific competitive motivations. In the Future Research Directions section, we offer potential boundary conditions for both these mechanisms.

RESOURCE SCARCITY AND THE VALUATION OF SELF-IMPROVEMENT BENEFITS

Thus far, we have theorized that resource scarcity can increase consumers' desire for self-improvement, and that, accordingly, those who are prompted with scarcity-related (vs neutral) thoughts will be more interested in products that offer self-improvement benefits. However, this does not necessarily imply that consumers experiencing incidental resource scarcity should be willing to pay more for products offering self-improvement benefits. It is possible that the predicted increase in interest may not translate into a higher monetary valuation of such benefits, especially given their resource-scarce situation.

Although prior research has demonstrated that resource scarcity increases (vs decreases) consumers' desire for products that can help restore (vs hinder) their personal control, little prior work also assessed their willingness to pay for such products. For instance, prior research has shown that economic recession cues increase consumers' desire for products that help attract romantic partners (Hill et al., 2012) and improve their professional appearance (Netchaeva & Rees, 2016). Financial deprivation has also been shown to increase consumers' preferences for higher calorie, satiating foods (Briers & Laporte, 2013) and material goods (vs experiences) that offer long-lasting utility (Tully et al., 2015). Resource scarcity has further been shown to increase consumers' interest in products associated with pride, as they help to bolster one's agency (Salerno & Escoe, 2020), and to decrease their interest in counter-hedonic products (e.g., horror movies), as they reduce their personal control (Yang & Zhang, 2022). However, consumers' monetary valuation of such compensatory products was not assessed in these papers.

Although little prior research has directly provided evidence for the effects of resource scarcity on consumers' willingness to pay, Goldsmith et al. (2020) offer indirect support. Specifically, they investigated the role of price in consumers' preferences for sustainable products promoted using either personal (i.e., saving money) or prosocial (i.e., saving the environment) benefits these products offered. The authors found that, when participants were experiencing resource scarcity, their purchase likelihood of the higher (vs lower) priced sustainable product increased when its personal (vs prosocial) benefits were highlighted. This finding provides indirect evidence that thoughts about resource scarcity can increase consumers' willingness to pay for products under certain conditions.

We draw from research in the domain of goals and valuation to predict that consumers experiencing an increased desire for self-improvement will be willing to pay more for products offering such benefits even when experiencing incidental resource scarcity. Research in this area has documented a *valuation effect*, such that when consumers have an active goal (e.g., to eat), they will spend more of their resources to acquire means to service that goal (e.g., food), as compared to consumers for whom that goal is not active (Brendl et al., 2003). This line of work suggests that if resource scarcity activates the desire for self-improvement, then consumers who are prompted with thoughts about scarcity should be willing to pay more for products that fulfill that desire.

We next present the results of a preliminary experiment that tests the effect of resource scarcity on consumers' monetary valuation of a product offering self-improvement benefits. The experiment leverages a neutral product (i.e., Post-it Notes) for which its self-improvement benefits are made salient versus not salient.

EVIDENCE THAT RESOURCE SCARCITY CAN INCREASE THE VALUATION OF SELF-IMPROVEMENT BENEFITS

This experiment provides initial support for our proposed effect of resource scarcity on the monetary valuation of products offering self-improvement benefits. Specifically, we demonstrate that associating a neutral product (i.e., Post-It Notes; Allard & White, 2015) with salient self-improvement benefits (vs not) increases consumers' willingness to pay when scarcity-related (vs neutral) thoughts are activated. We also leverage an incentive-compatible choice task adapted from Becker et al. (1964) to provide consequential evidence for our proposed effect.

Method. One hundred and seventy undergraduate students (61.8% female; M_{age} = 21.1; SD = 4.9) participated in a series of unrelated experiments as part of a 20-minute laboratory session in exchange for US$5. This study used a 2 (recall: scarcity vs control) × 2 (self-improvement benefit: salient vs not salient) between-subjects design. Participants first completed an episodic recall task used to activate thoughts about resource scarcity (Roux et al., 2015). In the scarcity condition, participants were asked to describe three or four episodes when they felt as if they "didn't have enough of something" or their "resources were scarce." They were next asked to pick two of the episodes they mentioned and describe each of them in detail, explaining what was lacking and what they experienced. In the control condition, participants were first asked to think about and write down three or four things that they did during the past week, and then to focus on and describe in detail two of these events. This manipulation was selected based on prior findings confirming that it is effective for eliciting feelings of scarcity, without influencing other factors (i.e., mood, affect, specific emotions; Roux et al., 2015). Two participants did not correctly complete the manipulation (i.e., they wrote irrelevant information) and were excluded prior to any analyses.

Next, participants completed an ostensibly unrelated product evaluation task. Specifically, they were shown a picture of a standard set of yellow Post-it Notes by 3M. Following Allard and White (2015), the product's self-improvement benefits were made salient (vs not) through the product description. Specifically, in the self-improvement benefit condition, participants were shown the following text below the picture of the Post-it Notes: "Sticky Notes for Effective Knowledge Retention! The Secret Weapon of those Wishing to Improve." Those in the no-benefit condition saw the same picture of the Post-it Notes; however, the text below the picture simply read "Sticky Notes." After reviewing the product and the description, all participants were asked to indicate whether they understood what the product was (options: "Yes" vs "No"). Two participants indicated they did not understand what the product was and were excluded prior to any analyses.

Participants were then instructed that the experimenters were interested in how much they would be willing to pay for the Post-it Notes. They were told that to measure this, they would be completing 20 binary choices. Within each choice, they would be asked to indicate whether they would prefer to receive the Post-it Notes or a certain amount of money (amounts ranged from $0.10 to $2.00 in

$0.10 increments). Further, they were instructed that at the end of the experiment, the computer would randomly select one of their choices, and they would receive the option they had selected for that choice (i.e., the Post-it Notes or a certain amount of money). This choice task was adapted from the original Becker et al. (1964) willingness-to-pay elicitation method.

In line with prior work (Becker et al., 1964), consumers' willingness to pay for the product was determined by the highest monetary value at which they would choose the product over the monetary alternative. Eleven participants provided inconsistent choices by switching back and forth between the Post-It Notes and the monetary amounts. Rather than excluding these participants, we used the monetary amount associated with their first switch in our analyses, as it provided the most conservative estimate of their willingness to pay. Of note, results remained unchanged when these participants are excluded. Last, participants completed a series of unrelated experiments, followed by a standard demographic questionnaire.

Results. A 2 (recall: scarcity vs control) $\times$ 2 (self-improvement benefit: salient vs not salient) between-subjects ANOVA revealed a significant interaction on willingness to pay for the Post-it Notes ($F(1, 162) = 4.78, p = 0.030, \eta_p^2 = 0.029$). There was no main effect of resource scarcity ($F(1, 162) = 1.15; p = 0.286$) nor salience of self-improvement benefits ($F(1, 162) = 1.82; p = 0.179$).

Pairwise comparisons further revealed that when the product's self-improvement benefits were made salient, participants prompted with scarcity-related thoughts were willing to pay more for the Post-it Notes ($M = \$0.64; SD = 0.54$) than those in the control condition ($M = \$0.42; SD = 0.40; F(1, 162) = 5.25; p = 0.023; \eta_p^2 = 0.031$). There was no significant difference in willingness to pay between the scarcity ($M = \$0.41; SD = 0.40$) and the control condition ($M = \$0.48; SD = 0.36$) when the product offered no salient self-improvement benefits ($F(1, 162) = 0.63, p = 0.429$). In addition, participants prompted with scarcity-related thoughts were willing to pay more for the product when salient self-improvement benefits were present (vs absent; $F(1, 162) = 6.19; p = 0.014; \eta_p^2 = 0.037$), whereas there was no difference in monetary valuation as a function of benefit salience among those in the control condition ($F(1, 162) = 0.35, p = 0.553$) (see Fig. 1).

The results from this experiment lend support for our prediction that considerations of resource scarcity increase consumers' monetary valuation of products offering self-improvement benefits using a consequential choice task. Furthermore, the results are consistent with our theorizing based on Cannon et al.'s (2019) self-regulatory model. That is, low mutability resource scarcity increases consumers' willingness to pay for products that help restore their diminished personal control, which include those that afford self-improvement benefits.

CONTRIBUTIONS AND IMPLICATIONS

The theorizing proposed in this chapter offers important contributions to existing theory. Firstly, it contributes to the literature on the antecedents of self-improvement by identifying a novel factor that can prompt this desire. Prior

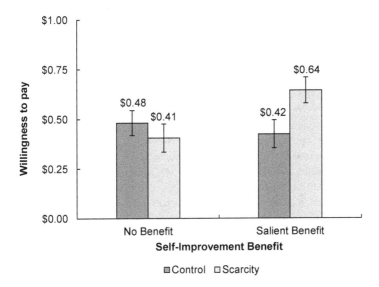

Fig. 1. The Effects of Resource Scarcity and Self-Improvement Benefit on Willingness to Pay. *Note:* − Error bars represent +/− 1 standard error.

research has found that past shortcomings or failures, upcoming challenges, self-construal (see Grewal et al., 2022 for a review), and feelings of guilt (Allard & White, 2015), among others, can prompt consumers' desire to self-improve. Extending this stream of research, we identify a factor that naturally varies among consumers, considerations of resource scarcity, as another antecedent to self-improvement. Our theorizing also offers practical implications for consumer behavior given the ubiquity of resource scarcity considerations.

Secondly, our theorizing helps further our understanding of the consequences of resource scarcity by identifying a novel outcome of resource scarcity. Prior work has proposed that resource scarcity that is low in mutability (i.e., no reasonable amount of effort will help directly address one's scarcity-related situation) prompts consumers to bolster their diminished personal control by pursuing control-restoration strategies, such as engaging in compensatory consumption or competitive behaviors (Cannon et al., 2019). Our theorizing contributes to this line of work by identifying self-improvement as another means through which consumers can bolster their diminished personal control.

Thirdly, our theorizing and preliminary empirical evidence offer novel insights about how considerations of resource scarcity impact consumption. Although prior research has demonstrated that resource scarcity can increase (decrease) consumers' preferences for products that help restore (hinder) their personal control (Briers & Laporte, 2013; Hill et al., 2012; Netchaeva & Rees, 2016; Salerno & Escoe, 2020; Tully et al., 2015; Yang & Zhang, 2022), little prior work also assessed their willingness to pay for such products (cf. Goldsmith et al., 2020). We extend this stream of research by demonstrating that consumers prompted with scarcity-related (vs neutral) thoughts are willing to pay more for products that offer salient self-improvement benefits. In doing so, we contribute to research demonstrating that resource scarcity can produce outcomes that benefit consumer welfare under certain conditions (e.g., Goldsmith et al., 2020; Roux et al., 2015).

In addition, the theorizing and empirical evidence provided in this chapter offer relevant practical implications. For instance, in contexts where scarcity-related cues are salient (e.g., economic recession, pandemic), marketers should highlight the self-improvement benefits that can be gained through their products or services. Doing so may be useful both to promote consumers' interest in the products and to offset their reticence to spend money during times of economic hardship. Similarly, marketing communications for products and services offering self-improvement benefits may be more effective when paired with content related to resource scarcity. For instance, online ads for self-improvement products could be placed within news articles about an upcoming economic recession or commodity shortage.

FUTURE RESEARCH DIRECTIONS

The theorizing proposed in this chapter offers fruitful avenues for future research. Firstly, researchers could further probe how considerations of resource scarcity impact the way in which consumers fulfill their desire for self-improvement. For instance, some self-improvement products available in the marketplace promise immediate, short-lived benefits (e.g., a beverage that increases mental focus after drinking it), whereas others offer incremental, longer term benefits (e.g., meditation exercises that increase mental focus over time). Prior research has shown that when faced with a self-threat, consumers tend to prefer solutions that allow them to feel better in the present (e.g., indulging) over pursuing their longer term goals (e.g., self-regulation; Crocker & Park, 2004). Future research could thus investigate if and when considerations of resource scarcity increase consumers' preference for products that offer more immediate (vs longer term) self-improvement benefits.

Another interesting extension would be to examine how resource scarcity shapes consumers' valuation of self-improvement benefits that are observable (e.g., enhancing one's appearance) versus unobservable (e.g., enhancing one's cognitive abilities). Prior work has demonstrated that resource scarcity can promote costly signaling behavior when it helps address compensatory or competitive motives (Hill et al., 2012; Netchaeva & Rees, 2016; Roux et al., 2015). However, prior research has also shown that lower income consumers' purchase decisions are judged more harshly (i.e., seen as less permissible) than those of their higher income peers (Hagerty & Barasz, 2020). Therefore, future research could investigate when and why resource scarcity may increase consumers' preference for products offering self-improvements benefits that are observable (e.g., for social signaling purposes) versus unobservable (e.g., to avoid social judgments of their monetary spending).

In addition, future research could investigate whether other forms of resource scarcity also impact consumers' desire for self-improvement. In this chapter, we focused on incidental forms of scarcity (i.e., everyday deficits in one's perceived levels of resources) as they are commonly experienced by consumers (Blocker et al., 2023). However, Blocker et al. (2023) argued that resource scarcity can take other forms: episodic (i.e., acute shorter lived deprivation; e.g., temporary layoff), conditional (i.e., enduring moderate deprivation; e.g., prolonged debt), and chronic (i.e., enduring acute restrictions; e.g., poverty). Consumers experiencing other forms of resource scarcity may also have an increased desire for self-improvement (e.g., Wang et al., 2023), but they may fulfill this need through different types of consumption.

Secondly, researchers could further probe how resource scarcity can impact the way in which consumers more generally attempt to restore their threatened personal control, to enhance our understanding of its effects on consumption (Cannon et al., 2019). For example, although enacting competitive motives prompted by resource scarcity in a "constructive" manner (i.e., maximizing one's absolute gains) is more socially acceptable and readily available in the market-place than doing so in a "destructive" way (i.e., maximizing one's relative gains, as discussed previously), some consumers may still prefer to derogate their rivals whenever possible. For example, during Black Friday, consumers may choose to sabotage other consumers' chances of acquiring products in limited supply through aggressive behaviors such as pushing and shoving (Kristofferson et al., 2017). Future research could thus investigate when and why some consumers may prefer constructive (vs destructive) strategies when experiencing resource scarcity (e.g., social value orientation; Roux et al., 2015).

Another interesting extension would be to examine the conditions that influence consumers' preferred control-restoration strategy when experiencing resource scarcity. Such strategies can take the form of compensatory consumption or competitive motives (Cannon et al., 2019), among others. For instance, both strategies may increase consumers' valuation of products offering self-improvement benefits for different reasons. A potential factor that could impact consumers' choice of control-restoration strategy may be whether the experienced resource scarcity is internally or externally attributed (Davis & Elaine Davis, 1972). For instance, resources such as money and time can be lacking due to internal (e.g., being unable to manage one's money or time well) or external factors (e.g., being assigned additional work or incurring unexpected expenses). Future research could investigate whether consumers' attribution of their experienced resource scarcity impacts their control-restoration strategy.

Finally, although prior research has demonstrated that resource scarcity can increase (decrease) consumers' preferences for products that help restore (hinder) their personal control, more research is needed to better understand when and why these shifts in preferences also impact consumers' monetary valuation of such products. Future research could identify other product benefits for which consumers experiencing resource scarcity may be willing to pay more, to develop a deeper understanding of its effects on consumer spending. In Table 2, we summarize the future research directions for resource scarcity both within the specific domain of self-improvement as well as in the more general domain of control restoration.

Table 2. Research Opportunities.

Domain	Research Questions
Self-improvement	• When and why do consumers experiencing resource scarcity prioritize immediate versus longer term self-improvement benefits? • When and why do consumers experiencing resource scarcity prefer products offering self-improvements benefits that are observable versus unobservable? • How do other forms of resource scarcity impact consumers' desire for self-improvement?
Control-restoration	• When and why do consumers experiencing resource scarcity prefer enacting their competitive motives in a "constructive" versus "destructive" manner? • Does the attribution (i.e., internal vs external) of their experienced resource scarcity impact consumers' control-restoration strategies? • Are there other types of product benefits that consumers experiencing resource scarcity would be willing to pay more for?

CONCLUSION

In summary, this chapter offers a more nuanced understanding of when certain vulnerability triggers (i.e., thoughts about resource scarcity) have the potential to motivate consumers to pursue positive outcomes. Our novel perspective suggests that the yin of hard times can be counterbalanced by its yang as consumers attempt to turn their vulnerability into personal growth. Although further research is necessary to establish the extent of the proposed theorizing and its boundaries, this chapter deepens our understanding of the effects of resource scarcity on consumption that affords self-improvement.

REFERENCES

Allard, T., & White, K. (2015). Cross-domain effects of guilt on desire for self-improvement products. *Journal of Consumer Research, 42*(3), 401–419.

Becker, G. M., DeGroot, M. H., & Jacob, M. (1964). Measuring utility by a single response sequential method. *Behavioral Science, 9*(3), 226–232.

Blocker, C., Zhang, J. Z., Hill, R. P., Roux, C., Corus, C., Hutton, M., Dorsey, J., & Minton, E. (2023). Rethinking scarcity and poverty: Building bridges for shared insight and impact. *Journal of Consumer Psychology, 33*(3), 489–509.

Brendl, C. M., Arthur, B. M., & Messner, C. (2003). The devaluation effect: Activating a need devalues unrelated objects. *Journal of Consumer Research, 29*(4), 463–473.

Briers, B., & Laporte, S. (2013). A wallet full of calories: The effect of financial dissatisfaction on the desire for food energy. *Journal of Marketing Research, 50*(6), 767–781.

Brock, T. C., & Brannon, L. A. (1992). Liberalization of commodity theory. *Basic and Applied Social Psychology, 13*(1), 135–144.

Cannon, C., Goldsmith, K., & Roux, C. (2019). A self-regulatory model of resource scarcity. *Journal of Consumer Psychology, 29*(1), 104–127.

Crocker, J., & Park, L. E. (2004). The costly pursuit of self-esteem. *Psychological Bulletin, 130*(3), 392–414.

Davis, W. L., & Elaine Davis, D. (1972). Internal-external control and attribution of responsibility for success and failure. *Journal of Personality, 40*(1), 123–136.

Fülöp, M. (2004). Competition as a culturally constructed concept. In C. Baillie, E. Dunn, & Y. Zheng (Eds.), *Travelling facts: The social construction, distribution, and accumulation of knowledge* (pp. 124–148). Campus Verlag GmbH.

Goldsmith, K., Roux, C., & Wilson, A. V. (2020). Can thoughts of having less ever promote prosocial preferences? The relationship between scarcity, construal level, and sustainable product adoption. *Journal of the Association for Consumer Research*, 5(1), 70–82.

Grand View Research. (2023a). *Fitness tracker market size, share & trends analysis report, 2023–2030.* https://www.grandviewresearch.com/industry-analysis/fitness-tracker-market. Accessed on October 11, 2023.

Grand View Research. (2023b). *GVR report personal development market size, share & trends report, 2023–2030.* https://www.grandviewresearch.com/industry-analysis/personal-development-market. Accessed on October 11, 2023.

Grewal, L., Wu, E. C., & Cutright, K. M. (2022). Loved as-is: How god salience lowers interest in self-improvement products. *Journal of Consumer Research*, 49(1), 154–174.

Griffith, E. (2020). People are panic-buying meat, toilet paper … And pelotons? https://www.nytimes.com/2020/05/06/technology/peloton-boom-workout-virus.html. Accessed on March 23, 2023.

Griskevicius, V., Ackerman, J. M., Cantu, S. M., Delton, A. W., Robertson, T. E., Simpson, J. A., Thompson, M. E., & Tybur, J. M. (2013). When the economy falters, do people spend or save? Responses to resource scarcity depend on childhood environments. *Psychological Science*, 24(2), 197–205.

Hagerty, S. F., & Barasz, K. (2020). Inequality in socially permissible consumption. *Proceedings of the National Academy of Sciences*, 117(25), 14084–14093.

Hill, S. E., Rodeheffer, C. D., Griskevicius, V., Durante, K., & White, A. E. (2012). Boosting beauty in an economic decline: Mating, spending, and the lipstick effect. *Journal of Personality and Social Psychology*, 103 (2), 275–291.

Khan, U., & DePaoli, A. (forthcoming). Brand loyalty in the face of stockouts. *Journal of the Academy of Marketing Science*.

Kristofferson, K., McFerran, B., Morales, A. C., & Dahl, D. W. (2017). The dark side of scarcity promotions: How exposure to limited-quantity promotions can induce aggression. *Journal of Consumer Research*, 43(5), 683–706.

Kruglanski, A. W., Shah, J. Y., Fishbach, A., Friedman, R., Chun, W. Y., & Sleeth-Keppler, D. (2002). A theory of goal systems. *Advances in Experimental Social Psychology*, 34, 331–378.

Mandel, N., Rucker, D. D., Levav, J., & Galinsky, A. D. (2017). The compensatory consumer behavior model: How self-discrepancies drive consumer behavior. *Journal of Consumer Psychology*, 27(1), 133–146.

Mullainathan, S., & Shafir, E. (2013). *Scarcity: Why having too little means so much.* Times Books.

Netchaeva, E., & Rees, M. K. (2016). Strategically stunning: The professional motivations behind the lipstick effect. *Psychological Science*, 27(8), 1157–1168.

O'Keefe, B. (2014). Tony Robbins, The CEO Whisperer. http://fortune.com/2014/10/30/tony-robbins-best-advice-executive-coach/

Ross, S. (2015). Vitaminwater has been Coca-Cola's best purchase. http://www.investopedia.com/articles/markets/081315/vitaminwater-has-been-cocacolas-best-purchase.asp

Roux, C., Goldsmith, K., & Bonezzi, A. (2015). On the psychology of scarcity: When reminders of resource scarcity promote selfish (and generous) behavior. *Journal of Consumer Research*, 42(4), 615–631.

Salerno, A., & Escoe, B. (2020). Resource scarcity increases the value of pride. *Journal of the Association for Consumer Research*, 5(4), 458–469.

Schlosser, A. E., & Levy, E. (2016). Helping others or oneself: How direction of comparison affects prosocial behavior. *Journal of Consumer Psychology*, 26(4), 461–473.

Sedikides, C., & Skowronski, J. J. (2000). On the evolutionary functions of the symbolic self: The emergence of self-evaluation motives. In *Psychological perspectives on self and identity* (pp. 91–117). https://doi.org/10.1037/10357-004

Shah, A. K., Mullainathan, S., & Shafir, E. (2012). Some consequences of having too little. *Science*, 338(6107), 682–685.

Sharma, E., & Alter, A. L. (2012). Financial deprivation prompts consumers to seek scarce goods. *Journal of Consumer Research, 39*(3), 545–560.

Sharma, E., Tully, S. M., & Wang, X. (2023). Scarcity and intertemporal choice. *Journal of Personality and Social Psychology, 25*(5), 1036–1054.

Tully, S. M., Hershfield, H. E., & Meyvis, T. (2015). Seeking lasting enjoyment with limited money: Financial constraints increase preference for material goods over experiences. *Journal of Consumer Research, 42*(1), 59–75.

Wang, Z., Jetten, J., & Steffens, N. K. (2023). Restless in an unequal world: Economic inequality fuels the desire for wealth and status. *Personality and Social Psychology Bulletin, 49*(6), 871–890.

Yang, H., & Zhang, K. (2022). How resource scarcity influences the preference for counterhedonic consumption. *Journal of Consumer Research, 48*(5), 904–919.

MARKETPLACE SOLUTIONS TO MOTIVATIONAL THREATS: HELPING CONSUMERS WITH FOUR DISTINCT TYPES OF VULNERABILITY*

Emily Nakkawita and E. Tory Higgins

Columbia University, USA

ABSTRACT

How can we better help consumers deal with threats to satisfying their basic motivational needs? When people fail to meet their fundamental needs for value, truth, and control effectiveness, they feel threatened. Are there products and services that can help consumers with these vulnerabilities? Based on a new 2 (prevention value vs. promotion value) × 2 (truth vs. control) motivated activity framework, we argue that different types of motivational threats produce distinct experiences of vulnerability, each of which can be resolved by engaging in unique compensatory activities. This proposal is especially relevant to marketers because brands can use this knowledge to create and promote product and service offerings that directly address these distinct kinds of vulnerability. In this review, we discuss four specific types of consumer threats and examples of branded solutions. We also suggest implications for marketers and open questions that warrant future research.

Keywords: Motivation; needs; threat; vulnerability; promotion; prevention; truth; control

---

*This research did not receive any specific grant from funding agencies in the public, commercial, or not-for-profit sectors.

The Vulnerable Consumer
Review of Marketing Research, Volume 21, 97–112
ISSN: 1548-6435/doi:10.1108/S1548-643520240000021007

INTRODUCTION

In the United States and elsewhere, recent years have seemed to present an especially broad range of threats to people's ability to satisfy their fundamental motivational needs. Some of these threats relate to the basic need of individuals to feel effective in understanding the world around them. For instance, political polarization in the United States has progressively increased over the past 50 years (Desilver, 2022), and as a result, people have needed to make sense of competing narratives about both what is right (e.g., when considering "culture war" issues from abortion rights to classroom curricula) and even what is true or real (e.g., when deciding if election results can be trusted). Other threats relate to individuals' basic need to feel effective in exerting control over their lives and livelihoods. For example, the COVID-19 pandemic hampered people's ability to effectively manage what happened in their lives, both by threatening their baseline state of health (e.g., when encountering the virus) and by limiting their ability to make progress in their social lives and careers (e.g., when facing government-imposed lockdown restrictions). How can we understand such diverse motivational threats? And how might marketers use such an understanding to help consumers address these threats and, in doing so, satisfy their fundamental needs?

Our view is that people experience vulnerability when the satisfaction of their basic motivational needs has been threatened. While different sets of needs have been proposed in the literature (e.g., Bagheri & Milyavskaya, 2019; Deci & Ryan, 2000; Maslow, 1943; McClelland, 1985; Murray, 1938), we draw from Higgins' (2012) theory of motivational effectiveness and posit that people fundamentally need to feel effective in three different aspects of their life pursuits: value, truth, and control. The need for value effectiveness can be satisfied by experiencing oneself as having desired results and not having undesired results; the need for truth effectiveness can be satisfied by experiencing oneself as establishing what is real or right; the need for control effectiveness can be satisfied by experiencing oneself as managing what happens in one's life. As we describe further in the sections that follow, fundamental needs to feel effective in these three domains work in combination to motivate distinct activities that facilitate their satisfaction. We propose that when individuals fail to effectively engage in such activities, they experience a motivational threat that manifests as feelings of vulnerability. These specific feelings will differ based on the type of motivational failure and may range from confusion to incompetence, insecurity, or the sense of being "stuck" in an undesirable status quo. More importantly, because these experiences of vulnerability result from distinct combinations of unsatisfied needs, each can be resolved in unique ways. Therefore, understanding which of these basic needs drive different types of everyday activities should provide insight into both why people feel vulnerable when these efforts are thwarted and how marketplace solutions might help consumers to remedy motivational threats (i.e., through targeted compensatory activity facilitated by products and services). This proposal is especially relevant to consumer psychologists and marketers because brands can use this knowledge to develop and promote offerings that help consumers to directly address these distinct kinds of vulnerability. In this article, we focus on four specific types of consumer threats and marketplace solutions.

A 2 × 2 FRAMEWORK OF MOTIVATED ACTIVITY

A new framework of motivated activity (Nakkawita & Higgins, 2021) provides novel insight into four unique ways in which consumers might feel vulnerable. This framework comprises two dimensions, each of which captures a fundamental motivational distinction.

Dimension 1: Prevention Versus Promotion Value

Regulatory focus theory (Higgins, 1997) describes two fundamental motivational systems that are both aimed at satisfying the fundamental need for value effectiveness, but in different ways. The *prevention* system aims to meet the value-related need for security. Given this focus, prevention motivation seeks to approach nonloss ("0") states and avoid loss ("–1") states (Higgins, 2018b). In contrast, the *promotion* system aims to meet the value-related need for growth. As a result, promotion motivation seeks to approach gain ("+1") states and avoid nongain ("0") states. Furthermore, research on regulatory fit (Higgins, 2000) reveals that unique goal pursuit strategies align with and sustain each of these systems: vigilant avoidance-oriented strategies fit a prevention focus, whereas eager approach-oriented strategies fit a promotion focus (Crowe & Higgins, 1997; Higgins et al., 1994). The motivated activity framework builds on this prior research, which had highlighted the broad strategic preferences of each regulatory focus, by identifying distinct goal pursuit *activities* that facilitate satisfaction of the basic needs that underlie each system.

Dimension 2: Control Versus Truth

As noted above, Higgins' (2012) theory of motivational effectiveness posits that in addition to value, people possess fundamental needs in the domains of truth (i.e., to feel effective in establishing what is real or right) and control (i.e., to feel effective in managing what happens in one's life). Similar to promotion and prevention value, the motivated activity framework identifies distinct goal pursuit activities relevant to these basic needs for truth effectiveness and control effectiveness.

Four Domains of Motivated Activity

Combined, these two dimensions produce four domains of motivated activity (Nakkawita & Higgins, 2021). Two of these domains encompass *truth-oriented* activities. In line with the prevention system's focus on vigilantly avoiding "–1" loss states and maintaining satisfactory "0" nonloss states, prevention-truth activities involve scrutiny and verification, such as assessing, reviewing, and verifying. These activities enable individuals to avoid mistakes and incorrect knowledge ("−1" truth states) and to approach certainty and accuracy ("0" truth states). The promotion system is motivated to satisfy the need for truth effectiveness in different ways. Given its focus on eagerly approaching "+1" gain states and avoiding "0" nongain states, promotion-truth activities involve knowledge growth and generation, such as imagining, discovering, and wondering. These activities enable individuals to expand their understanding of the world ("+1" truth states) and to avoid feeling a sense of mental stagnation ("0" truth states).

Prior research provides some initial evidence for these distinctions in the domain of truth. For instance, a prevention focus is associated with analytical problem-solving, such as accurately determining the answers to standardized testing questions involving logical reasoning (Friedman & Förster, 2005). Additionally, prevention motivates the use of deliberative reasoning in the process of making judgments (Avnet & Higgins, 2006; Cornwell & Higgins, 2016) and concerns with accuracy in tasks ranging from carefully connecting numbered dots to identifying errors while proofreading (Förster et al., 2003), all of which involve thoughtfully assessing information and ensuring that it is appropriate or correct (i.e., scrutiny and verification activities). In contrast, a promotion focus is associated with curiosity (Wytykowska & Gabińska, 2015). Promotion also motivates creative problem-solving, such as imagining possible solutions to scenarios during a sports game (Memmert et al., 2013) and generating new uses for objects (Friedman & Förster, 2005). Promotion-focused people demonstrate this kind of divergent thinking both in terms of the number of ideas they generate and in the breadth of such ideas (Beuk & Basadur, 2016), all of which involve expanding one's knowledge through learning and/or ideation (i.e., knowledge growth and generation activities).

The framework posits that a similar distinction between prevention- and promotion-focused goal pursuit activities emerges in the domain of *control-oriented* activities. Consistent with a prevention-focused concern with avoiding "−1" losses and maintaining "0" nonlosses, prevention-control activities involve status quo preservation, such as defending, protecting, and maintaining. These activities enable individuals to avoid states involving the absence or loss of a satisfactory status quo ("−1" control states) and to approach the maintenance of such states ("0" control states). In contrast, the promotion system motivates engagement in different types of control-oriented activities. Given its focus on eagerly approaching "+1" gains and avoiding "0" nongains, promotion-control activities involve movement and change, such as launching, accelerating, and progressing. These activities enable individuals to experience themselves as advancing and as efficiently effecting change ("+1" control states) and to avoid feeling mired in their current status quo ("0" control states).

Past research also provides initial evidence for these distinctions in the domain of control. For example, a prevention focus is associated with stability-oriented decisions to continue ongoing tasks rather than change-oriented decisions to switch to new tasks, whereas a promotion focus is associated with the opposite (Liberman et al., 1999). Additionally, a prevention focus predicts conservative political ideology as measured via self-reports (Cornwell & Higgins, 2013) and voting decisions for economic policies (Boldero & Higgins, 2011), as well as the preservation of interpersonal norms in the workplace (Zhang et al., 2011), all of which involve ensuring that current conditions persist (i.e., status quo preservation activities). In contrast, a promotion focus is associated with self-reported locomotion, which is the motivation to engage in movement and change (Higgins et al., 2008; Kruglanski et al., 2000), and with preferences for political change (Boldero & Higgins, 2011). The promotion system has also been shown to motivate speedy action that accelerates as the individual approaches their goal (Förster et al., 2003). This research indicates that the promotion system motivates individuals to advance quickly in their goal pursuits and to enact change (i.e., movement and change activities).

Beyond the prior work reviewed above, recent research by Nakkawita and Higgins (2021) that directly tested the motivated activity framework found that people share a common understanding of which truth- and control-oriented activities reflect a focus on prevention value versus promotion value. This research also found that activities that fit (vs. do not fit) an individual's regulatory focus are more accessible to them, both when regulatory focus is measured as a chronic individual difference factor and when it is induced within the course of a study. For a summary of the four activity domains within the motivated activity framework, as well as specific activities tested within this research, see Table 1.

MOTIVATED ACTIVITY, THREATS, AND VULNERABILITY

By advancing the field's knowledge of the specific activities that satisfy different combinations of unmet fundamental needs, this framework offers consumer psychologists and brand marketers a new lens through which they can conceptualize consumers' motivational threats and resulting experiences of vulnerability. More specifically, understanding the activities in which vulnerable consumers are motivated to engage allows marketers to offer tailored product- and service-based

Table 1. Motivated Activity Framework.

Prevention Value	Promotion Value
Truth-Oriented Activities	
Scrutiny and verification	Knowledge growth and generation
assess, examine, judge,	*discover, explore, imagine,*
review, scrutinize, verify	*invent, seek, wonder*
Control-Oriented Activities	
Status-quo preservation	Movement and change
defend, guard, maintain,	*accelerate, elevate, launch,*
preserve, protect, resist	*lead, progress, propel*

Source: Adapted from Nakkawita and Higgins (2021).

solutions that aid consumers in precisely addressing the distinct ways in which they feel threatened. In addition, this framework offers useful insight into how to frame both new and existing offerings most effectively within marketing communications.

It is worth noting that when thinking about vulnerability in the context of the basic needs represented in the framework, the prevention system may stand out as being particularly relevant as it is frequently the threat of a " -1 " reference point (i.e., a loss) that motivates people to pursue prevention-focused goals. With this said, it is useful to distinguish between prevention failures in the domains of control versus truth because different kinds of marketplace solutions are needed to help consumers remedy their vulnerability in each domain. Furthermore, marketers should also consider consumers' experiences of vulnerability that emerge due to promotion-related failures (i.e., "0" nongain reference points in the domains of truth and control). In fact, the original paper introducing regulatory focus theory explicitly emphasized that both systems allow for the experience of threat: "the threat of nonfulfillment (promotion threat) and the threat of committing mistakes (prevention threat)" (Higgins, 1997). In the following sections, we explore how consumers may experience vulnerability in each of the four domains due to the threat that results from failing to satisfy the underlying combinations of motivational needs, and we provide examples of relevant marketplace solutions.

Solutions for Prevention-Truth Threats

As noted above, one kind of threat to individuals' truth effectiveness is a "–1" loss state involving incorrect, mistaken, or uncertain knowledge, which produces an experience of vulnerability that can manifest as feelings of confusion or uncertainty. According to the framework, consumers who find themselves in such a threatening scenario will be motivated to engage in prevention-truth activities involving scrutiny and verification, such as reviewing, assessing, and judging. As a result, products and services that help individuals to validate and/or disconfirm their existing knowledge, and to reduce uncertainty regarding an issue, will support consumers in satisfying this combination of needs for prevention value and truth.

One source of prevention-truth ineffectiveness is the threat that results from making the wrong choice in the product or service decision-making process itself. Consumers who feel that they are vulnerable to making mistakes in this process may appreciate guidance in constructing their consideration set and in narrowing down their choices to determine which is right. For example, consider Wirecutter, the New York Times' product recommendation platform. Wirecutter provides subscribers with curated guides to product selection in a wide range of consumer domains, from robot vacuum cleaners to carry-on suitcases (New York Times, 2022). After a thorough testing and consumer interview process, Wirecutter editors create a short-list of products in the category of interest that are recommended at various price points (e.g., best overall; runner-up; budget and upgrade options). These top-level recommendations allow individuals lacking certainty (a "−1" truth state) about which option is most appropriate for them to make an informed judgment. Furthermore, for consumers interested in independently assessing their choice options even further, article footnotes provide detailed information comparing and contrasting the products that the Wirecutter team considered. By facilitating activities such as assessment and judgment, Wirecutter provides consumers with a solution for the threat they experience by failing to meet their needs for effectiveness in terms of both prevention value and truth.

Beyond services like Wirecutter that are expressly designed to help consumers avoid making the wrong choice in their decision-making processes, online retailers can help ease the same kind of prevention-truth threat by offering digital comparison tools within their e-commerce experiences. Such tools give vulnerable consumers the opportunity to easily review product or service options and avoid any incorrect decisions by carefully confirming which is most appropriate for them. For instance, Carnival Cruise Line's comparison tool provides consumers with a detailed overview of up to three of their ships across a variety of criteria, such as dining options, spa facilities, and entertainment schedules (Carnival Corporation, 2022). By facilitating such a careful examination of their offerings, Carnival helps their consumers to reduce their vulnerability in the domain of prevention-truth. Importantly, this kind of solution is not limited to the digital realm; brick-and-mortar retailers have long provided a similar service through expert sales representatives who can help shoppers to review product options in store.

Furthermore, people may also experience prevention-truth ineffectiveness in their life more broadly – outside of the consumer decision-making process – and savvy brands can directly provide remedies that help consumers to mitigate such threats and, thus, eliminate this feeling of vulnerability. For instance, consider the baby sleep product domain. For new parents interested in helping their children to sleep through the night, the range of potential solutions can be bewildering, and evaluating the benefits and drawbacks of each method can be a stressful, time-consuming process. Mistakes are particularly important to avoid for these parents, as the wrong decision can have deleterious consequences ranging from sleep deprivation to unsafe sleep situations for their babies. For these reasons, the creators of the SNOO smart bassinet offer customers one-on-one consultations with their team of baby sleep experts (Happiest Baby, 2022). These experts work with parents to review their current practices and determine the right way to help their children maintain a satisfactory sleep schedule. They also allow nervous new parents to verify that they are using the product correctly, thus helping them to satisfy their needs for prevention value and truth effectiveness.

Solutions for Promotion-Truth Threats

Although the solutions reviewed above help consumers to address threats that result from failures to satisfy needs related to truth and prevention value, different remedies are needed for consumers experiencing threats that result from failures to satisfy needs for truth and promotion value. More specifically, in this case, the threat is a "0" nongain state, which produces an experience of vulnerability that manifests as feeling of mental stagnation. Given this reference point, consumers who find themselves in such a threatening scenario will be motivated to engage in promotion-truth activities involving knowledge growth and generation, such as discovering, inventing, and seeking. As a result, product and services that help individuals to engage in curious exploration and imagination, and to avoid feeling mentally "stuck," will support these consumers in satisfying this combination of needs for promotion value and truth.

As in the domain of prevention-truth activities, one source of promotion-truth ineffectiveness is the consumer decision-making process itself. However, in the domain of promotion-truth, we suggest that individuals who experience a sense of promotion-truth vulnerability may be especially interested in discovering new products that spark their fancy. For this reason, product and services that facilitate this exploratory process should be especially appealing to these consumers. For instance, consider Pinterest, a social media platform that markets itself as being centered around "visual discovery" and that highlights to consumers that "you'll always find ideas to spark inspiration" (Pinterest, 2022). On Pinterest, people can explore beautiful images that other users have curated, and they can save these images to their own digital collections. By facilitating this process of discovery, Pinterest allows consumers who are bored with their current possessions but unsure of what to purchase next (a promotion threat nongain "0" truth state) to discover new fashions and home goods to add to their shopping list. In doing so, this platform provides consumers with a solution for the threat they experience by failing to meet their needs for effectiveness in terms of both promotion value and truth.

On a smaller scale, subscription services allow for a similar process of product exploration. For instance, the Brews Less Traveled Beer Club from Brewvana facilitates promotion-truth activities through subscribers' "discovering hand-selected beers from a new undiscovered beer city each month" (Brewvana, 2022). Similarly, beauty subscription service Birchbox helps consumers to learn about new hair and skin care products through a monthly package featuring a range of product samples (Birchbox, 2022). These kinds of subscription services have rapidly grown in popularity over the last decade (Emarsys, 2021), demonstrating strong consumer interest in this type of promotion-truth consumer experience.

Additionally, in recent years, brands have begun to help consumers to feel more effective in meeting their promotion value and truth needs by creating new digital tools that allow for imagination and invention. For instance, consider the IKEA Place augmented reality app (IKEA, 2022). This app enables consumers to bring their imagination to life by using their smartphone's camera to visualize what their home would look like with a piece of the brand's furniture in it. As another example, the Nike By You service allows consumers to create their ideal sneakers by exploring options, inventing custom designs, and ordering the unique pair of shoes that they created (Nike, 2022). By facilitating promotion-truth activities including ideation and invention, these branded experiences help consumers to move from the threat of remaining stuck in their "0" status quo to

"+1" truth states in which they have learned or created something new, thus satisfying their needs for both promotion value and truth effectiveness.

Solutions for Prevention-Control Threats

Just as in the domain of truth, consumers experience threat when they fail to satisfy their needs for control effectiveness in combination with different types of value. One such type of threat emerges when individuals' prevention value and control effectiveness are jeopardized by the potential or actual loss of a satisfactory current state, which would involve changing to a "−1" reference point. Such a threat would produce an experience of vulnerability that manifests as a concern about one's ability to effectively resolve such a state of insecurity. In response, according to the framework, consumers will be motivated to engage in prevention-control activities involving status quo preservation such as defending, preserving, and protecting. As a result, products and services that help individuals to actively secure and guard what they already have will help these consumers to satisfy this combination of needs for prevention value and control effectiveness.

Some brands provide consumers with prevention-control solutions pertaining to the purchase process itself. For instance, services like PayPal help consumers to ensure the security of their personal data (a satisfactory "0" control state) by handling payment transactions on third-party websites (PayPal, 2022). By using PayPal to complete their online purchases, consumers no longer need to feel uneasy about whether individual companies can safely manage their credit card or banking details; instead, PayPal is the only company that has access to this sensitive information. Fraud protection services provided by traditional credit card companies serve a similar purpose for consumer purchases conducted both on and offline. By facilitating activities such as securing and protecting, these services provide consumers with solutions to threats they experience by failing to meet their needs for effectiveness in terms of both prevention value and control.

Outside of the purchase process, a wide range of products and services help consumers engage in activities that mitigate prevention-control threats. One pervasive example of such a solution is insurance. Insurance companies offer consumers the ability to limit significant financial risks across a variety of domains ranging from their travel to their homes to their health through relatively smaller plan contributions. By allowing people to protect themselves from large to potentially catastrophic expenses, insurance plans offer a broader sense of security to consumers. For instance, State Farm describes that they enable individuals to "help safeguard the people and possessions that matter most" (State Farm, 2022). Home security systems serve a similar protective function. In doing so, these consumer goods serve as remedies to consumers' prevention-control threats and minimize their resulting experience of vulnerability.

Furthermore, a wide range of consumer offerings are aimed at facilitating the restoration or preservation of individuals' physical appearance. Both drugstore solutions like RoC anti-wrinkle creams and medical-grade cosmetic procedures like Botox injections help consumers to resist common signs of aging and to maintain their current looks (BOTOX Cosmetic, 2022; RoC Skincare, 2022).

Similarly, many weight loss products and fitness centers promise consumers to restore their bodies to a state of satisfactory wellness. For instance, the Back To You app claims to help postpartum mothers recover in order to "feel good in your own skin (again)" (The Wonder Weeks, 2022). By providing tools to pre-serve or recover a "0" status quo state, such offerings give consumers the chance to directly address threats to meeting their needs for prevention value and control effectiveness.

Solutions for Promotion-Control Threats

Finally, as in the domain of truth, a distinct set of solutions are needed for threats that consumers experience when they fail to satisfy needs related to control and promotion (vs. prevention) value. In this scenario, the threat to individuals' control effectiveness is a "0" nongain state that produces an experience of vulnerability that manifests as a sense of languishing. Given this reference point, consumers who find themselves in such a threatening scenario will be motivated to engage in promotion-control activities involving movement and change. As a result, products and services that initiate or accelerate progress toward some desirable "+1" end-state will help these consumers meet their combined pro-motion value and control effectiveness needs.

As in the domain of prevention-control, one source of promotion-control ineffectiveness can be the purchase process itself. Individuals who experience a sense of vulnerability in this domain may be especially interested in speedy, streamlined experiences. As a result, these consumers will likely find brands that offer a fast and easy shopping process to be particularly attractive. For example, Amazon offers an express purchasing option called Buy Now ordering, which enables consumers to purchase a product with a single click (Amazon, 2022). Furthermore, retailers that offer quick delivery options, such as same-day ship-ping, serve a similar motivational concern. By allowing consumers to accelerate the speed at which they can get a desired product into their hands, brands can help those frustrated by the typical purchase process (a threatening "0" control state) to satisfy their needs for effectiveness in terms of both promotion value and control.

Beyond the purchase process, branded offerings that facilitate physical movement and change will also help consumers to feel less vulnerable due to promotion-control threats, from fast cars to amusement parks offering roll-ercoaster rides. Additionally, products and services that help consumers to launch a new creative or business endeavor should also help consumers to meet their needs for promotion value and control effectiveness. For instance, the platform Squarespace enables people to quickly design and launch professional websites without needing to resort to a lengthy and potentially frustrating process working with a web developer. Squarespace's marketing clearly embodies promotion-control principles, describing that the platform allows individuals to elevate their website experiences by "build[ing] the ideal" and to propel their businesses forward by "learn[ing] fast, act[ing] fast" (Squarespace, 2022). Simi-larly, the online design tool Canva allows everyday consumers to quickly create attractive visual designs that can be used on a wide range of custom items for their personal lives and businesses, from event invitations and T-shirts to business cards and menus (Canva, 2022). By helping consumers to engage in promotion-control activities including elevating and launching, these products facilitate movement from the "0" status quo to "+1" control states in which they have taken positive and effective action, and thus satisfy both promotion value and control effectiveness needs.

IMPLICATIONS AND OPEN QUESTIONS

This new framework has important implications for consumer psychologists and brand marketers as it builds on the established distinction between prevention-focused strategic vigilance and promotion-focused strategic eagerness (Crowe & Higgins, 1997; Higgins et al., 1994) to identify specific goal pursuit activities that are particularly useful for consumers who seek to address different combinations of unmet motivational needs. Much of what is known about these prevention- and promotion-specific strategic preferences has emerged through research testing regulatory fit theory (Higgins, 2000). For instance, this work has shown that when people experience a fit (vs. nonfit) with their regulatory focus, their interest in product features increases (Werth & Foerster, 2007), they are willing to pay more for a product (e.g., Conley & Higgins, 2018), and they evaluate brands and advertising messages more positively (e.g., Lee & Aaker, 2004; Lee et al., 2010; Pham & Avnet, 2004). Furthermore, these kinds of effects emerge when examining the fit between individuals' motives and a range of consumer-relevant targets, including the decision-making process (Pham & Higgins, 2005), the retail environment (Conley & Higgins, 2018), and the product itself (Werth & Foerster, 2007). (For more thorough reviews of regulatory fit research that is relevant to consumer goal pursuit processes, see Higgins et al., 2020; Lee & Higgins, 2009.)

The multidimensional nature of the 2 × 2 motivated activity framework raises the intriguing possibility that people who simultaneously experience regulatory fit (vs. nonfit) on more than one motivational dimension might show stronger regulatory fit effects. In particular, each of the four cells represents a combination of two basic motivational needs with respect to which a person can experience regulatory fit: promotion value and truth, promotion value and control, prevention value and truth, or prevention value and control. Because representations are theorized to more strongly influence cognition and action when they have greater motivational relevance (Eitam & Higgins, 2010), we expect that consumer offerings and marketing messages that precisely fit individuals' areas of vulnerability on *both* of the framework's motivational dimensions (e.g., featuring the prevention-control activities that a service facilitates when advertising to people experiencing unmet prevention value and control needs) will be more compelling than offerings that only fit a single dimension (e.g., using messaging only featuring prevention value for people experiencing the same set of motivational threats). Similarly, rather than simply highlighting a product's general truth-oriented benefits (e.g., for business accounting software, as offering more effective financial oversight), marketers should consider framing it as delivering benefits related to either prevention-truth activities (e.g., as offering deeper scrutiny into financial records) or promotion-truth activities (e.g., as offering fascinating new insights from their financial records). We predict that this kind of precise-targeting messaging that addresses both motivational dimensions (promotion-prevention *and* truth-control) will be more effective in driving purchase decisions. Future research is still needed to test this hypothesis; with this said, such a finding would be highly relevant to marketers as it would indicate how they can more effectively impact consumers' interest in and willingness to pay for their products and services.

How might brands take advantage of this kind of multidimensional fit? Marketers will first need to determine which combination of motivational needs (i.e., which of the four cells in the 2 × 2 framework) their product or service helps consumers to satisfy. Some products and services may naturally function as a solution for just one of these four different types of multidimensional consumer threats. For instance, as described above, Amazon's Buy Now ordering option facilitates the activity of progressing, which satisfies unmet needs for promotion value and control, but it likely does not satisfy other combinations of needs (e.g., it doesn't allow for promotion-truth-oriented discovering, prevention-control-oriented defending, or prevention-truth-oriented scrutinizing). For these types of "single cell" offerings, brands will likely benefit from ensuring that their marketing communications clearly demonstrate to consumers its ability to help consumers meet their basic needs at that particular intersection of promotion versus prevention value *and* truth versus control.

Beyond marketing a product as meeting a *single* set of motivational threats (i.e., one multidimensional cell from the 2 × 2 framework as noted above), other brands may offer consumers the possibility of addressing *multiple* combinations of motivational threats (i.e., two or more multidimensional cells from the 2 × 2 framework). But is it possible to successfully market a product as simultaneously meeting more than one combination of unsatisfied motivational needs without diluting the effectiveness of the messaging? Although additional research is needed to test this proposition, we suggest that the implications for such brands may depend on whether these offerings help consumers to satisfy (a) both truth and control needs for a particular type of value, or (b) both promotion and prevention value needs for either truth or control. In the former case, because truth and control motives naturally work together to facilitate "going in the right direction" in the process of goal pursuit (Higgins, 2018a), one might expect that truth and control activities are less likely to be experienced by consumers as conflicting. In such a case, a mixed-messaging approach may allow consumers experiencing distinct motivational threats to each see their own needs addressed in the communications, without being negatively affected by the portion of the messaging that addresses the other kind of threat. For instance, while the consultations provided by makers of the SNOO bassinet address failures to satisfy needs for prevention value and *truth* as noted earlier, the bassinet itself may help consumers to dutifully maintain a healthy sleep schedule for their child, thus satisfying their needs for prevention value and *control*. For this reason, SNOO's marketing messaging might highlight to consumers that the brand helps them to both assess (prevention-truth) which sleep solutions are right for their family *and* preserve (prevention-control) their family's health and well-being through such solutions.

Would the same kind of "mixed messaging" approach work when the two cells include both promotion value and prevention value? We suggest that this scenario may play out differently. In contrast to the prior case involving truth and control threats for a single regulatory focus, we posit that brands that help consumers satisfy needs for both promotion *and* prevention value, along with either truth or control, may benefit from focusing on only a single cell within any given piece of marketing communications, as promotion value and prevention value motivate distinct, and frequently conflicting, eager versus vigilant goal pursuit strategies. For instance, consider the online course provider industry. One company, Coursera, markets their offerings using only promotion-truth messaging: "learn without limits" (i.e., indicating an opportunity to move from a "0" to "+1" state; Coursera, 2022). In contrast, competitor Khan Academy markets their offerings using both prevention-truth messaging ("fill gaps in their understanding": "−1" to "0") and promotion-truth messaging ("accelerate their learning": "0" to "+1" messaging; Khan Academy, 2022). We would suggest that the combined approach found within Khan Academy's messaging may in fact dilute its strength, although additional research is needed to test this hypothesis.

Furthermore, the motivated activity framework suggests that when companies consider their product development pipelines, they may benefit from ensuring that new brand and line extensions fall within the activity domains that are different from their original offerings – especially across the promotion versus prevention value dimension. In doing so, brands may be able to more effectively increase their market share as such products will appeal to distinct groups of consumers experiencing different types of motivational threats.

CONCLUSION

This review primarily focused on products and services that address consumer needs induced by specific threats in each of the 2 × 2 activity domains. However, it remains an open question whether these offerings will be just as appealing to people with a chronic prevention or promotion focus, even when not precipitated by a specific truth or control need. We would expect that without an inciting threat, consumers will find offerings from domains reflecting their chronic regulatory focus to be more attractive than offerings reflecting the opposing focus. For instance, we predict that chronically promotion-focused consumers will find both promotion-truth and promotion-control offerings to be more appealing than prevention-truth and prevention-control offerings. However, we also expect these promotion-focused consumers with a particular truth or control need will experience the strongest pull toward a product or service from the motivationally relevant domain. More research will be needed to investigate how these chronic and induced motives interact to influence the motivational relevance of these four domains, particularly when they are conflicting. We look forward to the results of this future work, as it should provide additional valuable insight to consumer psychologists and marketing practitioners as to how these distinct motives work together.

REFERENCES

Amazon. (2022). *Buy now ordering*. Amazon. https://www.amazon.com/gp/help/customer/display. html?nodeId=201889620

Avnet, T., & Higgins, E. T. (2006). How regulatory fit affects value in consumer choices and opinions. *Journal of Marketing Research*, *43*(1), 1–10. https://doi.org/10.1509/jmkr.43.1.1

Bagheri, L., & Milyavskaya, M. (2019). Novelty–variety as a candidate basic psychological need: New evidence across three studies. *Motivation and Emotion*. https://doi.org/10.1007/s11031-019-09807-4

Beuk, F., & Basadur, T. (2016). Regulatory focus, task engagement and divergent thinking. *Creativity and Innovation Management*, *25*(2), 199–210. https://doi.org/10.1111/caim.12182

Birchbox. (2022). *About Birchbox and our values*. Birchbox. https://www.birchbox.com/manifesto

Boldero, J. M., & Higgins, E. T. (2011). Regulatory focus and political decision making: When people favor reform over the status quo. *Political Psychology*, *32*(3), 399–418. https://doi.org/10.1111/j.1467-9221.2010.00814.x

BOTOX Cosmetic. (2022). *The story of BOTOX Cosmetic*. BOTOX cosmetic. https://www.botoxcosmetic.com/what-is-botox-cosmetic/botox-cosmetic-history

Brewvana. (2022). *Brews Less Traveled Beer Club*. Brewvana. https://brewvana.com/product/beer-of-the-month-club/

Canva. (2022). *About Canva*. Canva. https://www.canva.com/about/

Carnival Corporation. (2022). *Compare Carnival cruise ships*. Carnival Cruise line. https://www.carnival.com/cruise-ships/compare-cruise-ships

Conley, M. A., & Higgins, E. T. (2018). Value from fit with distinct motivational field environments. *Basic and Applied Social Psychology*, *40*(2), 61–72. https://doi.org/10.1080/01973533.2018.1434653

Cornwell, J. F. M., & Higgins, E. T. (2013). Morality and its relation to political ideology: The role of promotion and prevention concerns. *Personality and Social Psychology Bulletin*, *39*(9), 1164–1172. https://doi.org/10.1177/0146167213489036

Cornwell, J. F. M., & Higgins, E. T. (2016). Eager feelings and vigilant reasons: Regulatory focus differences in judging moral wrongs. *Journal of Experimental Psychology: General*, *145*(3), 338–355. https://doi.org/10.1037/xge0000136

Coursera. (2022). *Coursera | Degrees, certificates, & free online courses*. Coursera. https://www.coursera.org/

Crowe, E., & Higgins, E. T. (1997). Regulatory focus and strategic inclinations: Promotion and prevention in decision-making. *Organizational Behavior and Human Decision Processes*, *69*(2), 117–132. https://doi.org/10.1006/obhd.1996.2675

Deci, E. L., & Ryan, R. M. (2000). The "what" and "why" of goal pursuits: Human needs and the self-determination of behavior. *Psychological Inquiry*, *11*(4), 227–268. https://doi.org/10.1207/S15327965PLI1104_01

Desilver, D. (2022, March 10). *The polarization in today's Congress has roots that go back decades*. Pew Research Center. https://www.pewresearch.org/fact-tank/2022/03/10/the-polarization-in-todays-congress-has-roots-that-go-back-decades/

Eitam, B., & Higgins, E. T. (2010). Motivation in mental accessibility: Relevance of a representation (ROAR) as a new framework. *Social and Personality Psychology Compass*, *4*(10), 951–967. https://doi.org/10.1111/j.1751-9004.2010.00309.x

Emarsys. (2021, July 2). *Everything has changed: The rise of the subscription an on-demand economies.* Emarsys: An SAP Company. https://emarsys.com/learn/blog/the-rise-of-the-subscription-and-on-demand-economies/

Förster, J., Higgins, E. T., & Bianco, A. T. (2003). Speed/accuracy decisions in task performance: Built-in trade-off or separate strategic concerns? *Organizational Behavior and Human Decision Processes, 90*(1), 148–164. https://doi.org/10.1016/S0749-5978(02)00509-5

Friedman, R. S., & Förster, J. (2005). Effects of motivational cues on perceptual asymmetry: Implications for creativity and analytical problem solving. *Journal of Personality and Social Psychology, 88*(2), 263–275. https://doi.org/10.1037/0022-3514.88.2.263

Happiest Baby. (2022). *Got a question? Need help? We're here for you!* Happiest Baby. https://support.happiestbaby.com/hc/en-us/requests/new?ticket_form_id=360000194114

Higgins, E. T. (1997). Beyond pleasure and pain. *American Psychologist, 52*(12), 1280–1300. https://doi.org/10.1037/0003-066X.52.12.1280

Higgins, E. T. (2000). Making a good decision: Value from fit. *American Psychologist, 55*(11), 1217–1230. https://doi.org/10.1037/0003-066X.55.11.1217

Higgins, E. T. (2012). *Beyond pleasure and pain: How motivation works.* Oxford University Press.

Higgins, E. T. (2018a). Going in the right direction: Locomotion control and assessment truth, working together. In C. E. Kopetz & A. Fishbach (Eds.), *The motivation-cognition interface: From the lab to the real world; A Festschrift in honor of Arie W. Kruglanski.* Routledge.

Higgins, E. T. (2018b). What distinguishes promotion and prevention? Attaining "+1" from "0" as non-gain versus maintaining "0" as non-loss. *Polish Psychological Bulletin, 49*(1), 40–49. https://doi.org/10.24425/119470

Higgins, E. T., Nakkawita, E., & Cornwell, J. F. M. (2020). Beyond outcomes: How regulatory focus motivates consumer goal pursuit processes. *Consumer Psychology Review, 3*(1), 76–90. https://doi.org/10.1002/arcp.1052

Higgins, E. T., Pierro, A., & Kruglanski, A. W. (2008). Re-thinking culture and personality: How self-regulatory universals create cross-cultural differences. In R. M. Sorrentino & S. Yamaguchi (Eds.), *Handbook of motivation and cognition across cultures* (pp. 161–190). Academic Press. https://doi.org/10.1016/B978-0-12-373694-9.00008-8

Higgins, E. T., Roney, C. J. R., Crowe, E., & Hymes, C. (1994). Ideal versus ought predilections for approach and avoidance: Distinct self-regulatory systems. *Journal of Personality and Social Psychology, 66*(2), 276–286. https://doi.org/10.1037/0022-3514.66.2.276

IKEA. (2022). *Say hej to IKEA Place.* IKEA. https://www.ikea.com/au/en/customer-service/mobile-apps/say-hej-to-ikea-place-pub1f8af050

Khan Academy. (2022). *Khan Academy | Free online courses, lessons & practice.* Khan Academy. https://www.khanacademy.org/

Kruglanski, A. W., Thompson, E. P., Higgins, E. T., Atash, M. N., Pierro, A., Shah, J. Y., & Spiegel, S. (2000). To "do the right thing" or to "just do it": Locomotion and assessment as distinct self-regulatory imperatives. *Journal of Personality and Social Psychology, 79*(5), 793–815. https://doi.org/10.1037/0022-3514.79.5.793

Lee, A. Y., & Aaker, J. L. (2004). Bringing the frame into focus: The influence of regulatory fit on processing fluency and persuasion. *Journal of Personality and Social Psychology, 86*(2), 205–218. https://doi.org/10.1037/0022-3514.86.2.205

Lee, A. Y., & Higgins, E. T. (2009). The persuasive power of regulatory fit. In M. Wänke (Ed.), *The social psychology of consumer behavior* (pp. 319–333). Psychology Press.

Lee, A. Y., Keller, P. A., & Sternthal, B. (2010). Value from regulatory construal fit: The persuasive impact of fit between consumer goals and message concreteness. *Journal of Consumer Research, 36*(5), 735–747. https://doi.org/10.1086/605591

Liberman, N., Idson, L. C., Camacho, C. J., & Higgins, E. T. (1999). Promotion and prevention choices between stability and change. *Journal of Personality and Social Psychology, 77*(6), 1135–1145. https://doi.org/10.1037/0022-3514.77.6.1135

Maslow, A. H. (1943). A theory of human motivation. *Psychological Review, 50*(4), 370–396. https://doi.org/10.1037/h0054346

McClelland, D. C. (1985). *Human motivation.* Cambridge University Press.

Memmert, D., Hüttermann, S., & Orliczek, J. (2013). Decide like Lionel Messi! The impact of regulatory focus on divergent thinking in sports. *Journal of Applied Social Psychology*, *43*(10), 2163–2167. https://doi.org/10.1111/jasp.12159

Murray, H. A. (1938). Proposals for a theory of personality. In *Explorations in personality*. Oxford University Press.

Nakkawita, E., & Higgins, E. T. (2021). Motivating the journey: An integrative framework of prevention versus promotion goal pursuit activities. *PsyArXiv*. https://doi.org/10.31234/osf.io/eut2k

New York Times. (2022). *About us | Wirecutter*. New York Times. https://www.nytimes.com/wirecutter/about/

Nike. (2022). *Nike by you custom shoes*. Nike. https://www.nike.com/nike-by-you

PayPal. (2022). *Learn about security*. PayPal. https://www.paypal.com/us/webapps/mpp/security/learn

Pham, M. T., & Avnet, T. (2004). Ideals and oughts and the reliance on affect versus substance in persuasion. *Journal of Consumer Research*, *30*(4), 503–518. https://doi.org/10.1086/380285

Pham, M. T., & Higgins, E. T. (2005). Promotion and prevention in consumer decision making: State-of-the-art and theoretical propositions. In S. Ratneshwar & D. G. Mick (Eds.), *Inside consumption: Consumer motives, goals, and desires* (pp. 8–43). Routledge.

Pinterest. (2022). *All about Pinterest*. Pinterest. https://help.pinterest.com/en/guide/all-about-pinterest

RoC Skincare. (2022). *RoC skincare: Our story*. RoC Skincare. https://www.rocskincare.com/pages/about-us-roc-story

Squarespace. (2022). *About us*. Squarespace. https://www.squarespace.com/about/company

State Farm. (2022). *Triangle of protection*. State Farm. https://www.statefarm.com/insurance/triangle-of-protection

The Wonder Weeks. (2022). *Back to you—Full program app*. The Wonder Weeks. https://www.thewonderweeks.com/back-to-you-full-program-app/

Werth, L., & Foerster, J. (2007). How regulatory focus influences consumer behavior. *European Journal of Social Psychology*, *37*(1), 33–51. https://doi.org/10.1002/ejsp.343

Wytykowska, A., & Gabińska, A. (2015). The effect of emotions, promotion vs prevention focus, and feedback on cognitive engagement. *Polish Psychological Bulletin*, *46*(3), 350–361. https://doi.org/10.1515/ppb-2015-0042

Zhang, S., Higgins, E. T., & Chen, G. (2011). Managing others like you were managed: How prevention focus motivates copying interpersonal norms. *Journal of Personality and Social Psychology*, *100*(4), 647–663. https://doi.org/10.1037/a0021750

LEAVES IN THE WIND: UNDERDEVELOPED THINKING SYSTEMS INCREASE VULNERABILITY TO JUDGMENTS DRIVEN BY SALIENT STIMULI

Ryan Rahinel[a], Rohini Ahluwalia[b] and Ashley S. Otto[c]

[a]University of Oregon, USA
[b]University of Minnesota, USA
[c]Baylor University, USA

ABSTRACT

Humans engage in two types of processing. One system is the rapid, affect-based, and intuitive, "experiential" system, while the other is the relatively slower, cognition-based, and reflective, "rational" system. Extant work focuses on the consequences of having one system relatively dominant over the other. In the current research, we show that consumers who use neither system to a great degree (i.e., low-system consumers) are vulnerable to undesirable outcomes. Specifically, four studies demonstrate that these consumers face confusion in the process of making judgments due to their lack of processing inputs and resolve this confusion by making judgments that are implied by salient stimuli, regardless of the stimuli's diagnostic value. The result is an unbalanced, easily biased, and "blown away by the gust of wind" judgment process that both policymakers and low-system consumers should be vigilant to.

Keywords: Dual process; experiential system; rational system; low-system consumers; salience-driven decision making

The Vulnerable Consumer
Review of Marketing Research, Volume 21, 113–131
Copyright © 2024 Ryan Rahinel, Rohini Ahluwalia and Ashley S. Otto
Published under exclusive licence by Emerald Publishing Limited
ISSN: 1548-6435/doi:10.1108/S1548-643520240000021008

INTRODUCTION

It is now well accepted that two distinct types of information processing exist, one that is rapid, affect-based, and intuitive and the other slower, cognition-based, and reflective (Epstein, 1994; Evans, 2008; Kahneman & Frederick, 2002; Stanovich & West, 2000; Zajonc, 1980). Epstein and colleagues encapsulate these processing types in what they refer to as the experiential system and rational system, respectively (see Epstein, 1973; Epstein et al., 1996; Norris & Epstein, 2011; Pacini & Epstein, 1999). Extant work in this line of inquiry focuses on the independent outcomes of using each system, with, for example, the experiential system linked to creativity (Norris & Epstein, 2011), and the rational system linked to academic achievement (Epstein et al., 1996). These findings are made relevant by research showing that certain demographic groups (e.g., males and females) tend to be more rationally dominant or experientially dominant, respectively (Norris & Epstein, 2011), thus allowing for the greater prediction of decision-making outcomes across such groups.

In the current work, we explore the decision-making consequences of chronically using *neither* system, which is true for a significant proportion of consumers. Past studies have estimated that approximately 35% of adolescents and 25% of young adults fall into this category (Fletcher et al., 2012; Jokić & Purić, 2019). Furthermore, samples of older adults suggest that some individuals may also creep back into this category in their later years (i.e., 65+; Sladek et al., 2010). Does low-system usage make these consumers vulnerable? If so, in what ways? The current research provides new insights on how the lack of system usage can make consumers vulnerable in the marketplace and thus helps us better understand the vulnerabilities of the adolescent, young adult, and elderly populations, who are most likely to use neither system to a great degree.

THE EXPERIENTIAL AND RATIONAL SYSTEMS AND THE LOW-SYSTEM CONSUMER

The Experiential and Rational Systems

The experiential and rational systems are components of Epstein's Cognitive-Experiential Self-Theory (CEST), and they are built on Freud's psychoanalytic concepts of the id and ego, respectively (see, for reviews, Epstein, 1994; Epstein & Pacini, 1999). The key development in Epstein's conceptualization is the experiential system, which retains its roots as a primarily affective system but also includes other lower level processes such as automatic processing and concrete encoding, as well as higher order processes such as gut feelings and intuition (Pacini & Epstein, 1999). The experiential versus rational distinction is one of the broadest and most inclusive of the dual-system frameworks (Epstein & Pacini, 1999), as it subsumes many other dual process frameworks such as verbal versus nonverbal coding (Bucci, 1985), associative versus rule-based processing (Smith & DeCoster, 2000), and the related frameworks of central versus peripheral processing (Petty & Cacioppo, 1986) and heuristic versus systematic processing (HSM; Chaiken, 1980). In this way, the experiential/rational distinction is most similar to the system 1/system 2 distinction (S1/S2; Evans &

Stanovich, 2013; Kahneman & Frederick, 2002), although the experiential/ rational conceptualization adds both an evolutionary argument for the development of the experiential system and a theory of personality that provides scales for their measurement.

In our work, we leverage such scales to examine the joint influence of the two systems. Currently, CEST, HSM, and S1/S2 all allow for instances of joint influence, the nature of which is similar across the frameworks and is best described as a process of default intervention. In default intervention, the heuristic system, experiential system, or system 1 produces candidate outputs based on its constituent processes that are subsequently endorsed, revised, or replaced by the counterpart system (Chaiken & Ledgerwood, 2012; Evans, 2007; Pacini & Epstein, 1999). For example, as affect-based systems, both system 1 and the experiential systems are attracted to hedonic options (e.g., chocolate cake), but this natural inclination is sometimes dampened by the system 2 or rational system (respectively), and replaced with ostensibly healthier options (e.g., a fruit cup; Shiv & Fedorikhin, 1999). While this process represents co-occurrence of the systems, the joint influence that we study here represents the opposite: a nonoccurrence or lack of usage of both systems. Specifically, we study a subset of consumers who have chronically low usage of both systems, hereafter referred to as low-system consumers.

The Existence of Low-System Consumers

The existence of low-system consumers may be surprising to some, as although it is easy to imagine variance in the usage of the rational system, development and engagement of the experiential system is often thought of as universally common to the general population. Yet, in studies employing measures of experiential and rational system processing (including ours), the standard deviations for experiential and rational processing in both ours and many others' studies are highly similar (and directionally higher with experiential in some cases; Epstein et al., 1996; Witteman et al., 2009). Furthermore, the correlation between the measures of the two systems is often null and sometimes even weakly positive (Epstein et al., 1996; Norris & Epstein, 2011; Pacini & Epstein, 1999; Witteman et al., 2009; Wolfradt et al., 1999). Taking these two points together suggests four profiles in the population: (1) a rational-dominant group who employs their rational, but not experiential system to a great extent, (2) an experiential-dominant group, who employs their experiential, but not rational system to a great extent, (3) a high-system group, who employs both systems to a great extent, and (4) a low-system group, who employs neither system to a great extent. Indeed, work using clustering-based methods has further confirmed that all four categories are distinct segments in the population and are not merely statistical artifacts (Fletcher et al., 2012; Wolfradt et al., 1999).

Another reason the existence of low-system consumers may be surprising is that it is unclear why one may choose to not use at least one of the systems in processing stimuli. Consistent with the conceptualization of the experiential and rational systems, the scales designed by Pacini and Epstein (1999) to measure each of them capture both engagement with and ability for these systems. In other words, system usage is not a mere function of resource allocation to the systems; their development also exerts an influence in their usage. Thus, low-system individuals may simply have low ability in both systems. This is plausible given that the experiential system includes several higher order, noninnate processes (e.g., intuition, gut feelings, emotionality, empathy, creativity, esthetic judgment), which may not be accessible to all individuals or might not be as well developed in them. Some individuals may not have a wide emotional spectrum or be in touch with their inner feelings (Hogeveen & Grafman, 2021), others may lack emotional awareness (Lane & Smith, 2021), and some may not have developed their creativity, empathy or intuition (Pacini & Epstein, 1999). For instance, intuitive thin slice judgments, which develop with experience in a domain, correspond to the experiential system (Ambady et al., 2000). In the following section, we discuss how low-system consumers are posited to diverge from the other groups in their decision-making process.

SALIENCE-DRIVEN DECISION MAKING BY LOW-SYSTEM CONSUMERS

As the broadest of the dual-system frameworks, the experiential and rational systems together provide the full array of internal inputs that guide judgments and decisions in consumers' lives. As such, we propose that in facing decisions, the lack of internal guidance available to low-system consumers results in a sense of confusion. Indeed, prior research demonstrates that individuals faced with insufficiencies in internal guidance in particular domains (due to situational circumstances such as low knowledge or high task constraints) display indicators of confusion with respect to several processes common to decision making. For example, such situations may lead to erratic patterns of low-level perception (Reingold et al., 2001), uncertainty in encoding and categorization (Johnson & Mervis, 1997), and difficulties in translating benefit needs into attribute weights and choices (Dellaert & Stremersch, 2005). These difficulties with the sub-processes of decision making represent a sense of inadequacy in being able to sort through the internal and external information available for consideration (as a result of having neither processing system available), leading to the unfortunate dualism of having too much information yet nothing upon which to base one's judgment. We propose that, in response to these feelings of confusion, low-system consumers enact a specific strategy to produce a decision output.

Within the vast set of simplification strategies available to decision makers (see Broniarczyk & Griffin, 2014), we posit that low-system consumers are most likely to quell their confusion by relying on strategies that are salience-driven. We use the term salience-driven to denote strategies wherein the decision maker goes with a judgment or decision output that is implied in the decision context via salient stimuli and its resulting spreading activation. Spreading activation is an incredibly frugal process from a resource perspective (Collins & Loftus, 1975) and is therefore a good match to low-system consumers, who are chronically processing-constrained and do not have any other guidance on choosing inputs.

One reason this strategy may have been overlooked is that prior work on the experiential and rational systems and S1/S2 has used paradigms in which rational and irrational options are pit against each other, and spreading activation is unlikely to have impact. An illustrative example is available on the work by Epstein and colleagues on the ratio-bias phenomenon (Denes-Raj & Epstein, 1994; Pacini & Epstein, 1999), wherein individuals are given the chance to win money by drawing a red jelly bean from one of two bowls, one with more red beans but objectively worse odds (7 red beans out of 100) that appeals to the experiential system, and another that has fewer red beans but better odds (1 red bean out of 10) that appeals to the rational system. Paradigms such as these are certainly useful in testing processes related to default intervention; however, they diverge from commonly encountered judgment and decision environments that are richer in potential inputs and options, including those where spreading activation may impact outcomes.

Here, we employ paradigms in which many inputs are available, rationality is not represented by a "correct option," and a salient feature of the context can lead to spreading activation that suggests a particular option or direction of judgment. The salient feature may exist as an environmental context (e.g., a movie theater might imply the choice of popcorn among a variety of different options) or the decision context (e.g., making a judgment may be swayed toward a recent anchor value). As is evident by these examples, the salient stimulus need not contain any true diagnostic value for the judgment. All that is necessary is that the stimulus eases the decision confusion by steering the judgment toward an outcome via spreading activation. So long as this is met, the implied outcome will be used by low-system individuals to remedy the confusion brought upon by a lack of internal inputs and guidance.

At this point, one may wonder whether the proposed process is also exhibited by experiential-dominant consumers, as associative processing is a feature of the experiential system. Given the richness of these decision environments, which contain a variety of potential stimuli and internal inputs (in addition to the salient feature) that may attract the other properties of the experiential system, we expect the response to salient contextual features to be more muted for experiential-dominant consumers as compared to low-system consumers. As one example, even though popcorn might be the most salient snack option in a movie theater, an experiential-dominant individual might prefer an alternative snack that they have a strong internal affective response to. Indeed, our empirical approach allows us to test for this critical difference between low-system consumers and experiential-dominant consumers.

Overall, a salience-driven process makes low-system consumers particularly vulnerable. As we show in the following studies, salience can have a profound impact on food choices, which is important to both young people (who are the most likely to be in the low-system group) for whom the salience of unhealthy foods is high (Potvin Kent et al., 2019), and elderly (who are also likely to be low-system) for whom proper nutrition can help slow the decline of biological and physiological functions (Ahmed & Haboubi, 2010). Beyond food, salience-driven processes are arms-length from many potential negative outcomes via anchoring, such as overpayment (Simonson & Drolet, 2004), and poorer outcomes in negotiations (Galinsky & Mussweiler, 2001).

STUDY 1

In this study, we sought out initial evidence to support our proposition that low-system individuals are vulnerable decision makers. Specifically, we test whether low-system individuals are more likely to face confusion in decision making. We also test whether the experience of decision confusion heightens negative emotions during the decision-making process, as well as reduces decision satisfaction.

Method

Participants, Design, and Procedure

One hundred fifty-four individuals on Amazon MTurk completed the study. Participants first completed measures of experiential processing and rational processing. Participants then responded to measures of decision confusion, negative decision emotions, and decision dissatisfaction. Finally, participants were debriefed and thanked for their time.

Experiential and Rational Processing

To measure experiential and rational processing, we administered the REI-40 (Pacini & Epstein, 1999), which contains two separate 20-item subscales for the experiential (e.g., "I believe in trusting my hunches") and rational (e.g., "I have a logical mind") processing systems. Scales were anchored at 1 – *Definitely true of myself* to 5 – *Definitely not very true of myself* and separately averaged ($\alpha_{\text{experiential}}$ = 0.91; α_{rational} = 0.95).

Decision Confusion

We assessed how much confusion individuals felt in making decisions on the following items (1 – *Strongly disagree* to 7 – *Strongly agree*): "It is often hard for me to make up my mind about things because I don't really know what I want," "I tend to struggle with most decisions because I feel swayed in many different directions," "When making decisions, I often feel there is more information than I want to deal with," "When faced with a choice I often feel like I have nothing on which to base my decision" (α = 0.83).

Negative Decision Emotions

To measure negative decision emotions, we asked participants how often they felt the following emotions while making decisions (1 – *Never* to 7 – *All the time*): conflicted, confused, uncertain, overwhelmed, helpless, distressed, and nervous (α = 0.81).

Decision Dissatisfaction

To measure decision dissatisfaction, we asked participants the following two measures (both reverse coded; 1 – *Strongly disagree* to 7 – *Strongly agree*): "Once

I make a decision, I'm usually confident I've chosen the right option" and "I feel satisfied with most decisions that I make" ($\alpha = 0.84$).

Results

Preliminary Analysis
We correlated the experiential and rational subscales and, as expected, the two were not significantly correlated ($r = -0.06$, $p > 0.43$).

Main Analysis
We tested our hypotheses using regression models, which regressed each of decision confusion, negative decision emotions, and decision dissatisfaction on experiential processing, rational processing, and their interaction. Subsequently, we estimated the simple slopes for each processing style at $+/-1$ standard deviation of the other scale. The results are displayed in Table 1.

A comparison between rational-dominant individuals and low-system (low on both rational and experiential) individuals is given by the fourth column, which estimates the simple slope of rational processing for those low in experiential processing. The coefficients for all three dependent variables are significant and negative, indicating that low-system (vs. rational-dominant) individuals scored higher on all three measures. A comparison between experiential-dominant individuals and low-system individuals is given by the sixth column, which estimates the simple slope of experiential processing for those low in rational processing. The coefficients for all three dependent variables are significant and negative, indicating that low-system (vs. experiential dominant) individuals scored higher on all three measures. The comparisons for high-system individuals (given by the fifth and seventh columns) showed no significant differences between them and the system-dominant groups.

Table 1. Regression and Simple Slope Analyses in Study 1.

Dependent Measure	Standardized Coefficients (b)			Simple Slopes of Rational System ($+/-$ 1SD Experiential)		Simple Slopes of Experiential System ($+/-$ 1SD Rational)	
	Experiential	Rational	Interaction	Low Experiential	High Experiential	Low Rational	High Rational
Decision Confusion	-1.27**	-1.10***	1.35**	-1.17***	-0.36	-0.63***	0.04
Negative Decision Emotions	-1.10**	-1.01**	1.28*	-0.67***	-0.16	-0.25*	0.16
Choice Dissatisfaction	-1.33***	-1.14***	1.40**	-1.02***	-0.31	-0.58***	0.01

*$p < 0.05$, **$p < 0.01$, ***$p < 0.001$

Mediation Analysis
Bootstrapped mediation analysis (5,000 samples) using Model 8 of Hayes' (2018) PROCESS macro further showed that decision confusion mediated the interactive effects of processing systems on both decision dissatisfaction (indirect effect b = 0.27; 95% CI: 0.01, 0.53), and negative decision emotions (indirect effect b = 0.23; 95% CI: 0.03, 0.44).

Discussion
The results of this study confirm a key prediction of our framework. Specifically, low-system individuals reported higher levels of decision confusion than other individuals. Such confusion also led them to experience more negative emotions during decision making as well as be less satisfied with their decisions. As such, this study suggests that low-system individuals may be vulnerable to suboptimal decision outcomes and processes as a result of decision confusion. In the following three studies, we offer direct support of this vulnerability by demonstrating their greater reliance on nondiagnostic salient cues in decision making.

STUDY 2

In this study, we test our effect in the context of anchoring. Anchoring refers to overreliance on a salient first piece of information in judgment (Tversky & Kahneman, 1974). It is a robust effect with the ability to affect highly consequential outcomes such as willingness-to-pay (Simonson & Drolet, 2004), negotiated values (Galinsky & Mussweiler, 2001), and portion sizes (Mcferran et al., 2010). One of the most powerful explanations for anchoring relies on a salience-driven process known as selective accessibility, wherein an initial piece of information preferentially biases retrieval of anchor-consistent information via spreading activation (Strack & Mussweiler, 1997). Given that low-system consumers are more likely to use salience-driven processes that rely on spreading activation, we predict that low-system consumers will display larger anchoring effects than others.

Method

Participants, Design, and Procedure
One hundred fifty-one undergraduate students participated in exchange for course credit. This study was a 6 (judgment: length of Mississippi river, height of Mount Everest, monthly gas consumption, bars in city, professors in their University, babies born per day) × 2 (anchor value: high vs. low) × experiential processing × rational processing mixed design. Judgment was a within-subjects factor, anchor value was a between-subjects factor, and experiential processing and rational processing were measured continuous variables. In this design, a significant overall anchoring effect is given by higher (lower) judgment estimates in the high (vs. low) anchor value condition. Support for our core prediction is therefore given by such differences being larger for low-system individuals (vs. other groups).

Participants first completed the experiential and rational processing scales. They were then informed that the researchers were interested in their estimates of various facts related to people, places, and things. Participants were asked to make judgments related to six topics: length of Mississippi river, height of Mount Everest, monthly gas consumption, bars in city, professors in University, and babies born per day. Finally, participants were debriefed and thanked for their time.

Experiential and Rational Processing
Participants completed the same REI-40 (Pacini & Epstein, 1999) used in the previous study to indicate their experiential ($\alpha = 0.91$) and rational ($\alpha = 0.90$) processing.

Anchoring Manipulation and Dependent Measures
Typical of anchoring studies (Strack & Mussweiler, 1997), participants were first asked to indicate whether a focal estimate was greater or less than a low or high anchor value (e.g., "Is the length of the Mississippi river greater or less than [70 = low anchor condition] [2000 = high anchor condition] miles?"; see Table 2 for all anchor values used). Participants then indicated their own estimate of the actual value (e.g., for the first judgment: "How long is the Mississippi river (in miles)?"). This process was repeated for each of the six judgments, and the participants' own estimates served as the dependent measures.

Results

Preliminary Analysis
The experiential and rational subscales were not significantly correlated ($r = 0.01$, $p > 0.90$).

Main Analysis
Preliminary inspections of the estimates indicated that each judgment contained several outliers, so we log-transformed the estimates within each judgment. A mixed

Table 2. Anchor Values in Study 2.

Focal Estimate	Low Anchor Value	High Anchor Value
Length of Mississippi River	70 miles	2000 miles
Height of Mount Everest	2000 feet	45,500 feet
Average # of gallons of gas used by an American per month	10 gallons	80 gallons
Number of bars in (city where University is located)	10	125
# Of female professors at (University where study was conducted)	25	330
Average # of babies born per day in the United States	100	50,000

ANOVA with judgment (within-subjects repeated measure), anchor value (between-subjects), experiential (continuous IV), and rational (continuous IV) revealed a non-significant four-way interaction ($p > 0.38$), so we indexed the log-transformed estimates into an overall estimate score for each participant. We then used PROCESS model 3 (Hayes, 2018) to model a three-way regression of this estimate score on experiential processing, rational processing, anchor value (low = 0; high = 1), and all two- and three-way interactions. Every term in the model reached significance (all $ps < 0.01$), notably including the positive main effect of anchor value ($t(143) = 3.88$, $p < 0.001$), which indicates an overall replication of the anchoring effect.

Then, to test the core prediction of our framework, we tested the effect of anchor value separately at $+/- 1SD$ of experiential and rational processing, and then compared the magnitude of the anchor value effects between groups. Conditional effects of anchoring at $+/1$ SD of rational processing and experiential processing were significant for each group, indicating that every group engaged in anchoring to a significant degree (all high anchor Ms > all low anchor Ms; all $ts > 7.77$, all $ps < 0.001$; see Fig. 1).

To compare the magnitude of these effects between the groups, we used the conditional effects (i.e., difference between high and low anchor point estimates) and their standard errors to construct contrasts for low-system individuals versus each of the other groups. Indeed, low-system individuals had larger anchoring effects than each of the other groups (all $ts > 2.18$, all $ps < 0.04$), all of whom did not differ from each other (all $ts < 1$, *ns*).

Discussion

These results demonstrate the joint effect of processing systems on decision making in an anchoring context. Consistent with our predictions, low-system individuals

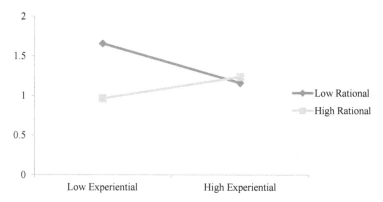

Fig. 1. Anchoring Effect by Experiential Processing and Rational Processing in Study 2. *Note:* The anchoring effect for each group reflects the standardized (within judgment) and summed (across judgment) point estimate for the high anchor group minus that of the low anchor group.

were more likely to allow their judgments to be influenced by a salient anchoring value, and as a result, displayed a larger anchoring effect than others. In the next study, we extend the effect into a consumer decision-making context.

STUDY 3

In this study, we test whether the decisions of low-system individuals are affected by the environmental contexts in which they are made. Environmental contexts can serve as a salient piece of information as spreading activation may imply a particular option. Here, we selected a context relevant to vulnerable consumers – namely [unhealthy] food consumption (Abelson & Kennedy, 2004; Hill & Peters, 1998). We selected food consumption as we contend that low-system individuals will be more (vs. less) susceptible to making unhealthy food choices when these options are contextually salient. To illustrate, being in a movie theater (vs. a mall) is likely to imply the choice of popcorn versus other snacks (e.g., chicken fingers or salad), since movie theaters and popcorn are highly associated. Therefore, since low-system individuals are likely to let salient inputs drive their decisions, we predict that they will be more likely to choose popcorn (vs. other snacks) when at the movie theater. We predict no differences between individuals when the options are not differentially associated with the environmental context (e.g., shopping mall).

Method

Participants, Design, and Procedure
Three hundred sixty-nine individuals on Amazon MTurk completed the study. We manipulated the environmental context of the decision between-subjects by altering the location described in the study. Specifically, participants were asked to imagine that they had arrived at one of two locations and decided to get a snack. Participants made a snack choice from three available options, completed measures of experiential and rational processing, and were debriefed and thanked for their time.

Environmental Context Manipulation
To manipulate the environmental context, participants were asked to imagine that they had just arrived at either a shopping mall or a movie theater at noon and had decided to get a snack. Participants were asked to choose between three snacks to have during the activity: popcorn, salad, or chicken fingers. Importantly, to select the three snacks, we conducted a pretest. Thirty-seven people were each asked the extent to which they associated a variety of snacks with shopping malls and movie theaters $(1 - Not\ at\ all$ to $7 - Very\ much)$. Shopping malls were rated to be equally associated with popcorn, salad, and chicken fingers $(M_{popcorn} = 4.84, M_{salad} = 4.68, M_{chicken} = 4.86$; repeated measures $F(2, 35) = 0.18, p > 0.83)$, but movie theaters were rated to be much more associated with popcorn $(M = 7.00)$ than either salads $(M = 4.68; t(36) = 27.65, p < 0.001)$ or chicken fingers $(M = 2.84; t(36) = 13.70, p < 0.001)$.

Experiential and Rational Processing
Participants completed the REI-10 (Epstein et al., 1996), which is a validated 10-item version of the REI-40 to assess experiential ($\alpha = 0.89$) and rational ($\alpha = 0.88$) processing.

Results

Preliminary Analysis
A correlation analysis did not reveal a significant correlation between the experiential and rational processing subscales ($r = -0.02, p > 0.73$).

Main Analyses
To test our hypothesis, we ran a logistic regression using Hayes (2018) PROCESS model 3 (2018) on food choice (0 = other, 1 = popcorn), with experiential processing, rational processing, environmental context (0 = mall, 1 = movies), and their two- and three-way interactions as predictors. Again, since popcorn is much more associated with movies than the other two options, we expect low-system individuals (vs. other individuals) to be more likely to choose popcorn when they are told they are going to see a movie, whereas we predict no differences between individuals when they are told they are going shopping at the mall, which is equally associated with all three options.

The only significant effects were those for activity ($z = 3.24, p < 0.01$), rational processing $\times$ activity ($z = -2.75, p < 0.01$), experiential processing $\times$ activity ($z = -2.98, p < 0.01$), and most importantly, the predicted three-way interaction ($z = 2.84, p < 0.01$). Two-way interaction contrasts showed that the experiential processing $\times$ rational processing interaction was significant in the movie condition ($b = 0.84, z = 2.81, p < 0.01$; see Fig. 2), but not in the control mall condition ($b = -0.15, z = -0.84, p > 0.40$).

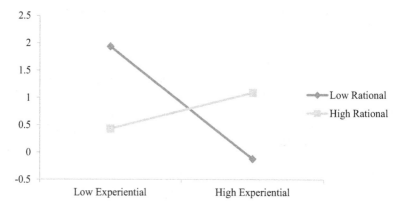

Fig. 2.   Log Odds Ratio of Popcorn Choice in Movie Condition by Experiential Processing and Rational Processing in Study 3.

Further decomposition of simple-simple slopes within the movie condition confirmed our predictions. Rational processing had a negative effect for those low in experiential processing ($b = -0.76$, $z = -2.08$, $p < 0.04$), indicating that low-system people chose popcorn significantly more than did rational-dominant individuals. Likewise, experiential processing had a negative effect for those low in rational processing ($b = -1.27$, $z = -2.93$, $p < 0.01$), indicating that low-system people chose popcorn significantly more than did experiential-dominant individuals. Additionally, rational processing had a positive effect for those high in experiential processing ($b = 0.61$, $z = 2.27$, $p < 0.03$), indicating that high-system individuals were more likely to choose popcorn than experiential-dominant individuals. The remaining simple-simple slopes in both the movie and control condition were all nonsignificant. In sum, when told they would be seeing a movie, low-system individuals were more likely to choose popcorn than other individuals. This effect did not emerge when participants were instead told they would be shopping at the mall.

Discussion

This study confirms our prediction that low-system individuals use a salience-driven process in decision making. Here, low-system individuals (vs. other individuals) were more likely to choose an option (i.e., popcorn) that was heavily implied by a salient environmental context (i.e., movie theater). Importantly, the effect of thinking style on snack choice did not emerge once the environmental context was changed (i.e., in the mall condition), which shows that the results were not driven by latent preferences for popcorn by low-system individuals. More broadly, the results suggest that low-system consumers are susceptible to suboptimal food choices when particular options are implied by a salient context.

It is important to note that an alternative explanation based on low involvement and heuristic processing is rather unlikely. That is, one might suggest that low-system individuals were not cognitively involved in the decision, which led them to use the learned heuristic that one eats popcorn when at the movies. However, heuristic processing is subsumed within the experiential system, and therefore, a heuristic-based process would have predicted a positive effect of experiential processing on popcorn choice in the movie condition. Here, we instead observed that experiential processing had a *negative* effect on popcorn choice in the movie condition when it was coupled with low rational processing, therefore providing strong evidence in favor of our theorizing. It is noteworthy that the negative effect of experiential processing in this setting is consistent with our theorizing. Experiential-dominant individuals are likely to be equipped with rich internal inputs in the domain of food choices (e.g., affective responses to the food options, cravings, etc.), making situational cues less relevant. In the next study, we test our effect in the context of complementary product choices.

STUDY 4

This study has two objectives. First, we extend the effect to a new consumer decision-making context: complementary choices. Complementary products are ones in which the availability or endowment of one increases the desirability of the other (Chakravarti et al., 1990; Martin & Stewart, 2001; Shine et al., 2007). In most cases, this joint desirability is because consumers wish to consume the products jointly (e.g., chips and salsa, peanut butter and jelly, etc.). This context is relevant to the current inquiry because complementary products are closely linked in memory (Samu et al., 1999), and since low-system consumers rely on salience-based spreading activation, in a subsequent choice task, they should be more likely to choose products that are complementary to a focal product encountered previously. Importantly, complementarity of products could also be a heuristic cue, but only in settings where joint consumption of the two products is anticipated. If joint consumption is not anticipated, then experiential-dominant consumers may be less likely to use it in their decision making, relying instead on other inputs including their internal affective responses.

Additionally, to fully establish the role of a salience-driven process in the effect, in this study, we leverage the notion that the effect of spreading activation for a given cue is likely to be attenuated when competing cues are activated (Collins & Loftus, 1975). Toward this end, the study also includes a separate condition wherein a short narrative activating competing concepts is inserted between the two product choice tasks. If our theory is correct, this condition should attenuate the anticipated effect of complementary products for low-system consumers.

Method

Participants, Design, and Procedure
Three hundred three undergraduate students participated in exchange for course credit. Participants were randomly assigned to a 2 (salience condition: high vs. reduced salience) × 2 (target category: crackers vs. frozen pizza). In the first set of choices, all participants were asked to imagine that they were at the grocery store to shop for several items for a *friend*. They were asked to choose one of three options in each of three categories: apples, gum, and a target category (crackers or frozen pizza). Next, they moved on to a second choice task. Participants in the reduced salience condition read a short narrative, whereas those in the high salience condition proceeded directly to the second choice set. As they began this task, all participants were shown the initial list of items they chose for their friend in the first set, then were asked to self-generate three additional items they would buy on the shopping trip for *themselves*. Note that since the three additional items were for oneself while the target category purchase made earlier was for a friend, there was no diagnostic value to selecting complements, since they would *not* be jointly consumed. We then assessed our core dependent measure (i.e., complementarity between initial target category purchase for friend and subsequent choices for oneself) and measures of experiential and rational processing before debriefing and thanking the participants.

Target Category Manipulation
We included two categories of products which have many (but different) complements associated with them – frozen pizzas and crackers. In the first task, participants chose between either three different frozen pizzas or three different types of crackers, for a friend. The other two categories they were asked to make a choice within have few complements associated with them. Including the target product category (pizzas vs. crackers) as a factor had no effect on the analyses, so we collapsed the data across the two target categories.

Salience Manipulation
To test the role of salience in the effect, we reduced the salience associated with the focal target category in one of the conditions. In the reduced salience condition, participants read a short narrative in between exposure to the target category in the first shopping task and the second task of choosing items for oneself. The narrative was designed to make two competing concepts salient: "breakfast foods" and "high school." These concepts are competing in that any spreading activation initiated by them should imply options associated with commonly eaten breakfast foods as well as foods that the participant consumed during their high school years. The increased salience of these latter categories should attenuate the effect of the target category for individuals relying on a salience-driven process (i.e., for low-system individuals). In the high salience condition, participants did not read this narrative and completed the additional item choices immediately after they made the target category choice.

Dependent Measure
Participants indicated via checkboxes which of their self-generated purchases for themselves, if any, they would consume with an item from their target category.

Experiential and Rational Processing
Participants completed the REI-40 to indicate their experiential ($\alpha = 0.93$) and rational ($\alpha = 0.93$) processing.

Results

Preliminary Analysis
A correlation analysis did not reveal a significant correlation between the experiential and rational processing subscales ($r = 0.06$, $p > 0.28$).

Main Analysis
We used PROCESS model 3 (Hayes, 2018) to regress the number of complements chosen on experiential processing, rational processing, condition (0 = high salience, 1 = reduced salience), and their two-and three-way interactions. All terms in the model reached significance, including the hypothesized three-way interaction ($t(295) = -2.02$, $p < 0.05$). Two-way interaction contrasts showed that the experiential processing $\times$ rational processing interaction was significant

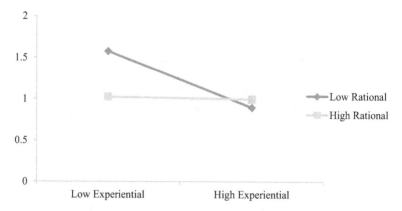

Fig. 3.   Number of Complements Chosen by Experiential Processing and
Rational Processing in the High Salience Condition of Study 4.

for those in the high salience condition ($b = 0.41$, $t(295) = 2.12$, $p < 0.04$), as
depicted in Fig. 3, but not for those in the reduced salience condition ($b = -0.04$,
$t(295) = -0.38$, $p > 0.70$).

Simple-simple slope analyses confirmed our core predictions. Rational processing had a negative effect for those low in experiential processing ($b = -0.44$,
$t(295) = -2.40$, $p < 0.02$), indicating that low-system individuals were more
likely to choose complements to the target category than were rational-dominant
individuals. Experiential processing had a negative effect for those low in rational
processing ($b = -0.54$, $t(295) = -2.70$, $p < 0.01$), indicating that low-system
individuals were more likely to choose complements to the target category than
were experiential-dominant individuals. The high-system individuals did not
differ from both the system-dominant groups (both $ps > 0.61$). All simple-simple
slopes in the reduced salience condition were also nonsignificant (all $ps > 0.18$).

Discussion

This study shows that low-system individuals are more likely to purchase grocery
items that are complementary to those most recently inserted in their shopping
basket. Since the effect is driven by the salience of recently chosen items, the effect
occurred even when the products were unlikely to be jointly consumed (e.g., one
of the products was for a friend), but was attenuated when a narrative reduced
the salience of the recently purchased item. These results therefore shed light on
the shopping processes of low-system individuals, as their minds seemingly flow
between related categories, even in the absence of any utility-based diagnosticity
between them.

GENERAL DISCUSSION AND CONCLUSION

Judgments and decisions are rarely made in a vacuum containing only diagnostic information and internal states. Rather, they are typically made in environments and contexts that may suggest suboptimal, biased, or irrelevant outcomes. Here, we identify a group of individuals – low-system consumers – who are particularly susceptible to salient suggestions from these sources. For these consumers, going with the judgment output that such information cues via spreading activation represents a way to quell the confusion that they face in decisions due to their lack of inputs.

From a theoretical perspective, one might wonder whether the notion of low-system consumers is local to the experiential/rational system or whether such consumers (and their corresponding decision outcomes) may also exist for other dual process theories that are more specific in nature. Although only the experiential/rational distinction provides the necessary scales to test such nonoccurrence in studies, we believe that the breadth of this framework is critical to the emergence of the effect, as the core argument for confusion comes from a lack of inputs upon which to make a judgment or decision. Thus, were scales to become available for other dual process frameworks, we expect these effects to be more likely to conceptually replicate for frameworks that are broader (vs. narrower), as they would represent coverage of greater (vs. fewer) decision inputs.

From the perspective of vulnerability, these findings suggest that low-system consumers should be vigilant to the influence of salient stimuli, and policymakers should deploy measures to protect low-system consumers from undesirable judgments and decisions where appropriate. While the odd purchase of a food item that shares little compatibility with the rest of one's cart because of an environmental context may not appear consequential in isolation, the classification of low-system processing signals a chronic phenomenon that applies to all decisions a consumer makes over the course of their life. Furthermore, the processes tapped into by our dependent measures often manifest in a variety of contexts, some of which are much more consequential than those in our studies. Anchoring, for example, can lead to overeating (McFerran et al., 2010), poorer outcomes in negotiations (Galinsky & Mussweiler, 2001), and heightened willingness-to-pay (Simonson & Drolet, 2004). These points are particularly important in light of the fact that low-system usage affects large groups of adolescents and young adults (Fletcher et al., 2012) as well as the elderly (Sladek et al., 2010). Such groups can ill afford decisions that lead to suboptimal utility.

REFERENCES

Abelson, P., & Kennedy, D. (2004). The obesity epidemic. *Science, 304*(5676), 1413.

Ahmed, T., & Haboubi, N. (2010). Assessment and management of nutrition in older people and its importance to health. *Clinical Interventions in Aging, 5*, 207–216.

Ambady, N., Bernieri, F., & Richeson, J. (2000). Toward a histology of social behavior: Judgmental accuracy from thin slices of behavioral stream. *Advances in Experimental Social Psychology, 32*, 201–271.

Broniarczyk, S. M., & Griffin, J. G. (2014). Decision difficulty in the age of consumer empowerment. *Journal of Consumer Psychology, 24*(4), 608–625.

Bucci, W. (1985). Dual coding: A cognitive model for psychoanalytic research. *Journal of the American Psychoanalytic Association, 33*(3), 571–607.

Chaiken, S. (1980). Heuristic versus systematic information processing and the use of source versus message cues in persuasion. *Journal of Personality and Social Psychology, 39*(5), 752–766.

Chaiken, S., & Ledgerwood, A. (2012). A theory of heuristic and systematic information processing. In P. A. M. V. Lange, A. W. Kruglanski, & E. T. Higgins (Eds.), *Handbook of theories of social psychology* (Vol. 1, pp. 246–266). SAGE Publications.

Chakravarti, D., MacInnis, D. J., & Nakamoto, K. (1990). Product category perceptions, elaborative processing and brand name extension strategies. In M. E. Goldberg, G. Gorn, & R. W. Pollay (Eds.), *North Atlantic advances in consumer research* (Vol. 17, pp. 910–916). Association for Consumer Research.

Collins, A. M., & Loftus, E. F. (1975). A spreading-activation theory of semantic processing. *Psychological Review, 82*(6), 407.

Dellaert, B. G., & Stremersch, S. (2005). Marketing mass-customized products: Striking a balance between utility and complexity. *Journal of Marketing Research, 42*(2), 219–227.

Denes-Raj, V., & Epstein, S. (1994). Conflict between intuitive and rational processing: When people behave against their better judgment. *Journal of Personality and Social Psychology, 66*(5), 819–829.

Epstein, S. (1973). The self-concept revisited: Or a theory of a theory. *American Psychologist, 28*(5), 404–416.

Epstein, S. (1994). Integration of the cognitive and the psychodynamic unconscious. *American Psychologist, 49*(8), 709–724.

Epstein, S., & Pacini, R. (1999). Some basic issues regarding dual-process theories from the perspective of cognitive-experiential self-theory. In S. Chaiken & Y. Trope (Eds.), *Dual-process theories in social psychology* (pp. 462–482). Guilford.

Epstein, S., Pacini, R., Denes-Raj, V., & Heier, H. (1996). Individual differences in intuitive-experiential and analytical–rational thinking styles. *Journal of Personality and Social Psychology, 71*(2), 390–405.

Evans, J. S. B. (2007). On the resolution of conflict in dual process theories of reasoning. *Thinking and Reasoning, 13*(4), 321–339.

Evans, J. S. B. (2008). Dual-processing accounts of reasoning, judgment, and social cognition. *Annual Review of Psychology, 59*, 255–278.

Evans, J. S. B., & Stanovich, K. E. (2013). Dual-process theories of higher cognition: Advancing the debate. *Perspectives on Psychological Science, 8*(3), 223–241.

Fletcher, J. M., Marks, A. D., & Hine, D. W. (2012). Latent profile analysis of working memory capacity and thinking styles in adults and adolescents. *Journal of Research in Personality, 46*(1), 40–48.

Galinsky, A. D., & Mussweiler, T. (2001). First offers as anchors: The role of perspective-taking and negotiator focus. *Journal of Personality and Social Psychology, 81*(4), 657.

Hayes, A. F. (2018). Partial, conditional, and moderated moderated mediation: Quantification, inference, and interpretation. *Communication Monographs, 85*(1), 4–40.

Hill, J. O., & Peters, J. C. (1998). Environmental contributions to the obesity epidemic. *Science, 280*(5368), 1371–1374.

Hogeveen, J., & Grafman, J. (2021). Alexithymia. *Handbook of Clinical Neurology, 183*, 47–62.

Johnson, K. E., & Mervis, C. B. (1997). Effects of varying levels of expertise on the basic level of categorization. *Journal of Experimental Psychology: General, 126*(3), 248–277.

Jokić, B., & Purić, D. (2019). Relating rational and experiential thinking styles with trait emotional intelligence in broader personality space. *Europe's Journal of Psychology, 15*(1), 140–158.

Kahneman, D., & Frederick, S. (2002). Representativeness revisited: Attribute substitution in intuitive judgment. In T. Gilovich, D. Griffin, & D. Kahneman (Eds.), *Heuristics and biases: The psychology of intuitive judgment* (pp. 49–81). Cambridge University Press.

Lane, R. D., & Smith, R. (2021). Levels of emotional awareness: Theory and measurement of a socio-emotional skill. *Journal of Intelligence, 9*(3), 42.

Martin, I. M., & Stewart, D. W. (2001). The differential impact of goal congruency on attitudes, intentions, and the transfer of brand equity. *Journal of Marketing Research*, *38*(4), 471–484.

McFerran, B., Dahl, D. W., Fitzsimons, G. J., & Morales, A. C. (2010). I'll have what she's having: Effects of social influence and body type on the food choices of others. *Journal of Consumer Research*, *36*(6), 915–929.

Norris, P., & Epstein, S. (2011). An experiential thinking style: Its facets and relations with objective and subjective criterion measures. *Journal of Personality*, *79*(5), 1043–1080.

Pacini, R., & Epstein, S. (1999). The relation of rational and experiential information processing styles to personality, basic beliefs, and the ratio-bias phenomenon. *Journal of Personality and Social Psychology*, *76*(6), 972–987.

Petty, R. E., & Cacioppo, J. T. (1986). The elaboration likelihood model of persuasion. In L. Berkowitz (Ed.), *Advances in experimental social psychology* (Vol. 19, pp. 123–203). Academic Press.

Potvin Kent, M., Pauzé, E., Roy, E. A., de Billy, N., & Czoli, C. (2019). Children and adolescents' exposure to food and beverage marketing in social media apps. *Pediatric Obesity*, *14*(6), e12508.

Reingold, E. M., Charness, N., Pomplun, M., & Stampe, D. M. (2001). Visual span in expert chess players: Evidence from eye movements. *Psychological Science*, *12*(1), 48–55.

Samu, S., Krishnan, H. S., & Smith, R. E. (1999). Using advertising alliances for new product introduction: Interactions between product complementarity and promotional strategies. *Journal of Marketing*, *63*(1), 57–74.

Shine, B. C., Park, J., & Wyer, R. S. Jr. (2007). Brand synergy effects in multiple brand extensions. *Journal of Marketing Research*, *44*(4), 663–670.

Shiv, B., & Fedorikhin, A. (1999). Heart and mind in conflict: The interplay of affect and cognition in consumer decision making. *Journal of Consumer Research*, *26*(3), 278–292.

Simonson, I., & Drolet, A. (2004). Anchoring effects on consumers' willingness-to-pay and willingness-to-accept. *Journal of Consumer Research*, *31*(3), 681–690.

Sladek, R. M., Bond, M. J., & Phillips, P. A. (2010). Age and gender differences in preferences for rational and experiential thinking. *Personality and Individual Differences*, *49*(8), 907–911.

Smith, E. R., & DeCoster, J. (2000). Dual-process models in social and cognitive psychology: Conceptual integration and links to underlying memory systems. *Personality and Social Psychology Review*, *4*(2), 108–131.

Stanovich, K. E., & West, R. F. (2000). Individual differences in reasoning: Implications for the rationality debate? *Behavioral and Brain Sciences*, *23*(5), 645–665.

Strack, F., & Mussweiler, T. (1997). Explaining the enigmatic anchoring effect: Mechanisms of selective accessibility. *Journal of Personality and Social Psychology*, *73*(3), 437–446.

Tversky, A., & Kahneman, D. (1974). Judgment under uncertainty: Heuristics and Biases: Biases in judgments reveal some heuristics of thinking under uncertainty. *Science*, *185*(4157), 1124–1131.

Witteman, C., Van den Bercken, J., Claes, L., & Godoy, A. (2009). Assessing rational and intuitive thinking styles. *European Journal of Psychological Assessment*, *25*(1), 39–47.

Wolfradt, U., Oubaid, V., Straube, E. R., Bischoff, N., & Mischo, J. (1999). Thinking styles, schizotypal traits and anomalous experiences. *Personality and Individual Differences*, *27*(5), 821–830.

Zajonc, R. B. (1980). Feeling and thinking: Preferences need no inferences. *American Psychologist*, *35*(2), 151–175.

"I DID NOT THINK OF MYSELF AS A 'CUSTOMER'": THE CONFLUENCE OF INTERTWINED VULNERABILITIES AMONG SUBSISTENCE CONSUMERS THROUGH MARKETPLACE LITERACY

Madhu Viswanathan[a], Lucy Joy Chase[a] and Maria Jones[b]

[a]University of Illinois Urbana-Champaign, USA
[b]Independent Researcher, USA

ABSTRACT

Vulnerabilities in subsistence marketplaces arise from the multifaceted deprivation that characterizes poverty. Associated with low income is low literacy, leading to vulnerabilities in terms of thinking, feeling, and coping. We review literature on vulnerability and on subsistence marketplaces, bringing out the confluence of vulnerabilities consumers in these contexts face. We also describe marketplace literacy, a way of addressing vulnerabilities and developing capabilities. We provide a case study of women in agriculture and conclude with a discussion of implications for research, education, and practice.

Keywords: Subsistence marketplaces; subsistence consumers; poverty; literacy; consumer vulnerabilities

The Vulnerable Consumer
Review of Marketing Research, Volume 21, 133–152
Copyright © 2024 Madhu Viswanathan, Lucy Joy Chase and Maria Jones
Published under exclusive licence by Emerald Publishing Limited
ISSN: 1548-6435/doi:10.1108/S1548-643520240000021009

INTRODUCTION

A low-literate, low-income woman living in a rural or urban setting around the world is vulnerable on many fronts in participating in the marketplace as a consumer. She is vulnerable in her social hierarchy through restrictions placed by her immediate family, particularly her husband and male elders. She must overcome societal norms to interact with people, including men, and to buy and sell. She is vulnerable due to the lack of skills and knowledge that will enable her to do so, and she is vulnerable in not knowing her rights in the marketplace. She is vulnerable, lacking in self-confidence, to be able to carry out her role as a customer (or as a seller or entrepreneur). She is vulnerable to local and global environmental impacts (inhaling smoke while cooking with firewood in enclosed spaces or impacted by natural disasters and climate change). These are vulnerabilities that come from individual, household, community, marketplace, societal, and macro-environmental levels. They stem from the multi-faceted deprivation that characterizes poverty. Among the associated factors is low literacy, which leads to vulnerabilities in terms of thinking, feeling, and coping.

We review literature on vulnerability, and the stream of work on subsistence marketplaces (Viswanathan, 2013, 2016; Viswanathan & Rosa, 2007), with a view to bringing out the confluence of vulnerabilities consumers face, as their deprivations are multi-faceted. We also discuss a research-based approach to marketplace literacy (Viswanathan et al., 2008, 2021), as a way of addressing vulnerabilities and developing capabilities that is based on this stream of work. We then provide an in-depth case-study of women in agriculture and apply the consumer vulnerability lens to both connect to and extend past work. We conclude with a discussion of implications for research, education, and practice.

VULNERABILITY

In this section, we provide a brief review of vulnerability from different perspectives. Merriam-Webster defines vulnerable as "capable of being physically or emotionally wounded" and "open to attack or damage." The word originates from the Latin word vulnus, which means "wound." Originally, the term was used only to refer to physical injury, but over time, it has come also to represent intangible injuries, such as emotional hurt or social degradation. Vulnerability can be seen as the state of being open to harm or injury, in a very broad sense. The origin of the harm or hazard is typically external to the vulnerable person and could arise from many different sources. An individual person or group of people may inflict harm on a vulnerable person. The government may enact restrictions or requirements that injure a person's ability to create an abundant life. Educational or social institutions may restrict a person's access to critical resources for growth and prosperity. The natural environment can pose existential threats to a vulnerable person's life, well-being, and livelihoods, especially with the mounting risks of climate-related and naturally-occurring severe weather and natural disasters (frequent floods, wildfires, severe drought, etc.).

Within a development context, vulnerability is often used to refer to populations that are assumed to be at naturally higher risk for harm. Women, children, and the elderly are often referred to as vulnerable populations, as well as impoverished people, without any reference to what these populations are actually vulnerable to (Bankoff et al., 2004). These broad categorizations lean on assumptions about who is vulnerable and the essence of vulnerability. A person living below the poverty line might well be rich in social networks, adaptability, and resourcefulness within their own environment and surprisingly well adept at providing for their own needs, whereas another person with the same financial means may be truly living at the edge of survival, frequently unable to meet their most basic needs of food, shelter, and safety. Broad categorizations about who is vulnerable need to be supplemented with more nuanced analysis, recognizing and identifying the particular vulnerabilities that some segments of these populations are susceptible to and the agency that individuals have to mitigate those risks.

In a 2012 report, The Intergovernmental Panel on Climate Change (IPCC) qualified vulnerability as resulting from a "lack of resilience and capacity to anticipate, cope with, and adapt to extremes and change," originating chiefly from environmental, social, and financial contexts (Cardona et al., 2012). Adaptability is a key to vulnerability, because any extreme change might be overcome by adaptation, responsiveness, and access to resources. The report also identified factors that can strongly influence vulnerability. These are cultural identity (race, ethnicity, and religion), gender, age, level of education, financial well-being and wealth, socioeconomic class or caste, health, and disability status. Such a diverse range of factors can have drastically different impacts on subsections of the population. The IPCC report, while focused primarily on vulnerabilities exacerbated by climate change, lends a comprehensive view of aspects of vulnerability relevant to consumers. Certain global processes are named as having a strong causal relationship with creating vulnerability, such as population growth, and socioeconomic inequalities.

Relevant to causal and associated factors of vulnerability is the concept of capability. The capabilities approach developed by Sen (1985) focuses on the actual freedoms people possess to fulfill their potential to do and to be (Robeyns & Byskov, 2020). It was proposed in contrast to more conventional development models which focus on per capita income and other finite measurements of well-being. Capabilities can be said to have an inverse relationship with vulnerabilities, allowing an individual to navigate the world with a lessened state of perceived and actual risk. Whereas many definitions of capability do not encompass the relationship to risk (Lindbom et al., 2015), it is important to consider capabilities as an essential component of risk abatement.

To truly understand vulnerability, it is useful to discuss it not only as a particular human condition but also as an emotional state. According to leading shame and vulnerability researcher, Brené Brown, vulnerability is "uncertainty, risk, and emotional exposure." It is neither good, nor bad, but instead represents the degree of openness a person allows toward feeling and emotion. As such, vulnerability is at the core of all human emotions (Brown, 2013). One can identify the feeling of vulnerability by imagining or remembering emotionally raw experiences in life, such as waiting for a response on a potential new job or promotion, loving someone and not knowing if they will love you back, standing up for yourself in an uncertain situation, or waiting for the results of a medical procedure. It is a feeling embedded in wants, desires, or needs, and importantly, in uncertainty; thus, being vulnerable translates to being fully exposed (Brown, 2013). As such, vulnerability is often seen as a negative emotion, a low-grade sense of fear and concern that an outcome may or may not be favorable.

Closely aligned with the feeling of vulnerability is the emotion of shame. Shame is defined as "an intensely painful feeling or experience of believing we are flawed and therefore unworthy of acceptance and belonging" (Brown, 2006). It is an emotion that one can experience as a result of our vulnerability, of not getting the job, being rejected from love, or discovering our health is failing. It is not unlike the feelings of shame sometimes experienced by those living in poverty, at not being able to meet one's own basic needs or the needs of one's family (Bilo, 2017). In Brown's study of shame resilience, participants described shame as "devastating, noxious, consuming, excruciating... and the worst feeling ever" (2006). In fact, researchers studying brain scans of people having recently experienced social and emotional rejection found that the same areas of the brain light up when experiencing social rejection as when someone is experiencing physical pain (Kross et al., 2011). Shame and vulnerability can literally be painful.

Yet, with vulnerability comes opportunity, the opportunity for love, for satisfying one's needs, the opportunity for growth and development, for making greater contributions to the community or society at large. And within oneself, emotional vulnerability is the key to human connection; indeed, different types of intimacy may not be attainable when vulnerable (Bouris, 2012). Vulnerability allows us to open up to all possibilities around us, physically, socially, and emotionally. Without this, our experience of the world would be greatly diminished. This view of vulnerability diverges greatly from the notion that vulnerability is a state of being experienced most severely, or even exclusively, by marginalized peoples. The conventional notion is that vulnerability denotes weakness and incapability, an inability to care or fend for oneself. This view invokes a moralistic and perhaps paternalistic sense of responsibility to protect or defend people deemed to be vulnerable. This contrasts with the more ontological approach, recognizing vulnerability as essential to human nature (Zagorac, 2017).

The wide set of factors in the vulnerability literature as well as specific realms such as emotional vulnerability also extend to the domain of consumers.

> Consumer vulnerability is a state of powerlessness that arises from an imbalance in marketplace interactions... arises from the interaction of personal states, personal characteristics, and external conditions within a context where consumption goals may be hindered, and the experience affects personal and social perceptions of self. (Baker et al., 2005)

This dynamic may be created due to a person's internal state, in which they are experiencing negative emotions (such as shame or lack of self-confidence). In turn, this may hinder them from experiencing the marketplace in a normative manner, or due to external factors, such as social, economic, or political patterns of discrimination or constraints. Consistent with past research (Baker et al., 2005; Bankoff et al., 2004), rather than to assume vulnerability in large swaths of the population, the subsistence marketplaces approach has used a bottom-up approach to examine vulnerabilities and strengthened beginning at the micro level.

SUBSISTENCE MARKETPLACES, MARKETPLACE LITERACY, AND CONSUMER VULNERABILITY

In this section, we discuss vulnerability from the vantage point of subsistence marketplaces, bringing out its intertwined nature as summarized in Fig. 1 and illustrated in Table 1. Our depiction covers how vulnerability plays out across roles, domains of subsistence, and functions, overlaying the earlier discussion on a variety of factors that impact types of vulnerability.

Subsistence Marketplaces

The stream of work on subsistence marketplaces partially reflected in the set of special issues and special sections on this topic has centered on consumer vulnerability through a variety of perspectives, albeit using different terminology. For instance, Corus and Ozanne (2012) bring out the importance of participatory approaches to understanding vulnerabilities. They note how even those most marginalized people may still participate in deliberative spaces under the right

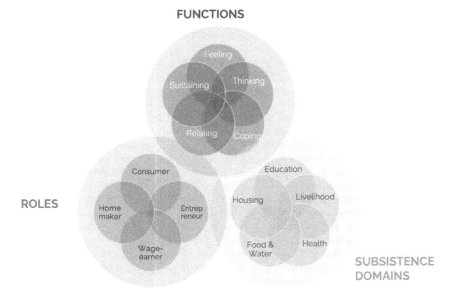

Fig. 1. Intertwined Vulnerabilities in Subsistence Marketplaces.

Table 1. Illustrative Examples of Work of Intertwined Vulnerabilities in Subsistence Marketplaces.

Papers	Authors	Topic	Geography	Roles	Functions	Domains
Understanding factors that influence purchases in subsistence markets	Chikweche and Fletcher (2010)	Purchase influencers	Zimbabwe	Consumer	Feeling, thinking	Food and water; health
Why art matters: Artistic consumer-entrepreneurship in subsistence marketplaces	Chakrabarti (2021)	Art	Mexico; Tanzania; Native American tribes	Entrepreneurs; consumers	Sustaining; relating	Livelihoods
The contextual value of social capital for subsistence entrepreneur mobility	Barrios and Blocker (2015)	Social capital	Colombia	Entrepreneurs	Coping	Livelihoods
Consumer well-being and social responsibility of subsistence entrepreneurs in subsistence marketplace	Azmat and Samaratunge (2020)	Social responsibility	Bangladesh; Sri Lanka	Consumer	Thinking; coping	Food and water
Understanding the dynamics between social entrepreneurship and inclusive growth in subsistence marketplaces	Azmat et al. (2015)	Social entrepreneurs	Bangladesh; Nepal	Entrepreneurs	Sustaining	Livelihoods
The institutional work of a social enterprise operating in a subsistence marketplace: Using the business model as a market-shaping tool	Aly et al. (2020)	Social entrepreneurs	Mozambique	Wage-earners; consumers	Sustaining	Housing
Fuel-efficient stoves for Darfur: The social construction of subsistence marketplaces in post-conflict settings	Abdelnour and Branzei (2010)	Fuel efficient stoves	Sudan	Consumer	Coping	Food and water; health

circumstances. At a more macro level, Toledo et al. (2010) examine how government programs impact perceived financial risk among entrepreneurs. Abdelnour and Branzei (2010) study the social construction of subsistence marketplaces in Darfur, a post-conflict setting, representing individuals and communities who are among the most vulnerable. The stream of work has examined vulnerabilities in different geographies (urban, rural, isolated tribal settings), domains (health, livelihoods, consumption, etc.), roles (consumers, entrepreneurs, homemakers, etc.), and functions (thinking, feeling, relating, etc.).

Our journey into understanding vulnerabilities in the stream of subsistence marketplaces begins at a minute level (Viswanathan, 2013; Viswanathan & Rosa, 2007). Our research and insights are where poverty and the marketplace intersect – relating to how individuals think, feel, cope, act, relate, and sustain – how individuals function as customers and entrepreneurs, buyers and sellers (see functions in Fig. 8.1). As the basis for our work, we unpack poverty as it relates to the marketplace, studying what it means to lack income, education, and exposure/experience. We describe these contexts in terms of inherent uncertainty in the most mundane of day-to-day activities and a lack of a margin of error, making subsistence consumers vulnerable in a variety of ways, connecting back to descriptions of vulnerability in terms of uncertainty and risk (e.g., Brown, 2006). We study vulnerabilities as well substantively in different domains of subsistence, health, livelihoods, and so forth (see domains in Figure). We also study vulnerabilities in terms of the material, cognitive, emotional, behavioral, social and so forth. The intertwined nature of the different subsistence domains, as well as different psychological aspects, is revealed with our holistic approach to subsistence marketplaces (Venugopal & Viswanathan, 2017; see Fig. 1).

Our insights cover thinking, emotion, and behavior. For example, we note the lack of education and difficulty in thinking beyond immediate, concrete terms, accentuated by the immediacy of urgent basic needs to be fulfilled. Our insights on thinking patterns can be best summarized in one phrase – the things we take for granted. Stated in terms of vulnerabilities, we take for granted the advantages we have in resource-rich settings, while often not aware of the vulnerabilities in subsistence marketplaces. Not only does this include material aspects, but also the richness of the words and concepts we use and think about as a result of literacy, education, and exposure. As a case in point, the women to whom we have provided education on marketplace literacy often speak of understanding broadly what a customer is, without thinking narrowly of themselves as a buyer. "I never thought of myself as a customer" is a powerful response we have heard. The notion of a customer is richly developed, multi-faceted and comes naturally for literate individuals – it covers identity and self-confidence, awareness of consumer rights, and an array of skills and knowledge.

Our insights on emotion highlight how mundane marketplace activities can lead consumers to celebrate or to despair. To lack literacy and be poor means that the woman in our opening example (or someone more generally) could be insulted by a shopkeeper for asking a question, be cheated constantly, be reprimanded for being poor or lacking an education or knowledge, or be publicly exposed at the counter for her inability to calculate and pay sufficient money

(Viswanathan, 2013; Viswanathan et al., 2005). Shame and vulnerability go hand-in-hand, as noted earlier (Brown, 2006). It means that psychological vulnerability, in terms of self-esteem, is very close to the surface with activities and interactions that literate consumers would not put any thought into. This follows from the attributions for negative experiences in marketplace interactions toward one's own state of poverty and low literacy (i.e., internal factors – Baker et al., 2005). This is on top of the humiliation she may face from her husband and others at a household level in order to get to the marketplace. On the other hand, to successfully negotiate the marketplace and get a good deal may be a cause to celebrate. This is because, what might be mundane transactions for many, may uplift aspects of her core identity. To be cheated means to be exploited for her vulnerability, relating to her lack of education, knowledge and resources, the cause of her day-to-day struggles. Although at the intersection of internal and external factors, psychological vulnerability here stems from low income and low literacy. Indeed, it is possible that low literacy, even more than low income, can accentuate feelings of vulnerability as it involves fundamental cognitive, emotional, and behavioral constraints that we expand on below.

Our insights on the marketplace highlight how being a human being and a customer are not mutually exclusive but instead blur together; transactions blur into relationships, products blur into immediate basic needs, marketplaces and communities blur into social milieus, and above all, customers may be poor in a material sense but can be rich in a social sense (Viswanathan et al., 2009). These contexts are intensely personal in some settings, a one to one interactional marketplace with fluid and responsive exchanges, enduring relationships that multiply value in small exchanges over time, and high interdependence and oral communications (Viswanathan et al., 2012). Although socially and emotionally risky, the marketplace social or relational environment can be rich with opportunities, a pathway toward capabilities to confront vulnerabilities. In fact, this one to one interactional environment, the centrality of having to be an entrepreneur to survive, and the immediacy of basic needs can lead to the development of capabilities. Being an entrepreneur is the other side of the coin of being a consumer in these settings, and vulnerabilities in these two roles gets intertwined (Viswanathan et al., 2010; see roles in Fig. 8.1), as brought out in the opening example. In this regard, the vulnerabilities of those with low income can be more stark in advanced economies, where a certain level of literacy is assumed in shopping environments, one to one interactions as a way to learn are much lower, and ironically, there is a lack of an entrepreneurial ecosystem that exists with more extreme poverty.

This stream of work has also examined from a bottom-up perspective what people in subsistence marketplaces try to sustain, as a counter-perspective to a top-down view of people, planet, and profit. Sustaining relates to the physical, the relational (to others and the local environment), and to growth, at least for the next generation (Viswanathan et al., 2014). If our journey starts at a minute or micro level, it then creates insights that go beyond. We are bottom-*up* in our perspective. Our insights are novel, because we begin at the level of individual life circumstances and vulnerabilities, developing a deep understanding of thinking, feeling, and coping, as well as self-confidence and development of identity as it relates to the marketplace. Noteworthy here is the confluence of intertwined vulnerabilities spanning thinking, feeling, and behaving (Fig. 8.1), reflecting deprivation on literally every front in the realms of life.

Unpacking Poverty and Marketplaces – Material and Cognitive Survival

Perhaps most relevant to consumer vulnerability and unique to our approach is our emphasis on unpacking poverty in terms of its association with low literacy. Thus, material poverty is accompanied by cognitive, affective, and coping constraints arising from low literacy. This lens is important in a number of ways. The very language we use, such as "consumer," "enterprise," "health," "nutrition," and so forth presumes a level of literacy and full development of underlying concepts. Lacking literacy means difficulty with abstractions and understanding causality. Such cognitive survivors buy the cheapest or the biggest items as a way to bypass complex calculations of information, reducing decisions to a single or a few attributes (concrete thinking; Viswanathan et al., 2005). They simplify complex notions, such as equating good health with not being in a hospital. They reduce complex marketplace activities into simple exchanges. Lacking know-why, they often focus on the "what" or the "how" of something, avoiding shops, checking expiry dates, etc., without gauging value in a fuller sense of give and get. Cause and effect are difficult, particularly when involving different degrees of abstraction, such as in the health or livelihood domain.

Subsistence consumers also engage in pictographic thinking, visualizing how they use products and buying corresponding amounts, or pattern-matching numerals and words between bus numbers or prescriptions and so forth (Viswanathan et al., 2005). Thus, subsistence consumers are vulnerable to cheating based on package sizes and actual amounts contained in them. Even calculations in a shopping situation can be pictorial, moving currencies mentally rather than computing abstractly, making buyers vulnerable to cheating in everyday transactions. Also relevant is a reliance on pictorial brand logos, creating vulnerability to counterfeit products.

We speak in the traditional marketing and psychology literature of cognitive misers who optimize or satisfice in their decision-making. But we would describe subsistence consumers more appropriately as cognitive survivors, as material resource constraints intertwine with cognitive and affective constraints. Cognitive misers "decide how to decide," devoting less effort to a habitual decision with less consequences (low involvement). Cognitive survivors may simply not be able to engage as much in meta-decision-making, which reflects know-why. The term, cognitive "survivors" is not meant in any way to downplay the extraordinary life-and-death consequences of survival per se. Rather, it is used to bring out the qualitatively different nature of thinking in these settings.

Such cognitive constraints are accentuated by the need for physical survival, leading to a variety of decisions that affect well-being. They are also accentuated by lack of exposure, making subsistence consumers vulnerable in marketplace interactions. For instance, in the health domain, rationing or foregoing healthcare by making the impossible tradeoff with livelihood and "necessities" is both material and cognitive. A similar example is in the financial or economic domain, borrowing money at higher interest rates from local moneylenders rather than accessing credit from formal money-lending institutions at lower interest rates (Banerjee & Duflo, 2007). The ability to think abstractly can lead to factoring in the longer-term impact of ill-health, as well as the complex combinations of factors that point toward vulnerabilities in this domain (e.g., high blood pressure, diabetes, and diet). This may lead to behavioral and other changes. But the vulnerabilities faced on the cognitive side compounded by the immediacy of survival make such considerations extremely difficult.

Also associated with being vulnerable in skills and knowledge is the lack of self-confidence and psychological vulnerability of engaging in the marketplace. Potentially being publicly exposed for having low literacy or the inability to complete tasks that are taken for granted by most consumers compromises subsistence consumers. In turn, they may choose, rather than to face these potentially very painful and shameful experiences (Brown, 2006), to pay a premium to shop comfortably in familiar settings with helpful employees. Vulnerabilities in being a consumer are blurred with those of being an entrepreneur as well. For instance, the lack of know-why and understanding of words and concepts, such as "enterprise," correspond to vulnerabilities as consumers. This is particularly germane, as these are a necessity rather than an opportunity for entrepreneurs for whom running a small microenterprise may be the only way to make a living.

Marketplace Literacy

As hinted above, we developed a marketplace literacy educational program (Viswanathan et al., 2008) that addresses the core issues above. The program is not about basic literacy (the capacity to read), but rather about using the social context to address thinking, feeling, and acting in the marketplace. We define marketplace literacy as skills and knowledge, as customers and as entrepreneurs. These two roles are two sides of the same coin in an exchange and the broader notion of marketplace literacy encompasses both. We employ a bottom-up approach in covering topics on generic marketplace literacy, consumer literacy, and entrepreneurial literacy. Traditional approaches in the economic realm that aim to empower women to confront their vulnerabilities focus on specific livelihood training and microfinancing. They address the issues she faces in a compartmentalized manner, when in fact a more holistic approach is essential. In fairness, these are not the only approaches. There are those that address the ecosystem in providing access to value chains and other linkages to employment and entrepreneurship. However, to empower her to cope with vulnerabilities means to address issues of her self-confidence and core identity at an emotional and motivational level, as well as her capacities at a cognitive level. It means fully understanding her life circumstances at a minute level and using this understanding to consider solutions at individual, community, and societal levels.

The woman we describe in the opening example may start a small food shop to survive because she knows *what,* to prepare food as she does at home and grew up learning about. But she needs to know *how,* to keep accounts or communicate. The what and the how are traditionally addressed in educational programs. But our journey began at the minute level of her life circumstances, providing insights about her thinking, feeling, acting, and relating patterns in the marketplace. At an intuitive level, these insights resonated with a focus on *why* she should do what she does. This led to a new-to-the-world educational program, one that began with the why or deeper understanding as a path to the how and what, an innovative educational program that came from innovative bottom-up research.

Our program uses the experiences of the woman we described at the outset as a starting point. Rather than convey business concepts top-down, we develop them bottom-up from people's own experiences. Our content is local and concrete, and our approach uses one skill that she has in abundance, the ability to relate socially to other women. For instance, we bring out the idea that customers and their needs are what make exchanges and businesses possible. But we do so by using a task where participants prioritize pictures of money, customers, producers, transporters, and shopkeepers in terms of what is most important to run a business. We set up simulated shops to purposefully cheat participants and then show how they got cheated on a host of issues. But we go beyond to place these issues in the umbrella of *give and get* and the notion of getting value in an exchange. Thus, we expand to a concept from concrete and intuitive aspects of exchange. In turn, the give and get is used in running an enterprise as well in terms of creating value or in being an employee. We then holistically develop this notion in other realms of life – sustainability, conservation, relationships, and life aspirations.

So how does our program benefit the woman described above? It helps develop self-confidence that she can be a better customer and perhaps an entrepreneur. Being a better customer comes with immediate benefits, money saved and better-quality products. We have observed how women go to their husbands and ask to take over buying functions, how they go to shop-keepers and threaten to switch, and how they believe they can run a small income-generating activity too. As they engage in these different activities, they are on a path to increasing self-confidence, along with awareness of rights, and skills and knowledge. We find the outcome of being a better customer to be nearly universal. Additionally, the outcome of starting a small enterprise or expanding an existing one occurs in one in four or five women, approximately, with the proportion increasing dramatically in extreme poverty. Starting an enterprise is not for everyone, and moreover, there may be obstacles placed, such as the husband not allowing it. These obstacles can be overcome over time perhaps with improved benefits to the household as customers, growing self-confidence, and a community level awareness that we begin to see in villages.

Empirically, we have shown the impact of marketplace literacy through randomized field trials, with positive impact on general well-being, confidence as consumers, decision-making, entrepreneurial intentions, and entrepreneurial startups (Viswanathan et al., 2021). In fact, some of the positive impact is higher for those with lower access, an external factor that leads to vulnerabilities (Baker et al., 2005).

Through the lens of the capabilities approach (Sen, 2005), we identify marketplace literacy as a critical capability required for subsistence individuals to overcome vulnerabilities, achieve important functionings, and, ultimately, improve their well-being. In the capabilities approach, the ends, or outcomes, have intrinsic importance whereas the means are instrumental to reach the goal of increased well-being (Robeyns, 2005). Well-being results from the expansion of individuals' freedom and opportunities to make choices that bring value to their lives (Sen, 1985). In contrast to conventional development thought that focuses on objective measures of income and education, Sen argues that well-being results from a combination of "functionings" and "capabilities." Functionings are comprised of activities and doings (e.g., negotiating price and checking product quality) and mental states and beings (e.g., being happy and confident). Capabilities are defined as the freedom and opportunity to choose to pursue these functionings among alternative choices. A central focus of the capabilities approach framework is an individual's sense of agency, or control over her decision for a better quality of life, which is necessary for carrying out functionings independently (Sen, 2005). Marketplace literacy is central to the capability to effectively function in the marketplace as consumers and entrepreneurs (Viswanathan et al., 2009). Beyond the notion of buyers and sellers, marketplace literacy encompasses marketing exchanges more broadly by focusing on value chains and the entire ecosystem that brings marketing to bear (e.g., interactions among consumers, sellers, wholesalers, and marketing agents). A consumer may use these capabilities for functionings such as choosing the right store, negotiating the right price, comparing products, assessing quality, and purchasing the right product. The "being" part of marketplace functionings includes becoming a confident consumer, with the ability to assertively acquire information and protect oneself from deception (Bearden et al., 2001) and acquiring the basic sense of self-confidence (and lack of shame) that a woman can adequately care for herself and her family (Brown, 2006).

The capabilities approach speaks to 'conversion factors', which include environmental factors (e.g., climate, geographical location) that may be necessary to convert capabilities into functionings (i.e., converting what people have into what they can do or be). Many such factors map on to vulnerabilities. For instance, access represents a critical environmental conversion factor in the capabilities approach framework (Robeyns, 2005). Whereas marketplace literacy is an internal capability, marketplace access represents an external factor. In the capabilities approach framework, conversion factors, as the name suggests, convert capabilities into functionings and well-being. In low-access settings, people face additional deprivation, and as a result, they may be forced to develop capabilities to overcome such constraints to survive (Hill, 1991). Internal marketplace literacy capabilities may work to overcome vulnerabilities in the face of deprivation and the urgency to meet basic consumption needs.

We also note that marketplace literacy could be viewed as an internal factor. In turn, it interacts with an external factor, such as access to markets. Indeed, lack of access to markets makes many consumers vulnerable on several fronts. Extending from tribal areas of Africa to the rural and urban United States, lack of access manifests in realms of healthcare and food.

Whereas we have covered a variety of issues relating to the content of marketplace literacy education, we note a variety of issues in reaching people and communities facing vulnerabilities. The very nature of these vulnerabilities makes this goal difficult, sometimes impossible. For instance, where women are not given access to education, recruiting participants by interacting with a variety of stakeholders has been critically important. We elaborate on these aspects elsewhere (Viswanathan et al., 2008; www.marketplaceliteracy.org).

CASE STUDY IN INTERTWINED VULNERABILITIES - WOMEN IN AGRICULTURE ACCESSING AGRICULTURAL TECHNOLOGIES[1]

In subsistence contexts, vulnerabilities do not occur in isolation as women's roles as consumers are intertwined with their roles as entrepreneurs, laborers, producers, homemakers, etc. (Figure). Vulnerabilities cut across domains of life and psychological elements (thinking, feeling, etc.). Women smallholder farmers living in the context of poverty in developing countries tend to encounter four structural drivers that underpin their marginalization: an inadequate asset base, poor access to services and infrastructure, weak political voice, empowerment, and institutional governance, and identity-based exclusion and social norms (Mittal et al., 2016). These align with the consumer driven definition and model of vulnerability developed by Baker et al. (2005). In this case, we bring out several themes of vulnerability both external and internal with a detailed example of women in smallholder agriculture and their ability to access, purchase and benefit from agricultural technologies.

According to the Food and Agriculture Organization, women account for 60%–80% of smallholder farmers and produce 90% of the food in Sub-Saharan Africa. However, women make up only 15% of landowners, receive less than 10% of credit, and receive only 5% of agricultural extension services. By closing these input gaps, productivity in women's fields could increase by 20%–30%, lifting 180 million people out of hunger (FAO, 2011). Though we know that women farmers can benefit from agricultural technologies, we need to better understand the numerous intertwined vulnerabilities they face in accessing, adopting, and benefiting from agricultural technologies. Vulnerabilities arise from external factors such as lack of land ownership rights, access to credit and information, that prevent women from investing in better tools (Doss, 2001). They also arise from internal factors, such as low literacy levels that create barriers in learning

---

[1]This case study has been developed from data collected as part of the Appropriate Scale Mechanization Consortium funded by the USAID Feed the Future Innovation Lab for Sustainable Intensification.

from field-trainings by public agricultural extension workers or trainers from local NGOs. Furthermore, women face intra-household barriers (Alwang et al., 2001; Theis et al., 2018). In many countries, negative socio-cultural perceptions are associated with women using agricultural machinery. This is further compounded by useful technologies that are not gender sensitive in design (Manfre et al., 2017). Below, we focus on specific vulnerabilities that women smallholder farmers face in their roles as agricultural producers and consumers of agricultural technologies.

External Factors

The distribution of resources, and especially access to land tenure, is an external factor that affects the everyday lives of women smallholder farmers and is beyond their control. An individual's land tenure depends on formal legal structures at the national level, mechanisms at a local or village level, and rules at a household level (Doss, 2001). However, in rural areas customary land tenure systems are dominant over statutory laws and national strategic policies. In Sub-Saharan Africa, women comprise 49% of agricultural labor, but only 15% of agricultural land holders (USAID, 2016). Even when women do own or control land, the quality is often lower and the amount less than that owned or controlled by men.

As Doss (2001) states, poorer farmers and those with least secure tenure are less likely to invest in or adopt new technologies. Lack of land ownership creates vulnerabilities in accessing credit which requires land deeds as collateral. Without adequate funds for capital investments, women-farmers are less likely than their male counterparts to buy and use fertilizer, drought-resistant seeds, sustainable agricultural practices, and other advanced farming tools and techniques that increase crop yields (Doss, 2001). Moreover, in many instances, land tenure is required to be considered to participate in agricultural training and development projects, making most women ineligible.

A typical female smallholder farmer in Burkina Faso is responsible for planting, among other farming tasks such as weeding, harvesting, and post-harvest activities. These agricultural tasks are in addition to child-care and household tasks, such as collecting water, cooking, and fetching firewood, all of which can take up to 16 hours a day (Jones, 2019). Specifically with respect to on-farm activities such as planting, many women farmers suffer from back pain from the hours of stooped labor, and physical exhaustion from hand planting. In addition to being labor intensive, time spent on hand planting creates conflicts with women's individual entrepreneurial efforts in harvesting shea and cashew nuts, and planting on their separate plots of land (Harrigan & Jones, 2020).

Internal Factors - Cognitive and Affective Constraints

In Burkina Faso, only 31% of adult women above the age of 15 are considered literate compared to 49% with adult males (World bank, 2021). Low literacy affects functional literacy, which includes the capability of applying various skills that stretch beyond reading and writing for sufficient daily functioning as an adult (Stewart & Yap, 2020). Furthermore, it leads to a variety of constraints in the marketplace, as noted earlier, such as concrete and pictographic thinking and, in a sense, cognitive survival. Men and women smallholder farmers need to have access to the information, skills, and tools they need to improve their yields and have economic growth (Manfre et al., 2013). However, low literacy levels create vulnerability for women smallholder farmers who tend to avoid attending information and training programs that discuss new technologies and methods. Lack of understanding or know-why prevents learning and learning how to learn. Understanding basic concepts and their relationships in agriculture as well in marketplace literacy are challenging (e.g., post-harvest-loss-prevention and consequences; value chain and selling alternatives). For instance, immediate financial needs may lead to borrowing on credit and giving harvested crops in return, preventing secure storage and sale timed for optimal market conditions. The latter requires understanding of how marketplaces work, from individual concepts such as value chains and relationships between them. Thus, the very notion of post-harvest prevention through proper storage may not arise due to a combination of low income and low literacy.

Compounding these cognitive factors are affective ones, such as lack of self-confidence due to low literacy, low exposure, socio-cultural norms and so forth. Women can be shamed for engaging in some agricultural activities. Despite the immense time-consuming amount of work done, women smallholder farmers are limited by strong socio-cultural norms. For example, a typical woman smallholder farmer in Bangladesh faces barriers in marketing and cannot sell in the marketplace. Their capabilities (Sen, 2005) are inhibited by cultural norms surrounding travel (i.e., cannot travel outside their communities without a male chaperone). Even when women sell agricultural produce to a local trader, they face the "unjust price" issue, receiving a lower price than what it could be sold for at the local market (Lee et al., 2022). Moreover, when a household is invited, women smallholder farmers tend to discredit their ability to understand educational events and do not participate in learning opportunities. This lack of access to extension services is further compounded by factors such as biases of extension providers who may not consider women as capable of making key farming decisions and leave them out of such activities.

Implications

The case study illustrates the intertwined nature of vulnerabilities across domains of life, across roles, and across psychological elements (Figure). It also illustrates the external and internal factors that can contribute vulnerabilities. Most importantly, it points to the need to move away from defining "vulnerable consumers" from a blanket categorization based on gender and gender-related capabilities. It also shows the need to move toward a nuanced view of vulnerabilities with a bottom-up perspective which helps one identify what makes one vulnerable – for example, lack of land ownership or lack of knowledge and education. Such nuanced understanding of vulnerabilities can enable policy makers and the private sector to take specific action steps to minimize vulnerabilities faced by women smallholder farmers in accessing mechanization.

Public policy efforts can be designed to move consumers from situational vulnerability to "normalcy" (Baker et al., 2005). In the context of agricultural mechanization, establishing women-only farmer groups to train women in new agricultural technologies is one approach that can address vulnerabilities arising from lack of access to training, information, credit, and training for low-literate consumers. For example, in women farmer's unions in Bangladesh, developed for the purpose of promoting mechanization, preliminary findings showed that women, including those traditionally facing many vulnerabilities, can take a lead in innovation processes with improved policy initiatives (Farnworth et al., 2019).

The private sector also plays an important role in minimizing vulnerabilities. Affordable financing mechanisms for accessing or purchasing equipment will enable both male and female smallholder farmers to purchase technologies. Ergonomically designed technology and convenient availability are among the attributes that can address vulnerabilities (Theis et al., 2019). In this regard, marketplace literacy education customized to agriculture and specific technologies is an important ingredient in enabling development of know-why in the agricultural realm and enhancing capabilities.

CONCLUSION

We note a number of aspects relating to the *what*, *how*, and *why* of consumer vulnerabilities. As noted, vulnerabilities for subsistence consumers span material, cognitive, emotional, and behavioral aspects in all domains of subsistence. Their deprivations and vulnerabilities are on multiple fronts, essentially all domains of subsistence. As such, they represent a confluence of vulnerabilities encompassing internal and external factors noted in Baker's framework. These vulnerabilities are intertwined and interactive, compounding the challenging circumstances that subsistence consumers face. In this regard, our approach relates to studying the entirety of subsistence holistically. Thus, we have unpacked poverty in terms of not only the material, but the cognitive, affective, behavioral, social, and cultural aspects.

Moreover, we study the multiple roles that consumers play in the marketplace, such as by being entrepreneurs themselves. Thus, we examine vulnerabilities as they play out broadly in marketplace interactions. The duality of consumer-entrepreneur roles and the related vulnerabilities from the latter when playing the former role is noteworthy.

We also emphasize the importance of studying both vulnerabilities and strengths or capabilities. Thus, the relational richness and one to one interactional environment leads to ways to overcome vulnerabilities through gaining marketplace literacy. This leads to a second aspect, how vulnerabilities in such contexts can be studied. We have employed a unique bottom-up approach focusing on both vulnerabilities and strengths or capabilities. We emphasize the term, marketplaces, here rather than markets, to bring out the need to understand these contexts in their own right, rather than as a means to an end. Understanding at the micro-level provides the basis to then examine vulnerabilities in day-to-day life at a granular level.

We have designed and delivered marketplace literacy to address the most fundamental vulnerabilities. We have also embarked on what we refer to as symbiotic academic-social enterprise (Viswanathan et al., 2020), sustained engagement in practice beyond the timeframe of a single project and enabling circular and highly integrated relationships between research and practice (as well as education). As such, we are able to continuously examine how vulnerabilities are overcome, in turn leading to other challenges. We are humbled by how marketplace literacy is one lever that women in these contexts amplify manifold in confronting multi-faceted vulnerabilities. We note a number of areas where the urge to overreach or overstate should be tempered. Vulnerabilities in poverty are accentuated by uncertainties in daily life and the lack of a margin of error. As such, multi-faceted vulnerabilities can manifest at any time and our solution is merely one ingredient. A much larger or more immediate vulnerability can overtake at any time. This is the nature of uncertainty and risk, all the more germane with the lack of a margin of error. Moreover, a variety of socio-economic inequalities can be insurmountable obstacles, such as lack of exposure, access, or safety for women due to sociocultural norms and other factors. As illustrated in the opening example, women are vulnerable on a multitude of fronts in subsistence marketplaces. Addressing their challenges would involve concerted effort on multiple fronts, with marketplace literacy being but one ingredient. We should also note that individual differences in such factors as the basic level of low to moderate literacy or of access and exposure to marketplaces lead to differences in outcomes as well. Unfortunately, such barriers may make it very difficult for some participants to be an entrepreneur or even an informed consumer.

Our research, while touching on a variety of vulnerabilities, specifically in subsistence marketplaces, is but one slice of the complex phenomenon. As literature in consumer behavior other areas have highlighted (Hill & Sharma, 2020); there are myriad intersections between such factors as race, gender, socio-economic status and so forth. Overlaying the internal and external factors and types of vulnerability, we highlight the need for studying this phenomenon in terms of roles, functions and domains of life.

In conclusion, we demonstrate the nuanced nature of vulnerabilities in subsistence marketplaces, emphasizing the need to examine interactions and interrelationships across domains of life, psychological elements, roles, and so forth. We do so by adopting a bottom-up approach to examining life circumstance holistically, beginning at the micro-level.

REFERENCES

Abdelnour, S., & Branzei, O. (2010). Fuel-efficient stoves for Darfur: The social construction of subsistence marketplaces in post-conflict settings. *Journal of Business Research*, *63*(6), 617–629. https://doi.org/10.1016/j.jbusres.2009.04.027

Alwang, J., Siegel, P., & Jorgensen, S. (2001). *Vulnerability: A view from different disciplines*. Special Discussion Paper No. 0115 23304. The World Bank.

Aly, H., Mason, K., & Onyas, W. (2020). The institutional work of a social enterprise operating in a subsistence marketplace: Using the business model as a market-shaping tool. *Journal of Consumer Affairs, 55*(1), 31–58. https://doi.org/10.1111/joca.12335

Azmat, F., Ferdous, A. S., & Couchman, P. (2015). Understanding the dynamics between social entrepreneurship and inclusive growth in subsistence marketplaces. *Journal of Public Policy and Marketing, 34*(2), 252–271. https://doi.org/10.1509/jppm.14.150

Azmat, F., & Samaratunge, R. (2020). Consumer Well-being and social responsibility of subsistence entrepreneurs in subsistence marketplace. *Journal of Consumer Affairs, 55*(1), 8–30. https://doi.org/10.1111/joca.12308

Baker, S. M., Gentry, J. W., & Rittenburg, T. L. (2005). Building understanding of the domain of consumer vulnerability. *Journal of Macromarketing, 25*(2), 128–139. https://doi.org/10.1177/0276146705280622

Banerjee, A., & Duflo, E. (2007). The economic lives of the poor. *The Journal of Economic Perspectives. 21*(1), 141–167. https://doi.org/10.1257/jep.21.1.141

Bankoff, G., Frerks, G., Hilhorst, D., & Cardona, O. (2004), The need for rethinking the concepts of vulnerability and risk from a holistic perspective: A necessary review and criticism or effective risk management (pp. 37–51). In *Mapping vulnerability: Disasters, development, and people.* Earthscan.

Barrios, A., & Blocker, C. P. (2015). The contextual value of social capital for subsistence entrepreneur mobility. *Journal of Public Policy and Marketing, 34*(2), 272–286. https://doi.org/10.1509/jppm.14.167

Bearden, W., Hardesty, D., & Rose, R. (2001). Consumer self-confidence: Refinements in conceptualization and measurement. *Journal of Consumer Research, 28*(1), 121–134. https://doi.org/10.1086/321951

Bilo, C. (2017). Psycho-socio consequences of poverty – Why it's important to talk about shame. https://socialprotection.org/discover/blog/psycho-socio-consequences-poverty-%E2%80%93-why-it%E2%80%99s-important-talk-about-shame. Accessed on June 19, 2022.

Bouris, K. (2012, November 27). Brené Brown: How vulnerability holds the key... Spirituality & Health. https://www.spiritualityhealth.com/articles/2012/11/27/bren%C3%A9-brown-how-vulnerability-holds-key-emotional-intimacy. Accessed on June 19, 2022.

Brown, B. (2006). Shame resilience theory: A grounded theory study on women and shame. *The Journal of Contemporary Social Services, 87*(1), 43–52.

Brown, B. (2013). *Daring greatly: How the courage to be vulnerable transforms the way we live, love, parent and lead.* Portfolio Penguin.

Cardona, O.-D., van Aalst, M. K., Birkmann, J., Fordham, M., McGregor, G., Perez, R., Pulwarty, R. S., Schipper, E. L. F., Sinh, B. T., Décamps, H., Keim, M., Davis, I., Ebi, K. L., Lavell, A., Mechler, R., Murray, V., Pelling, M., Pohl, J., Smith, A.-O., & Thomalla, F. (2012). Determinants of risk: Exposure and vulnerability. In C. Field, V. Barros, T. Stocker, & Q. Dahe (Eds.), *Managing the risks of extreme events and disasters to advance climate change adaptation: Special report of the intergovernmental panel on climate change* (pp. 65–108). Cambridge University Press. https://doi.org/10.1017/CBO9781139177245.005

Chakrabarti, R. (2021). Why art matters: Artistic consumer-entrepreneurship in subsistence marketplaces. *Journal of Consumer Affairs, 55*(1), 134–150. https://doi.org/10.1111/joca.12345

Chikweche, T., & Fletcher, R. (2010). Understanding factors that influence purchases in subsistence markets. *Journal of Business Research, 63*(6), 643–650. https://doi.org/10.1016/j.jbusres.2009.04.024

Corus, C., & Ozanne, J. L. (2012). Stakeholder engagement: Building participatory and deliberative spaces in subsistence markets. *Journal of Business Research, 65*(12), 1728–1735.

Doss, C. (2001). Designing agricultural technology for African women farmers: Lessons from 25 Years of experience. *World Development, 29*(12), 2075–2092. ISSN 0305-750X. https://doi.org/10.1016/S0305-750X(01)00088-2

Farnworth, C., Jafry, T., Rahman, S., & Badstue, L. (2019). Leaving no one behind: How women seize control of wheat–maize technologies in Bangladesh. *Canadian Journal of Development Studies/Revue Canadienne d'Études du Developpement.* https://doi.org/10.1080/02255189.2019.1650332

Food and Agriculture Organization. (2011). *Women in Agriculture: Closing the gender gap in development. The state of food and agriculture, 2010–2011*. Food and Agriculture Organization.

Harrigan, T., & Jones, M. (2020). "Now we can breathe." The impact of a mechanical maize planter on smallholder women farmers in Burkina Faso. *Feed the Future*. https://www.agrilinks.org/sites/default/files/media/file/Burkina%20Faso%20Planter%20Impact%20on%20Women_0.pdf

Hill, R. P. (1991). Homeless women, special possessions, and the meaning of "home": An ethnographic case study. *Journal of Consumer Research, 18*(December), 298–310.

Hill, R. P., & Sharma, E. (2020). Consumer vulnerability. *Journal of Consumer Psychology, 30*(3), 551–570.

Jones, M. (2019). *Gender assessment of early-stage seed planter technology in Burkina Faso*. Technical Report. https://agrilinks.org/sites/default/files/resources/jones_2019_planter_burkina_faso_tech_profile_final.pdf

Kross, E., Berman, M. G., Mischel, W., Smith, E. E., & Wager, T. D. (2011). Social rejection shares somatosensory representations with physical pain. *Proceedings of the National Academy of Sciences, 108*(15), 6270–6275.

Lee, H. B., McNamara, P. M., & Bhattacharyya, K. (2022). Does linking women farmers to markets improve food security? Evidence from rural Bangladesh. *Agriculture & Food Security, 11*(1), 33. https://doi.org/10.1186/s40066-022-00373-6

Lindbom, H., Tehler, H., Eriksson, K., & Aven, T. (2015). The capability concept – On how to define and describe capability in relation to risk, vulnerability and resilience. *Reliability Engineering & System Safety, 135*, 45–54.

Manfre, C., Rubin, D., Allen, A. M., Summerfield, G., Colverson, K. E., & Akeredolu, M. (2013). *Reducing the gender gap in agricultural extension and advisory services. How to find the best fit for men and women farmers*. Discussion Paper, Modernizing Extension and Advisory Services. United States Agency for International Development (USAID) project. https://www.meas-extension.org

Manfre, C., Rubin, D., & Nordehn, C. (2017). *Assessing how agricultural technologies can change gender dynamics and food security outcomes*. Cultural Practice Toolkit. USAID.

Merriam-Webster. (n.d.). Vulnerable definition & meaning. https://www.merriam-webster.com/dictionary/vulnerable. Accessed on June 19, 2022.

Mittal, N., Pereram, N., & Korkeala, O. (2016). *Leaving no-one behind in the climate and environment context. Evidence on demand*. DFID. https://assets.publishing.service.gov.uk/media/58483145e5274a130300005f/EOD_LNB_Learning_Materials_FINAL.pdf

Robeyns, I. (2005). The capability approach: A theoretical survey. *Journal of Human Development, 6*(1), 93–117. https://doi.org/10.1080/14649880520034266

Robeyns, I., & Byskov, M. F. (2020, December 10). *The capability approach*. Stanford Encyclopedia of Philosophy. https://plato.stanford.edu/entries/capability-approach/. Accessed on June 26, 2022.

Sen, A. (1985). *Commodities and capabilities*. North-Holland.

Sen, A. (2005). Human rights and capabilities. *Journal of Human Development, 6*(2), 151–161.

Stewart, C. R., & Yap, S.-F. (2020). Low literacy, policy and consumer vulnerability: Are we really doing enough? *International Journal of Consumer Studies, 44*, 343–352.

Theis, S., Krupnik, T. J., Sultana, N., Rahman, S.-U., Seymour, G., & Abedin, N. (2019). *Gender and agricultural mechanization: A mixed-methods exploration of the impacts of multi-crop reaper-harvester service provision in Bangladesh*. International Food Policy Research Institute.

Theis, S., LeforeMeinzen-Dick, N. R., & Bryan, E. (2018). What happens after technology adoption? Gendered aspects of small-scale irrigation technologies in Ethiopia, Ghana, and Tanzania. *Agriculture and Human Values, 35*. https://doi.org/10.1007/s10460-018-9862-8

Toledo, A., de la Paz Hernández, J., & Griffin, D. (2010). Incentives and the growth of Oaxacan subsistence businesses. *Journal of Business Research, 63*(6), 630–638.

USAID. (2016). *Fact sheet: Land tenure and women's empowerment*. https://www.land-links.org/issue-brief/fact-sheet-land-tenure-womens-empowerment/

Venugopal, S., & Viswanathan, M. (2017). The subsistence marketplace approach to poverty: Implications for marketing theory. *Marketing Theory*. https://doi.org/10.1177/1470593117704282

Viswanathan, M. (2013). *Subsistence Marketplaces*. eBook partnership, eText, and Stipes Publishing.

Viswanathan, M. (2016). *Bottom-up enterprise: Insights from subsistence marketplaces*. eBook partnership, eText, and Stipes Publishing.

Viswanathan, M., Baskentli, S., Gallage, S., Grigortsuk, M., Martin, D., & Subrahmanyan, S. (2020). A demonstration of symbiotic academic-social enterprise in subsistence marketplaces: Researching and designing customized sustainability literacy education in Tanzania. *Journal of Public Policy and Marketing, 40*(2), 245–261.

Viswanathan, M., Gajendiran, S., & Venkatesan, R. (2008). *Enabling consumer and entrepreneurial literacy in subsistence marketplaces.* Springer.

Viswanathan, M., Jung, K., Venugopal, S., Minefee, I., & Jung, I. W. (2014). Subsistence and sustainability: From micro-level behavioral insights to macro level implications on consumption and the environment. *Journal of Macromarketing, 34*(1), 8–27.

Viswanathan, M., & Rosa, J. (2007). Product and market development for subsistence marketplaces: Consumption and entrepreneurship beyond literacy and resource barriers. In J. Rosa & M. Viswanathan (Eds.), *Product and market development for subsistence marketplaces: Consumption and entrepreneurship beyond literacy and resource barriers* (pp. 1–17). *Advances in International Management Series,* Joseph Cheng and Michael Hitt, Series Editors. Elsevier.

Viswanathan, M., Rosa, J., & Harris, J. (2005). Decision-making and coping by functionally illiterate consumers and some implications for marketing management. *Journal of Marketing, 69*(1), 15–31.

Viswanathan, M., Rosa, J., & Ruth, J. (2010). Exchanges in marketing systems: The case of subsistence consumer merchants in Chennai, India. *Journal of Marketing, 74*(May), 1–18.

Viswanathan, M., Seth, A., Gau, R., & Chaturvedi, A. (2009). Internalizing social good into business processes in subsistence marketplaces: The sustainable market orientation. *Journal of Macromarketing, 29*, 406–425.

Viswanathan, M., Sridharan, S., Ritchie, R., Venugopal, S., & Jung, K. (2012). Marketing interactions in subsistence marketplaces: A bottom-up approach to designing public policy. *Journal of Public Policy and Marketing, 31*(2), 159–177.

Viswanathan, M., Umashankar, N., Sreekumar, A., & Goreczny, A. (2021). Marketplace literacy as a pathway to a better world: Evidence from field experiments in low-access subsistence marketplaces. *Journal of Marketing, 85*(3), 113–129. https://doi.org/10.1177/0022242921998385

World Bank. (2021). *Literacy rate, adult female (% of females aged 15 and above) Burkina Faso.* UNESCO Institute for Statistics. World Bank Data. Accessed on June 2022.

Zagorac, I. (2017). What vulnerability? Whose vulnerability? Conflict of understandings in the debate on vulnerability. *Facta Universitatis-Law and Politics, 15*(2), 157–169.

A CONSUMER VULNERABILITY PERSPECTIVE ON EVICTION

David Crockett[a], Lenita Davis[b] and Casey Carder-Rockwell[c]

[a]University of Illinois Chicago, USA
[b]University of Wisconsin Eau Claire, USA
[c]University of Arkansas-Little Rock, USA

ABSTRACT

Scholars, activists, and policymakers have paid increasing attention to housing instability, especially where eviction is a cause. Housing instability is a dynamic process rather than a discrete catastrophic event, and eviction imposes vulnerability on consumers. Even the threat of it can trigger the onset of a crisis. In this project, we deepen the understanding of eviction by exploring its use in property management practice. We begin by summarizing its definition and causes from a cross-disciplinary and still-evolving literature. We then provide an extended example of how eviction can be used to pursue strategic and financial goals using rental markets in Arkansas as an example. Arkansas is characterized by a quintessentially laissez-faire regulatory environment that imposes few restrictions on property owners. We conclude by posing questions that should be at the forefront of a vulnerability-focused, policy-oriented research agenda on eviction.

Keywords: Eviction; housing; housing instability; Rent burdened; vulnerable consumer

INTRODUCTION

In the popular imagination, housing instability (also insecurity) refers to forced displacement causing at least a temporary loss of shelter. But in truth, it is a dynamic process rather than a discrete catastrophic occurrence (DeLuca & Rosen, 2022). For many, it is experienced as an ongoing crisis that begins with

The Vulnerable Consumer
Review of Marketing Research, Volume 21, 153–165
Copyright © 2024 David Crockett, Lenita Davis and Casey Carder-Rockwell
Published under exclusive licence by Emerald Publishing Limited
ISSN: 1548-6435/doi:10.1108/S1548-643520240000021010

the mere threat. By the time threat materializes into "doubling up" (cohabiting) or a move to an emergency shelter, crisis may already be chronic and severe.

In the United States, since the Great Recession years of the early 2000s to early 2010s, and since the Supreme Court overturned the COVID-19 eviction moratorium (Liptak & Thrush, 2021), scholars, activists, and policymakers have paid increasing attention to forced displacement from housing, especially in the form of evictions and foreclosures. Treating it as a distinct object of analysis, they seek to better understand how it generates and exacerbates crisis in ways that intersect with poverty but are not wholly reduceable to it (Desmond, 2012). But with some notable exceptions, housing instability has been a matter of tangential interest to marketing and consumer researchers (cf., Hill, 2002, 1991; Hill & Stamey, 1990). This is an unfortunate oversight, both substantive and conceptual.

Substantively, acquiring adequate housing is a consumption act that directly affects life satisfaction (see Hill and Ramani, 2024). Further, the Office of the UN High Commissioner for Human Rights (2023) recognizes it as a human right and characterizes it as the "basis of stability and security for an individual or family." Yet housing instability from forced displacement, specifically tenant eviction, is an increasingly common outcome in the United States, one of the world's wealthiest economies. An estimated 7% of the US tenant population – roughly 2.7 million people – is threatened with forced displacement annually (Gromis et al., 2022). This is a fundamental consumer vulnerability based on Hill and Sharma's (2020, p. 554) definition: harm due to restricted access to and control over resources sufficient to function in the marketplace. Displacement most often results in lower quality, costlier housing (Desmond, 2012). Some preliminary evidence suggests that it also reduces durables consumption generally by worsening access to credit (Humphries et al., 2019). More distressingly, displacement is directly associated with increased exposure to premature death. To wit, Graetz et al. (2024) associate three displacement factors with double-digit percentage increases in all-cause mortality: a high rent burden, a large increase in rent burden, and a (prejudgment) eviction filing. In a similar vein, based on data from the National Violent Death Reporting System, Fowler et al. (2015) find that eviction- and foreclosure-related suicides doubled during the Great Recession years (2005–2010), from 88 to 176. Notably, that the three factors and nearly 80% of these suicides occur predisplacement strongly implicates displacement threat in exposure to premature death. Another source of exposure is neighborhood destabilization. Displacement makes neighborhoods more dangerous for the residents who remain. Semenza et al. (2022) associate eviction rates in Philadelphia neighborhoods with homicide specifically but associate other types of crime (e.g., robbery) with neighborhood poverty. These facts all suggest an urgent need for marketing and consumer researchers to focus scholarly attention on housing instability. Yet the disciplinary inattention to it is also a conceptual oversight, as the logics that govern rental housing markets appear to be undergoing a pronounced shift with financialization and digitization (see Fields, 2022). For this additional reason, displacement (especially eviction) warrants focused attention from marketing and consumer researchers.

Perceptions of what rental housing means and how rental markets should operate are grounded in competing "rights" and "commodity" logics (Patillo, 2013). People use logics, which are material and symbolic principles used to interpret reality (Thornton & Ocasio, 1999). Historically, commodity logic is more diffused throughout US housing markets, where ownership is openly privileged over tenancy in law and custom (Dreier, 1982, 1984). In most ways, the United States subjugates property's sheltering function to the whims of ownership.[1] Thus, it does not affirm the UN's claim that adequate housing is a human right. Such a right obligates states to ensure its provision. Instead, the US has long affirmed the rights of property; namely that an owner may sell it for use as shelter and may displace users at will subject to limitations. In the first two decades of the 21st century, the extent of this commodity logic's dominance over human rights logic is increasing, given skyrocketing rent burdens and the displacement that inevitably follows. Using data compiled by the real estate industry, Campisi and Baille (2022) report that the overall median monthly rent in the United States increased over 23% from July 2020 to July 2022. Beginning November of that year and over the ensuing 12 months, the National Eviction Lab reports over one million eviction filings across the 34 cities in 10 states that it tracks.

Marketing and consumer research are as well positioned as any discipline to generate conceptual insights into this apparent shift in market dynamics. Consequently, the purpose of this project is to explore some of the key policies, processes, and practices that would impose vulnerability in the form of displacement on consumers. Given space limitations, we forego a generalized discussion of housing instability and delimit our focus to eviction rather than foreclosure. Of course, to those displaced, the two are apt to feel similar. But foreclosure warrants its own distinct exploration because it involves competing claims on property ownership while tenancy does not. Thus, they are subject to different policies, processes, and practices. We also delimit our focus primarily to eviction's use as a management tool. In doing so, we depart from the more typical focus on antecedents to vulnerability or consumer (coping) responses to it. Rather, we take people's agency as given and, following Hill and Sharma (2020, Fig. 1), focus on the context in which vulnerability is imposed on others. We seek to explore that imposition in the context of property management, where it occurs in pursuit of strategic and financial goals. We conclude by posing questions that should be at the forefront of a vulnerability-focused, policy-oriented research agenda on eviction.

WHAT IS EVICTION?

A discussion of eviction should begin with tenancy, its presumed opposite state. Tenancy emerged in the United States as a meaningful legal and sociocultural

---

[1]Contrast this with the strict limits placed on property owners in other contexts. States routinely limit claims to natural resources located on private property (e.g., precious metals, oil, protected species, etc.). Likewise, local governments use zoning and eminent domain powers to restrict the ways and purposes for which property can be used.

identity with the application of English common law to sharecropping (Hatch, 2017). Due in no small part to this history, rental agreements still generally offer fewer legal protections to tenants than mortgage-backed deeds offer to homeowners. Where the "homeowner" is revered and openly favored in tax codes, the tenant is broadly and persistently stigmatized as lower in status, even morally inferior (Dreier, 1982; Hatch, 2017). Obviously, the extent can vary. The Manhattan high rise tenant is not stigmatized at all while the rural mobile home owner is stigmatized heavily (e.g., Saatcioglu & Ozanne, 2013). But among tenants, eviction stigma does not vary. It is universally legible as a marker of "last place" or lowest status, a fact reinforced by the demographic composition of those most threatened by and living with eviction (Crowell, 2022; Desmond, 2016). Graetz et al. (2023, p. 3, Fig. 2) estimate that Blacks, while comprising just over 18% of renters in the US, account for over 51% of those threatened with eviction and over 43% of actual evictions.

As noted, contemporary research on eviction has broadened beyond a limited initial focus on the moment forced displacement materializes to encompass the entire process of rent burden and arrearage. In this process-oriented view, eviction begins when the threat of it becomes salient (Garboden & Rosen, 2019). In this view, tenancy and eviction are not conceptual negations on opposite sides of a notice or court filing. Rather, they are mutually reinforcing sets of policies, practices, and processes. Interested actors can marshal them to protect tenants from displacement threat or to enhance the threat. For instance, a tenant receiving a government rent subsidy may benefit from robust enforcement of tenant protections because they also receive routine visits from a social worker. An unsubsidized renter with no visiting social worker may be less able to access those protections. So, should they, for instance, advocate for needed repairs, a landlord might raise their eviction threat by vigorously sanctioning them for minor rental agreement violations (e.g., noise), thereby creating a pretext for an eviction filing. In other words, eviction is a messy process insofar as it is commonly multi-sited and multivocal (Desmond, 2016). Eviction filings in court can come to a swift resolution or none at all, and even the former does not always neatly comport with any particular notion of justice. Indeed, some eviction filers hope to avoid court judgment. Instead, they use court filings as leverage to extract rent, fees, and other concessions (Garboden & Rosen, 2019). Moreover, landlords can use eviction filings in conjunction with an array of widely available digitized property management tools to increase their leverage (Fields, 2022). Consider that in 2023, the US Department of Justice joined a class action lawsuit that accuses RealPage, creator of a popular algorithm-driven property management tool, of using it to facilitate price-fixing among landlords (see Vogell, 2023).

Much recent eviction scholarship situates it (and housing instability) into the broader, meso-level process of neighborhood mobility (DeLuca & Rosen, 2022). A longstanding assumption is that mobility to better resourced residential environments is a key tactic for alleviating household disadvantage. Moving to a neighborhood with even modest comparative resource advantages can have outsized effects on well-being. Consequently, scholars are most attentive to movement from high-disadvantage neighborhoods to better resourced ones. To illustrate, Manduca and Sampson (2019) show that growing up in high-disadvantage Chicago-area census tract neighborhoods – those characterized by exposure to concentrated violence, incarceration, and lead – predicts low intergenerational income mobility and high adult incarceration. They attribute 20%–60% of the racial disparity in these outcomes to differing rates of exposure to high-disadvantage conditions. Racial disparities persist at every income level because Chicago neighborhoods are racially segregated to such a degree that virtually all majority-Black census tracts are exposed to these hazards while hardly any majority-White ones are. Unfortunately, by far the most common mobility type is to other high-disadvantage neighborhoods or worse-resourced ones, and eviction is the primary impetus for such moves (Desmond, 2016; Hartman & Robinson, 2003). We summarize recent scholarship from multiple disciplines that pivots around this central insight.

What causes eviction? A rental agreement violation causes eviction in the narrowest sense, but this belies the notion that eviction is better understood as the process of evicting (Garboden & Rosen, 2019). Baker (2021) highlights research across a range of disciplines that offer economic, political, and technological explanations for a variety of forced displacement types including eviction. Economic explanations are typically macro-structural and emphasize displacement's central role in wealth accumulation (e.g., Harvey, 2004). To illustrate, contemporary financialized mortgages link the house-as-property to global financial markets, where investors pursue ever-greater returns (Baker, 2021, p. 799). Eviction empowers property owners with the flexibility to alter direction to align themselves with such pursuits. That may be through converting traditional rental property into Airbnb-style short-term rentals that can cannibalize the former (Li et al., 2022). Political explanations, like economic ones, are typically macrostructural and focus on the state's wide-ranging role in facilitating or restricting wealth accumulation (Baker, 2021). Where they have implications for tenants and landlords, this can involve the content of legislation/regulation and enforcement. It can also involve those persons or groups targeted by the state for restriction or for its largesse. Technological explanations for displacement, which emphasize how displacement occurs, are closely associated with a process-oriented view. They focus on the mundane objects and practices that perform the work, such as court documents, software tools, platforms, and systems design (Baker, 2021, p. 805).

How does eviction happen? A common line of inquiry in eviction research explores the practice of evicting by drawing attention to observable settings and practices that better unpack the process. To illustrate one such practice, consider that landlords with the same tenant base can be differently prone to "serial filing." This refers to having a high-frequency or high-likelihood of submitting an eviction filing in court. In some markets, a comparatively small proportion of landlords initiate most eviction filings (Gomory, 2022; Rutan & Desmond, 2021). Further, as noted, many serial filers do not necessarily seek tenant removal. Rather, they use filing as leverage to alter the terms of a rental agreement to extract fee revenue or discourage tenants from lease renewal, which can maximize rent increases (Crowell, 2022; Leung et al., 2021). Ethnographic and interview-based approaches that focus on interpersonal interactions are likely best suited to uncovering such leveraging tactics (Desmond, 2012; Garboden & Rosen, 2019). However, analysis of archival data like court filings can show the prevalence of serial filing by landlord type. Gomory (2022) documents two to three times the rate of serial filing among corporate (vs. small) landlords, and that such filings are commonly over smaller amounts of money in arrears. A proliferation of corporate owners managing widely dispersed properties increasingly utilize digitized products that systematize the management function; a phenomenon Fields (2022) labels the "automated landlord." Thus, serial filing is increasingly likely to be algorithm-driven rather than emergent from interpersonal interaction with tenants. Nevertheless, nonserial filing remains a stronger predictor of eviction and is most prevalent among small landlords (Immergluck et al., 2020). When these landlords file, they are more apt to be seeking resolution in court rather than leverage, which makes displacement a more likely outcome. Given the high eviction rates cited elsewhere, it should not surprise that Black neighborhoods have substantially higher nonserial filing rates, net other factors. Additionally, investor-owned properties have high nonserial filing rates. For instance, in Detroit, a city hard-hit by the foreclosure crisis, where demand for affordable single-family housing well exceeds the supply, investor owners are turning foreclosed/distressed houses into rental properties. Many have favored a high-tenant-turnover model, which can be quite lucrative (Seymour & Akers, 2021).

To sum, the study of eviction as a process has the potential to carry on the long-standing tradition of marketing and consumer research in the public interest. Accounting for the full process – inclusive of public policy and managerial practices that generate harm for renters through displacement and limiting mobility – has clear implications for researchers interested in consumer vulnerability. Likewise, a consumer vulnerability perspective that privileges understanding the context that produces constraint, per Hill and Sharma (2020), rather than merely describes who is constrained and by how much, can deepen our understanding of the eviction process. An explicit accounting of the role that (local) rental markets play in the eviction process is only beginning to emerge. To illustrate it, we turn next to a brief exploration of eviction at it unfolds in the state of Arkansas.

EVICTING AS A SOCIAL PROBLEM: AN ILLUSTRATION FROM ARKANSAS

We outline a few features of rental markets in Arkansas that we consider to be vulnerability imposing on renters. We focus specifically on features of the state's regulatory environment to help illustrate.

Given space limitations, we highlight only features of the regulatory environment that formally oversee tenancy and shape property management in ways that impose vulnerability on renters. As this is not intended to be a formal case analysis or evaluation, we do not represent Arkansas as in any way "typical" of US rental markets (even presuming such a thing exists). Rather, we chose the state because it illustrates a quality of interest quite well. Its prevailing regulatory features are vulnerability imposing because they allow eviction threat to be relatively easily triggered. The state government's approach to regulating rental markets is quintessentially laissez-faire. Fewer than 10 state-level laws regulate rental markets, and they largely limit landlord obligations and liability. Additionally, the largest local rental markets do not feature stronger tenant protections, as in some states with large population centers.

Hatch (2017) introduces a typology of policy archetypes that regulate rental markets that conform to three distinct approaches to state law: protectionist (favors tenants), probusiness (favors landlords), and contradictory (favors both). Laws and regulations governing rental markets cover one or more of: pricing (e.g., rent control, security deposit ceilings), health/safety (e.g., warranty of habitability, utility shutoff), rental unit possession (e.g., lease duration, reasonable access), and discrimination. Hatch (2017, p. 110, Fig. 5) identifies 13 "protectionist" states with comprehensive tenant protection, 17 "probusiness" states with limited tenant protection, and 20 "contradictory" states that usually favor tenants in health/safety and (dis)possession but display no discernible pattern in pricing or discrimination. Arkansas is probusiness. Notably, and perhaps surprisingly, based on available data from the Eviction Lab, Arkansas has among the lowest displacement rates despite a high poverty rate (14%) and high rent burden, averaging 29.5% of income in 2016 (Dewitt, 2020).

Pricing regulation and extracting revenue premiums. As noted, the threat of eviction can create opportunities for extracting revenue above monthly rent. Arkansas' probusiness regulatory environment, as established by Arkansas Code §17 and 18, the Residential Landlord-Tenant Act of 2007, facilitates such opportunities, typically as penalties for arrearage and other damages with no reciprocal duty to initiate repairs or maintain property (Arkansas Code of 1987). Although penalties for non-/late payment and damages can be found in any regulatory environment, Arkansas allows landlords and tenants to agree to any terms not expressly prohibited by law and prohibits few. Although the Act, which regulates tenant evictions statewide, does not grant rental agreements the formal status of adhesion contracts whose provisions can be modified by the offering party, it gives landlords broad latitude to set penalties or other provisions except where plainly forbidden or unreasonably one-sided. Tenants are free to negotiate these terms but must ultimately accept agreements subject to them or "as is."

To illustrate, consider the security deposit, which is a key rental agreement provision, and typically collected at or before occupancy. They protect landlords from property damage and are usually subject to tenant protections from wrongful forfeiture. Thus, per the Arkansas Attorney General website, they are capped at the value of two months' rent. But the Act gives landlords wide latitude to claim deposits at the time of displacement, as outlined in §18-16-301 to §18-16-306, based on property damage or other violations of a rental agreement in the landlord's determination. They have 60 days from the time of displacement to return the deposit to the tenant, less any portion seized for accrued unpaid rent and any itemized list of damages. The Act considers a landlord compliant if they send the deposit (less itemized deductions) to the tenant's last known address, which may be the residence most recently vacated. The deposit is forfeited to the landlord 180 days from the date of payment, assuming a "reasonable effort" to find the tenant.

The penalties for landlords who violate their obligation can be substantial, including liability to the tenant for twice any wrongfully withheld amount, plus court costs, and tenant's attorney's fees. However, these penalties only apply to landlords acting in bad faith. In fact, the obligation to return a tenant's security deposit in 60 days applies only to large landlords – those with at least five dwellings available for rent that are not owner managed (Porter, 2023). Tenants renting from the modal small landlord who self-manages one or a few properties are not entitled to deposit protections. They must initiate a lawsuit to recoup a wrongfully withheld deposit.

Possession, health/safety regulation and cost reduction. The landlord-favoring regulatory environment in Arkansas is further evidenced in the enforcement of health and safety protections. To wit, Arkansas is one of only a few states with no implied warranty of habitability, and it only partially complies with the Uniform Residential Landlord and Tenant Act (URLTA) of 1972. The Act, drafted by the National Conference of Commissioners and on Uniform State Laws (1972), is a sample law intended to be adopted by states. It was established to standardize landlord-tenant law and rental market experiences across the states that to date has been adopted in whole or in part in fewer than 30 states (National Center for Healthy Housing, 2008). URLTA does not expressly renounce commodity logic but pushes it to clearly define landlords' and tenants' respective rights and obligations.

Per an overview by the National Center for Healthy Housing (2008), URLTA requires landlords to provide basic services to ensure the habitability of rental property, including the maintenance of all electrical, air-conditioning, and plumbing systems, among other facilities and appliances, and the removal of waste products. It establishes an implied warranty of habitability that requires landlords to act to make and keep premises habitable. This includes compliance with applicable housing/building codes, repair and upkeep of the entire premises including common areas, maintenance of electrical, plumbing, HVAC, and sanitary systems, waste and rubbish removal, and water. Moreover, collection of rent is contingent on fulfillment of these obligations. Where landlords do not comply, tenants are protected through various remedies, including termination of lease, withholding rent, making necessary repairs, and deducting cost from rent, and others. Likewise, URLTA and its 2015 revision (RURLTA) stipulates appropriate conduct for tenants and requires their compliance with explicit-stated landlord rules. Landlord remedies include eviction and recovery of damages but require due process.

The Arkansas Residential Landlord-Tenant Act of 2007 only adopts URLTA's pro-landlord provisions and none of its tenant protections. The Act plainly copies URLTA's tenant obligations to maintain the property but imposes no duty on landlords to perform repairs or otherwise ensure habitability for the tenant. Following an extensive review of landlord-tenant law in Arkansas, and in other US states relative to the provision in URLTA, the Arkansas Non-Legislative Commission on the Study of Landlord-Tenant Laws (2012, 19) noted in their report that "Arkansas does not recognize the right of tenants to safe, habitable conditions... a landlord has no duty of repair unless the landlord expressly agrees to such in the lease."

The laissez-faire commodity logic underlying Arkansas' approach to regulating rental markets is based on the presumption that market forces are sufficient to discipline landlords whose offers do not meet acceptable standards. In other words, if potential tenants find a dwelling unsuitable, they will not live in it. Thus, an implied warranty of habitability would pervert local rental markets by imposing undue costs on landlords and raise rental rates in a low-income state. The low average rent in Arkansas – The World Population Review estimates rent at $745/mo for a 1-bedroom apartment in 2022 – reflects its low median income (as rent burden is still high). However, the existence of implied warranties of habitability in other low average rent states (below $700/month) like West Virginia, Montana, and Oklahoma severely undermines this argument. Arkansas was the only state where landlords had no implied warranty of habitability prior to 2019. The state relied instead on existing local housing codes that require landlords to maintain properties. However, such codes exist only in the state's largest cities. Even there, regulatory response to code violations is typically prolonged. Meanwhile, tenants have little recourse other than court if they are threatened with retaliatory eviction, which is not expressly prohibited by law.

The regulatory environment in Arkansas is not replicated everywhere, but features of it are present in many rental markets across the United States. It is a startling illustration of a status quo, where high rent burdens trigger eviction threat and property owners are incentivized to raise that threat even further with little on the horizon to inspire hope of change. Moreover, the question of what is to be done is no simple one. While we would support full adoption of the RURLTA standards, this alone is unlikely to solve the crisis. Thus we move next to a policy research agenda that raises the question of what is to be done for specific audiences (i.e., scholars and policy makers) and offers a few suggestions in response.

A BEHAVIORAL AND POLICY RESEARCH AGENDA ON EVICTION

For scholars generally, explorations of eviction remain in their infancy. Given this, we keep our suggested policy research agenda brief and broad in scope. That agenda is centered on three areas that cut across disciplinary approaches and research traditions.

Vulnerability-Related Behaviors and Practices

For consumer researchers interested in exploring evictions, much more work is needed to understand the experience of living with rental debt, which was not our focus in this project. Many renters spend at least some time in arrears or have other rental agreement violations. How do they, especially those with low income, understand rental debt? How do they account for it and prioritize it relative to other obligations? What strategies do they use to mitigate its impact? Consumer researchers have produced significant work on the management of debt that can help generate insights. Likewise, for scholars interested in managerial practice, how do tenant protections like rent control impact landlord behavior by type (small vs. corporate)? How do we understand the purposes for which they raise eviction threat? That is, under what conditions is it for revenue extraction, behavior modification, or tenant turnover? In that same vein, for landlords who rarely if ever file for eviction, how do they manage arrearage? How do recently emerging investor-owners of foreclosed properties compare? A few scholars cited in this article have begun to address these questions, but more work is needed.

Public Policy Research on Evictions

At present, rental markets are largely regulated locally. Yet, the municipal-level public policy that shapes vulnerability-inducing market conditions has not been well explored. Because local rental market environments vary so widely, in some crucial respects, "eviction" is contingent rather than the same phenomenon everywhere all the time. There is still much to understand about basic features of rental markets, many of which are shaped directly by public policy. To wit, what is a landlord obliged to do based on what a given market's implied warranty of habitability covers? How are municipalities addressing the emergence of short-term rentals and the threat they pose to the traditional rental housing supply? The city of Little Rock, Arkansas, for instance, recently passed an ordinance limiting the number of short-term rentals licenses it will grant and raising their cost (Garza, 2023). Additionally, how do these rental market features inform the comparative experience of eviction for tenants and landlords?

Finally, what is the process of rental market regulation and law? How are the political and economic interests of various marketplace actors transformed into regulation and law? To our knowledge, there have been few inquiries into this important topic since Hatch (2017). We know little of how the comparative power of tenants and landlords materialize as actualized or failed attempts at regulation? To wit, since the early 2000s, Arkansas legislators made multiple unsuccessful attempts to introduce an implied warranty of habitability into state law. Efforts in 2005 and 2007 led to passage of the 2007 act regulating rental markets, but it excluded the warranty (Wood, 2017). The Non-Legislative Commission on the Study of Landlord-Tenant Laws issued its comprehensive report in 2012, which included a recommended implied warranty of habitability. But numerous subsequent legislative proposals based on those recommendations died in the House Insurance & Commerce Committee (Wood, 2017).

In 2021, the Arkansas legislature passed Act 1052, which "sets forth implied habitability standards for all lease or rental agreements (with a few exceptions) entered into or renewed after November 1, 2021." Arkansas landlords are now expected to make available: hot and cold running water, potable drinking water, electricity, sanitation, and sewage that conforms to applicable building and housing codes, roofing, and HVAC. They are further expected to review and update their contract terms to reflect this new standard. This law falls well shy of the Commission's 2012 recommendations insofar as it does not cover some rental agreements (e.g., rent-to-own leases), expressly prohibit retaliatory evictions, permit renters to withhold rent for repairs, or require working smoke detectors. A question of interest to public policy researchers is where were the legislative veto points in prior bills and in what ways (and to what extent) were they overcome? More generally, what levers can lessen the asymmetries between landlords and tenants?

CONCLUSION

The asymmetric power favoring landlords in rental markets highlights the importance of both institutional and interpersonal features of context that gives rise to consumer vulnerability. Property-holding interests are legitimized by legislation, case precedent, and strong political lobbying efforts to resist reform. But evicting happens through management practices embedded in interpersonal interactions that are routinely raced and gendered. The ordinary functioning of rental markets – not the extraordinary actions of villainous landlords – manufactures consumer vulnerability through displacement and its threat. Because shelter is a foundational component of consumer well-being, displacement in the form of eviction is a wicked social problem. Scholars cited in this article and advocates at the grassroots have claimed that existing solutions prioritize maintaining the rental market status quo at the expense of housing people. In line with the dominance of commodity logic over human rights, even governmental rental assistance programs routinely shift administrative and other burdens onto assistance seekers. Their reliance on pre-existing stores of knowledge about programs, means-testing, and complex application processes all prevail on scarce or nonexistent resources to appease fears of moral hazard. More policy-focused research is needed to better understand how vulnerability is generated, maintained, and exacerbated in rental markets and how its impact on consumers can be effectively mitigated.

REFERENCES

Arkansas General Assembly. (2007). Arkansas Residential Landlord-Tenant Act of 2007. *Arkansas Code*. https://casetext.com/statute/arkansas-code-of-1987/title-18-property/subtitle-2-real-property/chapter-17-arkansas-residential-landlord-tenant-act-of-2007

Baker, A. (2021, August). From eviction to evicting: Rethinking the technologies, lives and power sustaining displacement. *Progress in Human Geography, 45*(4), 796–813. https://doi.org/10.1177/0309132520910798

Campisi, N., & Baille, K. (2022, August 26). Why the U.S. rental housing crisis is so dire – Forbes advisor. *Forbes*. https://www.forbes.com/advisor/personal-finance/rental-housing-costs-rise/

Crowell, A. R. (2022, April). Renting under racial capitalism: Residential segregation and rent exploitation in the United States. *Sociological Spectrum. 28*, 1–24.

DeLuca, S., & Rosen, E. (2022). Housing insecurity among the poor today. *Annual Review of Sociology, 48*, 1–20.

Desmond, M. (2012). Eviction and the reproduction of urban poverty. *American Journal of Sociology*, *118*(1), 88–133.

Desmond, M. (2016). *Evicted: Poverty and profit in the American City*. Crown Publishers.

Dewitt, E. (2020, June 17). Eviction rates in every state. *Stacker*. https://stacker.com/stories/4233/eviction-rates-every-state

Dreier, P. (1982). The status of tenants in the United States. *Social Problems*, *30*(2), 179–198. https://doi.org/10.2307/800517

Dreier, P. (1984). The tenant's movement in the United States. *International Journal of Urban and Regional Research*, *8*(2), 255–279. https://doi.org/10.1111/j.1468-2427.1984.tb00611.x

Fields, D. (2022, February). Automated landlord: Digital technologies and post-crisis financial accumulation. *Environment and Planning A: Economy and Space*, *54*(1), 160–181. https://doi.org/10.1177/0308518X19846514

Fowler, K. A., Matthew Gladden, R., Vagi, K. J., Barnes, J., & Frazier, L. (2015, February). Increase in suicides associated with home eviction and foreclosure during the US housing crisis: Findings from 16 national violent Death reporting system states, 2005–2010. *American Journal of Public Health*, *105*(2), 311–316. https://doi.org/10.2105/AJPH.2014.301945

Garboden, P. M. E., & Rosen, E. (2019, June 1). Serial filing: How landlords use the threat of eviction. *City & Community*, *18*(2), 638–661.

Garza, J. (2023, June 21). New regulations are coming to short-term rentals in little rock. *THV11.com*. https://www.thv11.com/article/news/local/short-term-rentals-little-rock/91-3c55defe-8486-4136-99f9-82b04d5a868b

Gomory, H. (2022). The social and institutional contexts underlying landlords' eviction practices. *Social Forces*, *100*(4), 1774–1805.

Graetz, N., Gershenson, C., Hepburn, P., Porter, S. R., Sandler, D. H., & Desmond, M. (2023). A comprehensive demographic profile of the US evicted population. *Proceedings of the National Academy of Sciences - PNAS*, *120*(41), e2305860120–e2305860120. https://doi.org/10.1073/pnas.2305860120

Graetz, N., Gershenson, C., Porter, S. R., Sandler, D. H., Lemmerman, E., & Desmond, M. (2024, January). The impacts of rent burden and eviction on mortality in the United States, 2000–2019. *Social Science & Medicine*, *340*, 116398. https://doi.org/10.1016/j.socscimed.2023.116398

Gromis, A., Fellows, I., Hendrickson, J. R., Edmonds, L., Leung, L., Adam, P., & Desmond, M. (2022). Estimating eviction prevalence across the United States. *Proceedings of the National Academy of Sciences*, *119*(21). https://doi.org/10.1073/pnas.2116169119

Harvey, D. (2004). The 'new' imperialism: Accumulation by dispossession. *Socialist Register*, *40*. https://socialistregister.com/index.php/srv/article/view/5811

Hatch, M. E. (2017, January). Statutory protection for renters: Classification of state landlord–tenant policy approaches. *Housing Policy Debate*, *27*(1), 98–119.

Hill, R. P. (2002). Service provision through public-private partnerships: An ethnography of service delivery to homeless teenagers. *Journal of Service Research*, *4*(4), 278–289. https://doi.org/10.1177/1094670502004004005

Hill, R. P. (1991). Homeless women, special possessions, and the meaning of 'home': An ethnographic case study. *Journal of Consumer Research*, *18*(3), 298–310.

Hill, R. P., & Ramani, G. (2024). Vulnerability and consumer poverty: An explication of consumption adequacy. *Review of Marketing Research*, *21*, 25–48.

Hill, R. P., & Sharma, E. (2020). Consumer vulnerability. *Journal of Consumer Psychology*, *30*(3), 551–570.

Hill, R. P., & Stamey, M. (1990). The homeless in America: An examination of possessions and consumption behaviors. *Journal of Consumer Research*, *17*(3), 303–321.

Humphries, J. E., Mader, N. S., & Tannenbaum, D. I. (2019, August). *Does eviction cause poverty? Quasi-experimental evidence from Cook County, IL*. National Bureau of Economic Research. https://www.nber.org/system/files/working_papers/w26139/w26139.pdf

Immergluck, D., Ernsthausen, J., Earl, S., & Powell, A. (2020). Evictions, large owners, and serial filings: Findings from Atlanta. *Housing Studies*, *35*(5), 903–924.

Leung, L., Hepburn, P., & Desmond, M. (2021). Serial eviction filing: Civil courts, property management, and the threat of displacement. *Social Forces, 100*(1), 316–344.

Li, H., Kim, Y., & Srinivasan, K. (2022). Market shifts in the sharing economy: The impact of Airbnb on housing rentals. *Management Science, 68*(11), 8015–8044. https://doi.org/10.1287/mnsc. 2021.4288

Liptak, A., & Thrush, G. (2021, August 27). Supreme Court ends Biden's eviction moratorium. *The New York Times*. https://www.nytimes.com/2021/08/26/us/eviction-moratorium-ends.html

Manduca, R., & Sampson, R. J. (2019). Punishing and toxic neighborhood environments independently predict the intergenerational social mobility of black and white children. *Proceedings of the National Academy of Sciences - PNAS, 116*(16), 7772–7777. https://doi.org/10.1073/pnas. 1820464116

National Conference of Commissioners and On Uniform State Laws. (1972). *The Uniform Residential Landlord-Tenant Act of 1972 (URLTA)*. National Conference of Commissioners. https:// bloximages.chicago2.vip.townnews.com/bgdailynews.com/content/tncms/assets/v3/editorial/d/ 8f/d8f433ac-89a4-11e6-b3aa-ffc366bf6836/57f2ba62666ae.pdf.pdf

National Council for Healthy Housing. (2008). *Uniform Residential Landlord-Tenant Act (Overview)*. https://nchh.org/resource-library/Uniform%20Law%20Commission%20-%20URLTA.pdf

Office of the UN High Commission on Human Rights. (2023). *The Human Right to Adequate Housing*. OHCHR. https://www.ohchr.org/en/special-procedures/sr-housing/human-right-adequate-housing

Patillo, M. (2013). Housing: Commodity versus right. *Annual Review of Sociology, 39*, 509–531.

Rutan, D. Q., & Desmond, M. (2021, January). The concentrated geography of eviction. *The Annals of the American Academy of Political and Social Science, 693*(1), 64–81. https://doi.org/10.1177/ 0002716221991458

Saatcioglu, B., & Ozanne, J. L. (2013). Moral habitus and status negotiation in a marginalized working-class neighborhood. *The Journal of Consumer Research, 40*(4), 692–710. https://doi. org/10.1086/671794

Semenza, D. C., Stansfield, R., Grosholz, J. M., & Link, N. W. (2022, April). Eviction and crime: A neighborhood analysis in Philadelphia. *Crime & Delinquency, 68*(4), 707–732.

Seymour, E., & Akers, J. (2021, January 1). Building the eviction economy: Speculation, precarity, and eviction in Detroit. *Urban Affairs Review, 57*(1), 35–69.

Thornton, P. H., & Ocasio, W. (1999). Institutional logics and the historical contingency of power in organizations: Executive succession in the higher education publishing industry, 1958–1990. *American Journal of Sociology, 105*(3), 801–843.

Vogell, H. (2023, November 16). *DOJ backs tenants in price-fixing case against big landlords and Real Estate Tech Company*. ProPublica. https://www.propublica.org/article/doj-backs-tenants-price-fixing-case-biglandlords-real-estate-tech

Wood, R. (2017, May 7). Renters have few rights under Arkansas law. *Arkansas Democrat Gazette*. https://www.arkansasonline.com/news/2017/may/07/renters-have-few-rights-under-arkansas-/

INDEX